Dragonfly Eyes

CAO WENXUAN

Translated by Helen Wang

WALKER BOOKS

Dragonfly Eyes

Published by arrangement with Phoenix Juvenile and Children's Publishing Ltd

First published in the English language 2021 by Walker Books Ltd 87 Vauxhall Walk, London SE11 5HJ

2 4 6 8 10 9 7 5 3 1

Text © 2016 Cao Wenxuan
English translation © 2021 Helen Wang
Cover illustration © 2021 Benji Davies

The right of Cao Wenxuan and Helen Wang to be identified as author and translator respectively of this work has been asserted by them in accordance with the Copyright, Designs and Patents Act 1988

This book has been typeset in Berkeley Oldstyle

Printed and bound by CPI Group (UK) Ltd, Croydon CR0 4YY

British Library Cataloguing in Publication Data:
a catalogue record for this book is available from the British Library

ISBN 978-1-4063-7825-2

www.walker.co.uk

MIX
Paper from responsible sources
FSC® C020471

CHAPTER 1

The Café

Ah Mei looked different from other children; she *was* different. Wherever she went, silent eyes stared at her from all directions. She would appear a little shy and embarrassed, but inside she would feel a deep swelling of pride. She would rise very subtly onto her tiptoes, push her slender neck forward and raise her head. Then her little white face would turn very subtly, scanning the crowd, as though searching for someone.

People stopped talking the moment they saw her, as though caught by surprise, as though while taking a stroll by the river, mindlessly watching the flow of the water, a sudden chill had swept up from the surface. One by one, they stopped, until they were all standing there, spellbound – countless pairs of eyes watching her every move, without a moment's thought as to how it might make her feel.

It was as though this little girl had floated down from heaven, and the people around her were caught in a trance.

Ah Mei had known this gaze for as long as she could remember, this combination of surprise, curiosity, fascination and appreciation that followed her wherever she went.

And she knew it was because of Nainai.

Nainai was French. Born in the famous port city of Marseilles, she had grown up by the bright blue Mediterranean Sea. Nainai was her grandmother, and without Nainai, Ah Mei wouldn't exist.

Ah Mei lived in Shanghai. At least, she lived there until she was thirteen.

From the time Ah Mei came into this world to the year Nainai passed away, when Ah Mei was fifteen, Nainai never stopped telling her stories about her life with Yeye, stories filled with adventure and romance. Nainai poured her heart and soul into the tales, even when Ah Mei was still very young. She didn't stop to wonder if Ah Mei could understand or not – as long as those bright little eyes kept watching and blinking, Nainai would carry on talking, her soft-spoken Shanghainese dotted with beautiful French words. Eventually, she'd remember that Ah Mei probably couldn't understand what she was saying. Then she'd laugh, and continue telling the stories anyway, pouring her heart and soul into them once again. Deep down, she knew she was telling the stories for her own benefit. She'd talk as she pushed Ah Mei's pram into Beijing West Road, as she held Ah Mei's little hand while they walked slowly beneath the apricot trees, and as she lay down on the bed with Ah Mei, their two heads sharing the same pillow. She told the stories in no particular order, and she repeated them too often to count. But for Ah Mei, it was like hearing a new story every time, and she was constantly asking, "What happened next?" They were like shiny beads each offering a glimpse of the bigger story.

Over the years, Ah Mei strung the shiny beads together, and the sequence of events began to take shape in her mind. But there were gaps, and it was clear that Nainai was holding back certain parts. As Ah Mei got older, she could guess what they were. She understood, in a naïve kind of way, that there were some things that Nainai did not feel comfortable sharing with her. She would never forget Nainai's look of embarrassment when those awkward moments arose. Then Ah Mei would peer into Nainai's deep blue eyes, and wag her finger playfully before running it down Nainai's nose. Nainai would pretend to bite at the finger, then pinch Ah Mei's cheeks, or hug her so tightly she could hardly breathe. As soon as Ah Mei tried to pull away, Nainai would giggle and let go. Nainai laughed differently from all the other ladies Ah Mei knew. Nainai had been in Shanghai for a long time – she belonged there and spoke Shanghainese fluently – but when she laughed, she was French.

Du Meixi was born into a wealthy family, a very wealthy family. Their money came from the family silk business, which reached halfway round the world to Europe. It was Du Meixi's father who had set his sights on Europe, and, to that end, had entrusted the running of the Shanghai business to his cousin, and got on the boat himself. Having travelled the length and breadth of Europe, he had finally settled in France, and established the European side of the business in Lyons. It had flourished and expanded: his Chinese silk company became well-known in Europe and its products were highly sought after.

When Du Meixi was twenty-five, his father had wanted him to join him in Lyons and take charge of the business there. He had refused, on the grounds that he was still grieving for his late wife, who had died of an illness. His father knew that was not the real reason: it was he who had insisted on the marriage, but Du Meixi had never been happy. He had always been a strict father, but this time he would not force his son against his wishes. He simply turned around, and, with his back to Du Meixi, sighed and said, "As you wish."

The past few years had been oppressive for Du Meixi. He had felt sad all the time, sometimes even desperate. But he had realized that his old life was over, and was determined now to start a new life. With a friend's help, he cast aside everything from his old life, and, holding his head high and pushing out his chest, he climbed aboard a steamer and became a sailor. The ship belonged to a French company, and sailed back and forth between Shanghai and Marseilles all year round.

Du Meixi loved being at sea. He was enthralled by the boundlessness of the water, the wind driving the clouds across the sky, the continuous rise and fall of the waves that rolled over the surface of the water, the islands in the distance floating like mirages, the gulls dancing in the spray behind the boat, the fish leaping in the brilliant moonlight, the merging of sea and sky. He had never known air so fresh. The world had never seemed so deep or so vast. Life on the steamer was simple, yet full of all kinds of unexpected danger. His previous life seemed even duller in comparison. Doused in the salty tang of the sea, he was happier than he had ever been. He learned the skills he needed on the job, and soon rose to assistant helmsman, and then to second in command.

Meanwhile, the family silk business continued to flourish and expand. It had spread across Europe as smoothly as a cloud floating across the sky. And now, having covered Europe, it was heading towards the Americas.

But Du Meixi, by nature drawn to freedom and a life free of restriction, was still not interested.

His father looked up at the sky and sighed. As long as the family in Shanghai were looking after Du Meixi's children – a little boy and a little girl – then he could spend the rest of his life drifting about in the wind and the waves, if that was what he wanted.

Du Meixi's steamer docked at Marseilles. He had been there many times, and knew what to expect.

It took several days to unload a full ship, and once unloaded, the ship would need to stay in dock while a series of inspections and repairs were carried out. This meant he would have time on his hands and could go and enjoy himself. Marseilles is an ancient port, with a history going back thousands of years. There are traces of the past everywhere. They catch your eye, and before you know it, you are caught in a daydream, lost in thought. It happens time and time again, and you never tire of it.

The cobbled streets – some wide, some narrow, some long, some short, some winding, some straight – were lined on both sides with little shops selling an assortment of items from all over the world. The seamen wandered aimlessly in and out of these little shops, not to buy anything, just to pass the time. Of course, they were much more interested in the restaurants. They had been at sea for weeks, and the food on board was bland and monotonous. Here, in Marseilles, as soon as they saw food their eyes lit up and their mouths started watering. The sight of Parma ham, sliced wafer-thin, whetted their appetite. The aroma of calamari, lightly fried with parsley and garlic, tickled their tastebuds from a hundred steps away. Pasta with scallops, in a squid and fish sauce, stopped looking strange when the delicious smell reached their nostrils. But what they really looked forward to every time they came ashore was bouillabaisse, the rich fish soup for which Marseilles is famous all over the world. Made with at least four different types of fish cooked slowly to draw out their flavour, it is probably the best soup in the world. No matter how difficult things get, when people eat bouillabaisse they feel life is worth living.

Du Meixi and a few other seamen had spent the whole day strolling around town. They could see from the sky that it was getting late, so they went into a very small restaurant. Naturally, they ordered bouillabaisse. As a huge pot of the soup was brought to their table, the group bent their heads over it. The flavours were intense, and when Du Meixi ate his first spoonful, he closed his eyes and sighed with delight, "Ah! This soup is delicious! My tongue's almost hanging out of my mouth!" There was a round of slurping. Naturally, they ordered wine – how could they not! They were seamen, after all, and seamen have a natural affinity with alcohol. And this was Marseilles. They spent the evening eating and drinking, and by the time night had fallen and the sky was dark, they could neither see straight nor walk straight – all except Du Meixi, who had resolved to stay sober. He knew they were in no fit state to roam around town, so he had everyone link arms, and he led them back to the ship. Then he waved goodnight from the shore, and went for a late walk. He had always thought that the true face of a town, its soul, reveals itself only at night, and that this was especially true in a city like Marseilles which held so many secrets.

Du Meixi wandered down streets that were thousands of years old, walking slowly over uneven cobbles.

Eventually, feeling a little tired, he loosened the collar of his coat, and stepped inside a café on a street corner. He could never have imagined that his entire life would change the moment he stepped inside that café.

Du Meixi was tall, and well built. As he walked towards an empty seat, the golden glow of the candlelight swept his shadow over a Frenchwoman who was sitting in the corner.

She had a cup of coffee in front of her, and was reading a book. She felt the black wings of his looming shadow glide over her, and instinctively looked up. She saw his face. He saw only the empty seat.

He sat down and ordered a cup of coffee.

The Frenchwoman sitting in the corner glanced up at the Chinese sailor. His weatherbeaten face was the colour of old bronze and in the flickering candlelight there was a slightly cool sheen to it. There were bags under his eyes, but the eyes themselves shone with life beneath black bushy eyebrows. His hair was black, and a little dry and scruffy, like wild grass. The tiny table seemed out of proportion beside his large body. His open collar made his chest seem even broader, a chest that was the same attractive bronze colour as his face. And as the Frenchwoman studied him, she could not help smiling.

He was not exactly handsome, she thought, but rather majestic – in the way that a statue is majestic.

Du Meixi was tired. It felt good to sit down and relax, and he drank his coffee with a mind free of all thoughts.

The Frenchwoman watched him from behind her book.

As Du Meixi stirred his coffee, he started to reflect. *I have plenty of time. Should I pay a visit to my father?* he wondered. He realized that deep down he missed his father. The spoon went round and round, clinking against the side of the cup, and it was not long before his eyes started to moisten and mist over.

The Frenchwoman kept her eyes on her book, as though she had already forgotten about him.

Du Meixi turned his head to look out of the window, and finally noticed the Frenchwoman, at the very same moment that she happened to glance up at him.

Their eyes met, crashing in the quiet of the café.

The Frenchwoman remained in the café until very late. Du Meixi stayed even later. He spent the entire time after she had left staring at her empty seat.

The next day, at the same time, Du Meixi returned to the little café on the corner of the street. As he stepped inside, he saw the Frenchwoman. She was sitting in the same seat as before.

He greeted her with a quick nod, and she smiled in return, rather shyly.

For three days in a row, Du Meixi went to the café at the same time every night. Before going inside, he would walk around the neighbourhood for a while, wondering if she'd be there again. Of course not, he told himself. But when he opened the door, he would see her straight away, as though she had been sitting there for years. He gave her a little wave, and she gave a little wave back.

He noticed that she was always reading the same book, and always seemed to be reading the same page.

One day he arrived early, but the Frenchwoman was still there before him. This time, however, she was leaning against the railing outside the café, as though she was waiting for him.

Many, many years later, when Nainai told this story to Ah Mei, the little girl would blink at her and ask, "Were you waiting for Yeye? Or was he waiting for you?" And Nainai would say, "He was waiting for me, of course."

"But Yeye says you were waiting for him."

"That's men for you. They're not always very good at remembering the important things."

When doubt flashed across Ah Mei's eyes, Nainai would say, "Who do you believe? Me or him?"

Without even pretending to weigh up her choices, Ah Mei would answer immediately, "I believe you, Nainai!"

Sometimes Yeye would be standing near by, listening to every word. He wouldn't offer any protests, just a smile, as he handed Nainai a cup of freshly made coffee.

From there, Yeye and Nainai's story developed very smoothly. There were no cliffhanging moments, no twists and turns. They walked along the coast of the bright blue Mediterranean from early morning to late at night; they went to Provence and saw fields of lavender stretching to the horizon.

Nainai did not take Yeye home to meet her family right away, but she did take him to a small wood, where she pointed to a distant house with a red-tiled roof and a garden. "That's my house," she said. And Yeye took her on board his ship.

All in all, they spent fifteen days together. During those fifteen days, they walked and walked. It was a beautiful journey of love.

One day when Ah Mei was eleven, she was secretly reading a novel under the desk at school and came across the expression "love at first sight". At the time, the teacher was writing words and phrases on the blackboard and asking the students to use them in sentences. Ah Mei mentally added "love at first sight" to the list, and in an instant had written: "The day Yeye and Nainai met in a café in Marseilles, it was love at first sight."

On the sixteenth day, Yeye and Nainai met at the café again. They sat there, facing one another, for a very long time.

On the seventeenth day, they set out for Lyons.

CHAPTER 2

Yeye's Port

When Océane appeared in front of Du Meixi's father, it felt as if a curtain had been swept open, and a dazzling shaft of sunlight had come flooding in through the window. Du Meixi's father almost lost his balance, and was ready to raise his hands to shield his eyes. Océane was twenty.

The big bright lounge was suddenly filled with youth and promise, so much so that for a while Du Meixi's father forgot to look at his son. He hadn't seen him for a very long time, but instead of examining him head to toe, he was looking at this young woman. "Her eyes are so blue!"

"This is Océane," said Du Meixi.

His father quietly repeated the name to himself: "Oh-say-ann… Oh-say-ann…"

"Like the sea," Du Meixi explained.

"No wonder her eyes are so blue."

The older man took a good look at Océane. She tried to sidle behind Du Meixi. Her naturally rosy cheeks had turned a very bright red.

"She doesn't seem very French. She seems more Chinese than French." Du Meixi's father was beaming. He could barely contain his delight.

When Du Meixi moved aside so that Océane was standing in front of his father, she tried to hide behind him again. This time, he slipped his strong arm behind her and gave her a gentle push, so that she was standing in front of his father.

She felt uncomfortable at first, but as they talked, she began to relax.

Eventually, the conversation turned to Du Meixi's future. "You're not going to keep drifting about at sea all year and leave Océane behind, are you?" his father asked.

"I've handed in my notice."

Du Meixi's father was astonished by the power that this young woman held over his son. "You know, I tried so hard to persuade you," he said, shaking his head, "but it wasn't enough. I couldn't make you change your mind. And now, this French girl comes along and just like that she brings you to shore. Incredible!" He looked at Du Meixi, at the hard life that was written in his son's face, and felt a rush of emotion. *I can see that these past few years have not been easy for you,* he wanted to tell his son.

"I've found my port," said Du Meixi, looking at Océane. "Here she is."

His father let out a long breath. "Does this mean I can go back to Shanghai?"

Du Meixi smiled.

His father couldn't have been happier. "It looks as though

I'll be able to say goodbye to Lyons after all."

"If you feel confident enough…"

"You've changed your mind so suddenly! I'm still trying to get used to the idea," Du Meixi's father teased.

"Yes, it's all happened very quickly," said Du Meixi, glancing at Océane.

Du Meixi's father walked over to the window, opened it and gazed out at the blue sky over Lyons. "All right," he said, looking back at his son. "But it will be hard to leave this place."

"Then stay."

"No," said Du Meixi's father. "You have your own lives to live, and I don't want to be in the way." Du Meixi having found Océane was like the story of the Prodigal Son. His son had come home, and that was all he had ever wanted.

That evening, Du Meixi's father called his son into his bedroom, opened the wardrobe and took out a beautiful little sandalwood box. He lifted the lid and carefully opened up the cream-coloured silk that was wrapped around two knobbly little balls. He took them out and lay them in the palm of his hand. When he held them up to the lamp, they glowed different colours.

The effect was magnificent.

"Look at these!" said Du Meixi's father.

The strange little balls were about two centimetres in diameter, and slightly oval. One was a dark blue colour, patterned with white rings, and within each white ring was a light blue ring, which glowed more brightly than the darker blue. And in the middle of each light blue ring was a small magenta ball. The other one was a red colour, also patterned with white rings, but within each white ring was a green ring, and a little orange ball.

"They look like eyes," said Du Meixi.

His father nodded. "Dragonfly eyes – that's what they're called." He looked at the two beads in the palm of his hand. "They're made of glass. The earliest ones appeared in Western Asia and Egypt in 2500 BC, then they spread to China. The imperial family and the nobility adored them. It was a complex process to make even one of these beads, and there was such a demand for them that at some point in the Warring States period, Chinese glassmakers started to produce them. They created beads that were quite different from those of Western Asia, Egypt and the Mediterranean. Can you see all the different layers? Don't they look like dragonfly eyes?"

Du Meixi's father held his hand up to the lamp again. The beads seemed to come to life, twinkling as they caught the light, like a dragonfly that has landed and is turning its head.

"They're precious, aren't they?" Du Meixi asked.

"Priceless," said his father. "I got them from a collector a long time ago. I want you to have them."

"You want to give them to me?"

Du Meixi's father shook his head. "No, I want you to give them to Océane. Find a good jeweller, and have these two beads strung together with gemstones to make a necklace. On the day of your marriage, give the necklace to Océane. I like this girl. I liked her from the moment I saw her." Du

Meixi's father looked at the beads in his hand. "It's strange. I could easily have left these in Shanghai, but for some reason I brought them with me to Lyons, as though I was meant to give them to you both here. It must be fate."

Within a few days, Du Meixi's father had handed over his European business to his son and was on his way back to Shanghai. Before leaving, he said only one thing to Du Meixi: "You're right: you've found your port."

CHAPTER 3

Nainai is a Boat

Yeye and Nainai met in 1925.

Their first son was born in the spring of 1927, their second in the autumn of 1929. Ah Mei's father arrived in the summer of 1931, and her aunt in the spring of 1933. The family lived in Lyons. Occasionally they would go to Marseilles for a few days, and whenever they went, Yeye and Nainai would leave the children with Nainai's parents and walk arm in arm to the little café on the corner. They would sit there for two or three hours, sometimes longer, not saying much, just lingering over their coffee, watching the world go by.

By this time, Nainai could already speak some Chinese, and could say Yeye's name perfectly, with the correct pronunciation and tones:

"杜梅溪! Du Meixi."

Nainai loved the sound of his name, and said it as often as she could, sometimes loudly, sometimes quietly, sometimes drawing it out, sometimes in a soft whisper.

As well as speaking French, the children were also fluent

in Chinese – or, rather, Shanghainese. Yeye had arranged for a home tutor to come all the way from Shanghai, to live with them and teach the children Chinese.

The silk business continued as usual, and life was peaceful and prosperous for the family. Although Yeye still missed Shanghai and his family, he was like a mature tree that had put down roots and had gradually grown accustomed to the sky, sunshine and rain in Lyons. If, for the first few years, he'd felt he didn't really belong, those feelings had long since faded. And now, each time he took Océane and the children back to Shanghai, it felt strange and unfamiliar. The children, on the other hand, found life in Shanghai new and exciting, although they knew that it was not their city. They belonged in France.

Yeye had already broached the subject with his father on a few occasions – that he might stay in France for the rest of his life.

His elderly father proved to be surprisingly open-minded, and told Yeye, "I can continue looking after things in Shanghai for a while. The business is important, but you must put Océane and the children first."

So Yeye devoted his attention to the business in Europe, and to family life with Nainai and the children in Lyons. It was a lovely life, poetic even. Then, in November 1937, the Japanese occupied Shanghai, and everything changed. Dark clouds spread all over the world, shrouding everything in darkness. Anxiety and terror gripped millions of people. Soon Hitler's planes would be flying in formation like flocks of birds, bombing Europe.

The news from Shanghai, when it got through, was disheartening and depressing. Yeye's father had held on for a long time, but eventually succumbed to illness. Various relatives tried to keep the family business afloat, but it was heading downhill before their eyes.

War had made transport difficult, gradually cutting off supplies of goods. The demise of the silk business in Europe appeared imminent. It was still holding up in Shanghai, and in China generally, but even there things were becoming difficult. Yeye suddenly became very aware that he was his father's only son, and that his family was in China. In every telegram that arrived from Shanghai, he could hear his father, who no longer had the strength to do as he wished, calling him from the bottom of his heart – calling him to hurry back to Shanghai as soon as he could, to take over the family business that was struggling to survive, and to keep it alive, however weak the flame, so that when the cloud lifted and the sun came out, he could breathe new life into it once again.

Yeye started to feel restless and anxious.

He was so distracted that even when he'd finished the steak on his plate, he continued cutting into the imaginary meat with his knife and fork.

Nainai watched him, without saying a word.

At night, Yeye tossed and turned. Unable to sleep, and worried about disturbing Nainai, he would eventually slip out of bed, tiptoe downstairs to the lounge, and lie uncomfortably on the sofa.

Meanwhile, Nainai lay awake in the darkness of their bedroom.

Finally, the day came. "Océane..." Yeye hesitated for a while, then continued. "I'm thinking of going back to Shanghai for a while."

"We'll all go." Nainai seemed to have thought it through already.

Yeye shook his head. "No, you stay here with the children, and wait for me to come back."

At this point, Nainai took Yeye's hand and led him to another room. She gave the door a gentle push. Yeye was startled to see six enormous bulging suitcases waiting there.

Nainai told Yeye to go and lift one of the suitcases.

Yeye picked up one, then another, and could feel how full they were. He looked at his wife in disbelief.

"I've packed for the whole family," said Nainai.

Yeye was still shaking his head.

"I love Shanghai," said Nainai.

"But Shanghai has fallen," protested Yeye.

"And Paris won't fall soon?"

Yeye shook his head again. "Let me think about it."

"I'm a boat, and you're my port," said Nainai.

Yeye laughed. "From the first day I met you, I've always known you were my port."

"So now it's your turn to be the port," said Nainai.

Before leaving France, Yeye and Nainai went to the tiny café in Marseilles one more time.

They sat quietly in the warm candlelight. Over a decade had passed, and everything in the café seemed a little older and a little shabbier, but the candlelight was the same as it had always been.

Yeye looked at Nainai the entire time.

There were lines on her face now, and her skin had lost the glow and suppleness of youth. But her spirit was still there, and her girlish shyness still showed itself from time to time, even after four children.

She was wearing the necklace with the two dragonfly eyes. All the different colours glowed in the candlelight.

"Océane…" Yeye said her name softly.

A light blush spread over Nainai's face.

Yeye's big hands grasped hers. "Océane, there's still time to change your mind."

Nainai shook her head.

"We can't see what life will be like in the future. The road ahead may be filled with thorns – danger, even," said Yeye.

Nainai looked down at the dragonfly eyes. "You said these bright eyes would protect against evil."

Yeye gripped her hands, and as he looked at the dragonfly eyes he nodded.

That day they sat in the café for a very long time, until they were the only remaining customers. They said goodbye to the owner, now bent in the back, and reluctantly went on their way.

It was the last time they ever set foot in the café.

CHAPTER 4

The Blue House

Nainai led the children through a crowd of onlookers into the bright and spacious European-style house. It was the autumn of 1939.

Wutong leaves were blowing about in the wind all over Shanghai. This was by no means an unfamiliar sight for Nainai, because the same kind of tree grows all over France, and every autumn you can see wutong leaves falling wherever you go. But this did not make the place feel any more familiar to Nainai.

For the first few days, she kept walking over to the window, or standing on the doorstep, looking out at the brown fallen leaves. Her thoughts drifted between Lyons, Marseilles and Shanghai. She felt a twinge of sadness, but mostly she felt excited: she was looking forward to the future.

She could never have imagined that she would spend the rest of her life at this house.

Their new home was three storeys high, and had been designed by a famous German architect. The roof tiles, doors and windows were blue, the colour of the sea, and the walls were white. It seemed fresher, cleaner and brighter than the other European-style houses on the road. This sea-blue was Nainai's favourite colour, as though fate had chosen this house for her, and it had been waiting for her to arrive.

On their first day in Shanghai, Nainai had gone to visit Yeye's father in hospital.

Yeye's father was as thin as a piece of paper. You could barely see there was a human body beneath the pristine white sheet of his sickbed.

When Yeye's father saw Nainai, his eyes opened as wide and as bright as two round bells. He reached out with his shaky hands covered in age-spots, and grasped her hands. He held them gently for a long time, then, in very rusty French, said, "Océane, I'm so sorry, I'm so sorry…"

Nainai leaned towards him. "Shanghai's my home too. I've come home, to be by your side."

Yeye's father's eyes did not leave her.

One by one, Nainai pushed the children to their grandfather's bedside. Four children.

"Thank you, Océane, for blessing me with these grandchildren." He smiled in contentment, and a little dribble fell from the corner of his mouth.

Nainai quickly wiped it away with a towel that was by his pillow.

A week later, the whole family went to the hospital. Yeye's father was nearing the end of his life.

This time, Yeye's father could barely open his eyes. But he managed to open them up a crack, which was enough to see the necklace around Nainai's neck, and the two dragonfly eyes. He pulled his hand out from under the cover, and, shaking, reached towards the necklace.

Nainai understood. She lowered her head until the two dragonfly eyes were resting in his thin, pale hands. "Thank you for giving them to me," she said.

Weakly, Yeye's father instructed her: "Océane, don't ever let them leave you."

Nainai nodded.

Sapped of all strength, Yeye's father's hands dropped away, but his eyes never moved from Nainai's face.

"Perhaps he's trying to tell you something," said Yeye.

Nainai turned her head so that her left ear was by Yeye's father's mouth. His words seemed to come from deep in his soul. "Océane, look after them…"

Those were his last words. She would remember them through the decades that followed.

At dusk that day, Yeye's father quietly slipped away from a world in which gunfire might ring out at any moment.

Soon after this, Nainai met Yeye's children from his first marriage: a son and a daughter.

The first time they saw Nainai they were hesitant and dubious. She looked so different. They felt distant and shy.

Nainai also felt shy. But she leaned forward, and stared into each of their faces, then said gently, "You can call me Mama, or Océane."

That evening, a smiling Nainai said to Yeye, "Du Meixi, now there are six children, we need to reconfigure the family.

Let's do it the Chinese way, and number them by age!" she said, opening her arms wide. "Imagine them all in a line!"

Yeye nodded. "Good idea."

And with that, she counted them out on her fingers: "Lao Da, Lao Er, Lao San, Lao Si, Lao Wu, Lao Liu." Yeye's son and daughter from his first marriage were the first and second, and the children Nainai had borne were the third, fourth, fifth and sixth.

It was only natural, then, that over a decade later, Ah Mei would call her aunts and uncles in the Chinese way too.

Lao Da	老大	was Ah Mei's Dabo	大伯	(Oldest Uncle)
Lao Er	老二	was Ah Mei's Dagu	大姑	(Older Aunt)
Lao San	老三	was Ah Mei's Erbo	二伯	(Uncle No. 2)
Lao Si	老四	was Ah Mei's Sanbo	三伯	(Uncle No. 3)
Lao Wu	老五	was Ah Mei's Baba	爸爸	(Father)
Lao Liu	老六	was Ah Mei's Xiaogu	小姑	(Younger Aunt)

Nainai was firm but fair with the children, and within a matter of days, the six of them came together as a family. They had their own bedrooms, but they didn't like being alone, and usually stayed together, running about and having fun, upstairs and downstairs, indoors and outdoors. Every now and then, the two servants, Mrs Hu and Mrs Song, would mutter as they dodged the charging children, "One of these days, the little devils are going to bring the ceiling down."

Nainai had been learning Shanghainese, and could now understand everything she heard. When she saw the children tearing around the house, she would smile at Mrs Hu and Mrs Song as if to say, *What can you do?*, but there was contentment and joy in her eyes. There were also times when she would have to tell the children off. When they were playing, arguments would break out, and sometimes tears, too. Nainai would listen patiently to everyone's complaints. She would always find something they hadn't thought of, and, as if by magic, they would all be friends again. All day long, the six children called out "Mama!" and from the moment the first child woke to the moment the last child fell asleep, she was constantly going upstairs and downstairs, and in and out of rooms. She would open the oldest child's curtains in the morning – "Lao Da, the sun's at the window, could you think about getting up?" – and at night she would tuck the youngest child in bed, whisper goodnight, then quietly leave the room, closing the door behind her.

When Yeye sat in his recliner on the verandah, watching the children as they chased around the garden, calling out to one another and laughing, he would look for Nainai. And when he found her, he would say with his eyes, *Thank you, Océane!*

By this time, it was not unusual in Shanghai to see a Japanese army truck or two driving along the road, the back filled with Japanese soldiers standing ready for action, rifles poised, bayonets glinting, the flag with the rising sun flapping at the front. Wailing sirens went off day and night, spreading fear through the city.

Nainai instructed Mrs Hu and Mrs Song: "Whenever the children leave the house, for whatever reason, they must look neat and tidy, and ready for the day." She told the children: "If you see Japanese people when you go out, you must not be afraid. Don't look at them. Keep your head up and your chest out, and carry on walking. The roads are Chinese, and so are you."

Sometimes the children would go out as a group. Although they all looked different, you could see from the way they stayed together that they were a family. They walked hand in hand, the two eldest children keeping the others in order, their energy and confidence breathing fresh air into the deathly pall that hung over Shanghai, boosting the morale of all who saw them.

Nainai firmly believed that the darkness in the world could not last for ever, and that sooner or later the Japanese would be driven out of China. If they didn't go home voluntarily, the Chinese would drive them into the sea.

Although Yeye and Nainai had been together for many years, she knew almost nothing about his silk business. Now they were in Shanghai, what she needed to do was turn the Blue House into a home, and create a sanctuary for Yeye, where he didn't have to worry about anything.

She knew only too well how hard it was for him to keep production going. It was clear that he was aging faster than she was – his hair seemed to have gone grey overnight. Nainai couldn't help feeling sad. She was determined to keep their family home shipshape, and she devoted herself to the children and their education. They went to the best schools in Shanghai, and though times were hard, no matter how chill the wind, or how harsh the rain, she was determined that the children would grow stronger and more resilient by the day. She would show Yeye that when circumstances were better they would all have a bright future ahead.

Yeye was out all day long. In addition to the business side of the company, the Du family still had three mills producing silk: one in Shanghai, one in Suzhou and one in Wuxi. Yeye spent long days at work in Shanghai but often travelled to see the mills in Suzhou and Wuxi too. These trips lasted several days, and each time he went away, he would feel bad about leaving Nainai on her own again. But each time, she would reassure him, "Don't worry about us, we'll be fine."

Whatever storms were raging around it, the Blue House stood firm and strong under the grey Shanghai sky.

Every time Yeye came home to the Blue House, he would think of the ship pulling into Marseilles or Shanghai – it was that same feeling of pulling into port, of having been at sea for a long time, buffeted by the wind and the waves, then finally coming into a calm bay, mentally and physically exhausted, knowing that he could now relax.

But it was taking a lot longer for circumstances to improve than Yeye or Nainai had imagined.

In fact, the situation was getting worse. One of the family's once prosperous silk mills was teetering on the brink of collapse. With the silk business hanging by a thread, the mill was gasping for breath. As a result, life was growing harder and harder. But Nainai carried on caring for her children calmly and cheerfully, with the devoted assistance of Mrs Hu and Mrs Song. When Yeye came home, the Blue House was always full of joy and laughter. If he was weary, someone always brought him a strong cup of coffee or a hot towel – if not Nainai, then Mrs Hu or Mrs Song. The gramophone was always playing, filling the house with music.

Yeye had begun to notice how lined Nainai's face had become. At times she looked quite haggard. And in those moments, Yeye felt so sorry. He would walk over to her, and gently wrap his strong arms around her waist. And she would look up at him and smile – a smile of affection and pain.

The wartime troubles grew more and more intense. Then, finally, the fighting came to an end. And when peace was restored, Yeye and Nainai suddenly realized that their children had grown up.

"Their wings are strong," Nainai told Yeye. "When the time comes to leave the nest, don't hold them back, let them be free!"

In the following few years, the four eldest children left home. They settled down and soon had children of their own.

The youngest moved out too, although she didn't settle down and start a family. Xiaogu, Ah Mei's aunt, played the piano exceptionally well and became a music teacher at a primary school.

That left only one child at the Blue House. In 1952 Lao Wu got married, and a year later, Ah Mei arrived, the only granddaughter.

Nainai was smitten. Of all her grandchildren, she loved Ah Mei the most.

Everyone could see that Nainai adored Ah Mei. They thought it was normal that she should feel this way, because they had all produced little rascals, and had been longing to see a little girl in the family. Nainai teased her grandsons: "You're so naughty, how can you be my favourites? Of course I like Ah Mei the best." The boys' parents didn't mind, and neither did the boys themselves, because they knew that Nainai loved them – it was just that she had a particularly soft spot for Ah Mei. They all loved Ah Mei, and always wanted to pick her up. Nainai would be on edge watching her clumsy grandsons with her only granddaughter, and when they pretended to drop her, to give Nainai a scare, she would rush over to snatch Ah Mei from them and tell them to scarper.

There was another reason why Nainai loved Ah Mei so much, and that was because, out of all of her grandchildren, Ah Mei looked the most like her. Everyone agreed. Nainai could see a hint of blue in the baby's eyes, and a glint of gold in the colour of her hair. But these were minor things – the main similiarity was in Ah Mei's profile, and even her expressions.

"It's incredible!" said Xiaogu.

When Ah Mei's parents suggested that they moved out of the Blue House, Nainai said, "You can go if you like, but Ah Mei's staying here."

Ah Mei's parents had smiled at each other, and stayed at the Blue House. It wasn't until Ah Mei was twelve that they eventually moved into a home of their own.

CHAPTER 5

Jumpers

There were many things that Ah Mei would not understand until she was grown up.

Long before Ah Mei came into this world, the silk business and silk factories that the Du family had established in Shanghai, Suzhou and Wuxi had ceased to belong to the family. Yeye didn't seem particularly bereft or upset about this, and he certainly wasn't frustrated or bitter. Both inside and outside the family, people were under the impression that he had willingly and voluntarily handed everything over to the state, and he had seemed extremely calm when he did so, as though he had been waiting years for that day to come.

Life at the Blue House was growing harder by the day.

Before, no one had worried about money at home, but now, Nainai had to think about it constantly. Money was getting tighter all the time. Very reluctantly, Yeye had to let Uncle Ding, the housekeeper, go. Uncle Ding had been with the family for decades, and when the time came to say goodbye, Yeye honoured him with a glass of wine, and, clasping his hands together, made a deep bow of respect to him. By the time he was upright again, and the two men were face to face, both of them were in tears. Not long after that, he had to let Uncle Wang, the gardener go. Uncle Gao, the driver, had left of his own accord two years earlier: Yeye had handed over both cars to the state along with the factories, and with no car to drive, Uncle Gao felt he couldn't stay and live off the family. The situation made Nainai think of a river full of fresh water, constantly flowing all day and all night, then the water stops flowing in but keeps flowing out, until finally there are only puddles left on the riverbed, glistening before they dry up too.

Nainai would spend several days deciding whether or not to buy a length of cloth. She'd think it over, and then over again, and eventually decide against it: old clothes would do, as long as they were clean.

Each Sunday, the whole family gathered at the Blue House to spend the day with Nainai. In addition to Ah Mei, there were nine other grandchildren, all of them boys. They all called her Nainai, including Dagu's two boys, who should really have called her Waipo (which is what maternal grandmothers are usually called).

One particular Sunday, the boys were shouting "Nainai, Nainai!" non-stop, and Nainai was answering non-stop, without knowing who she was answering.

The children were having great fun in the garden.

Nainai sat on a chair on the verandah, with three-year-old Ah Mei on her lap.

Seeing the boys chasing around the garden, shouting and

making a lot of noise, Ah Mei kept trying to slip down from Nainai's lap. But Nainai's long arms gently hauled her back and held her in place while Ah Mei wriggled and waved her little hands at the boys.

"Ah Mei, come and play!" the boys shouted. They all loved her. Some of them called her Ah Mei and some of them called her Dolly, because whenever they went out, people would gasp in surprise, "Oh! A Western doll!"

Dabo's son, Daoge, came over to the verandah. "Nainai, please can you lend Ah Mei to us for a while?"

"What do you think she is? A toy?" said Nainai. "I'm not going to let her play with you! You boys are wild, and rough. If you're not careful, you'll hurt her." And she jiggled her granddaughter on her knee. "Ah Mei's staying right here with her grandmother, aren't you? Look at those boys, Ah Mei, they're all dirty." And she waved him away. "Off you go. Go and play."

Daoge ran back to the huddle of boys, calling over, "Nainai said no. She won't let Ah Mei play with us."

Nainai watched her grandchildren, and as she watched, she started to hatch a plan: "Autumn's coming, I'll knit each of them a jumper." She could see that the clothes they were wearing were old, and that two of her grandsons were wearing clothes that had been patched.

Nainai felt a pang in her heart.

She was determined that her grandchildren should all wear nice clothes. She decided to knit a jumper for each grandchild – French-style.

But when Nainai opened the wardrobe and took out

the metal cash box, she was overcome with anxiety. There weren't many coins in it, and if she took some out to go and buy wool, there would only be a few left, and then how would the family manage? She counted the coins twice, looked at them once more, then again to be sure, and finally put the pitiful things back in the metal box, and put the box back in the wardrobe.

Nainai closed the wardrobe door, but she didn't close her mind to the idea of knitting jumpers for her grandchildren. The idea wound itself round and round inside her head.

A few days later, Nainai took Ah Mei to the department store on Nanjing Road. She stood in front of the wool counter, looking carefully at the choice in front of her. Although the colours were rather drab, she pictured all the jumpers she could knit for the grandchildren. She was determined, even with these colours, to knit the most beautiful jumpers in the world.

The saleswoman's attention was drawn first to Nainai, and then to Ah Mei, who was in Nainai's arms, and for a while she forgot all about selling. When the salespeople at the other counters saw Ah Mei, they hurried over. Though a little shy at first, Ah Mei was also curious, and peeped out at them.

"Such a beautiful child!"

"Look at her eyelashes, they're so long!"

"Her eyes are so deep."

"The bridge of her nose is so high."

"She has such a pretty chin, too."

"Are you related?" one of the saleswomen asked Nainai,

immediately thinking it was a pointless thing to ask in Chinese, and never expecting Nainai to answer "I'm her grandmother", not only in Shanghainese, but in a very Shanghainese manner.

The salespeople were taken completely by surprise.

Then one of them clapped her hands and opened her arms towards Ah Mei. Ah Mei opened her arms in response, leaned towards the woman and let herself be lifted from Nainai. Everyone laughed. Then the saleswoman sat Ah Mei on the counter, and the others gathered round.

Nainai couldn't stop smiling.

Finally, the saleswoman remembered that Nainai was a customer, and, moving along behind the counter, asked, "Would you like to buy some wool?"

Nainai had been clutching her purse the whole time. She nodded.

"What kind of wool? And how much do you need?" the saleswoman asked.

Nainai pointed to the different wools, and told her how much she needed of each. But when the saleswoman started to take the wool out, Nainai stopped her. "I'm sorry, I need to double-check." Nainai had changed her mind, but she was finding it difficult to take her eyes off the wool.

Eventually, she picked up Ah Mei, and, saying, "Sorry…" a few times, started to walk away from the counter. She didn't turn back. Feeling awkward and embarrassed, she hurried out of the store, holding Ah Mei tight.

A tram came rumbling past. Ah Mei, intrigued and a little scared, hooked one hand tightly round the back of Nainai's neck, and pointed at the tram with the other. "Nainai!" she said, wanting her grandmother to look at the tram too.

Nainai nodded, though she seemed rather distracted.

The metal tram tracks in the middle of the road glinted in the sunlight. A constant stream of pedestrians walked past Nainai, but she didn't notice them flashing by, one shadow after another. Nainai was thinking about the worryingly small amount of money they had, about all of her grandchildren, and about jumpers, all the jumpers she had planned, one for each child.

Nainai had already written to her two sisters in France, hoping that they might be able to send some money, and although she hadn't gone into detail, the message was clear enough: she and her family had hit hard times. But there had never been any reply. She doubted that the letters had ever arrived in France – their journey had probably been interrupted somewhere.

That evening, after handing a sleeping Ah Mei back to her mother, Nainai opened her wardrobe and took out one of her jumpers. She gave it a shake, then held it against herself, and took a good look in the mirror. She gave a sigh, and then a laugh.

Nainai held the jumper under the lamp, and searched for a loose end. She worked it free, and then, as she pulled on the thread, the jumper began to unravel.

Very soon, Nainai had four large balls of wool.

The following day, Nainai unravelled another of her beautiful jumpers. It took her longer this time: she kept slowing down, sometimes pausing with indecision. Then, her mind made up, she'd set to, and work the thread faster than before, watching the beautiful jumper disappear before her eyes. She was about to unravel a third jumper when Mrs Hu and Mrs Song stepped in.

"If you stop me, how will I ever get enough wool to knit ten jumpers?"

When Yeye heard what was happening, he said, "No problem. You can have my jumpers."

Nainai thought about it, then nodded. "All right."

Nainai asked Mrs Hu and Mrs Song to wash the unravelled wool and hang it out to dry. Then one Sunday, when the children were at the Blue House, she took their measurements, made a note of their heights, and started to knit the jumpers to the styles and patterns she had been planning in her head.

Nainai knitted non-stop, barely noticing if it was night or day. Sometimes, she would knit half a jumper, and decide it was not turning out as she had imagined. Without a moment's hesitation, she would unravel it and start again. Mrs Hu and Mrs Song watched with mixed emotions. They felt sorry for Nainai, but didn't understand why she was unravelling a perfectly good piece of knitting.

"It was beautiful!"

"But not beautiful enough," said Nainai, shaking her head.

When Nainai finished a jumper, she didn't give it to the designated child straight away, but hung it up on a clothes hanger next to the other ones, which she stopped to admire from time to time.

Mrs Hu and Mrs Song would also take a break from their work now and then, and go and look at the jumpers. They had never seen such beautiful jumpers before, and could think of no better word to express their admiration.

"Beautiful!"

"So beautiful!"

Nainai was delighted to hear their praise.

Nainai knitted and knitted. But there was still not enough wool. Just as she was planning to unravel another of her jumpers, her daughter, Xiaogu, turned up at the house with four big balls of wool. She held them up to show Nainai. Her mother knew at a glance where they had come from. "You've unravelled the jumper that I knitted for you?"

"Mama, you can't unravel all your jumpers. You need to keep one or two for yourself," said Xiaogu.

"But you loved that jumper!" Nainai looked at the four balls of wool in Xiaogu's hands. She felt a pang in her heart as tears welled up in her eyes. She tried to focus on the four enormous fluffy balls of wool.

Nainai knitted for several days in a row. When she was too tired to keep sitting up straight in a chair, she moved to her bed, and with her back supported, she carried on knitting. Finally, the ten jumpers were ready. As there was some wool left over, Nainai took out a small amount of money, went to the store and bought a little more wool, enough to knit an extra sleeveless vest for Ah Mei.

She knitted through the night to finish the vest, falling asleep in her chair just before dawn.

*　*　*

And then Sunday came.

When the children put on the jumpers that Nainai had made for them, the whole world seemed to change – it was so colourful, so bright, so beautiful.

Mrs Hu and Mrs Song stood, gaping in awe. They had never seen anything like it.

Ah Mei's jumper was patterned, and it looked even more eye-catching surrounded by the boys' jumpers. She knew it was beautiful. She wore that patterned jumper with the sweetest smile on her face and looked lovelier than ever.

In their new jumpers, the children didn't race around the garden and make their usual racket. They were worried the jumpers might get dirty, and all of them seemed a bit awkward, not quite sure what to do with their hands and feet.

Nainai could see this. She laughed and said, "Come on, let's go out!"

And so they went out, with Nainai leading the way.

It was autumn now, and the sunlight was almost blinding. The wind was blowing off the Huangpu River, and the wutong trees lining both sides of the road were beginning to drop their leaves. The children walked behind Nainai, the leaves swirling around them, this colourful little procession breaking through the bleakness and chill of the Shanghai autumn.

CHAPTER 6

A Wet Afternoon

Yeye still worked at the silk company, although he was no longer the boss, just an ordinary employee. People at all levels of the company were very polite to this "easy-going" and "open-minded" old man, and Yeye seemed happy with the situation, except for the low wage he received every month. In reality, his pay was quite high compared with the other workers', but it was almost nothing compared with the rolling flow of money he'd known in the past. He made some adjustments. He had been a cigar smoker before, but now he smoked a pipe. Tobacco wasn't expensive, but even so, Yeye had to use it sparingly. Each month, he kept only a small amount of money for himself, and handed the rest to Nainai. And each time he handed his pitiful pay to Nainai, he would say the same thing: "Océane, I'm sorry." And she would smile and say, "It's enough." She would count it out, then take a few coins and tuck them into Yeye's jacket pocket. "Get some decent tobacco – I can't stand the smell of that cheap stuff," she'd say, waving her hand in front of her nose. "It's just awful."

Nainai found a job as an editor for a publishing house, proofreading translations of novels from French into Chinese. She'd return from work with a huge stack of paper, then put on her glasses and check the translations carefully, losing all track of time, and working late into the night.

She also looked after Ah Mei until she was old enough to go to school.

Ah Mei was a sensible girl, and when Nainai was working, she would either go to the market with Mrs Hu, or play quietly by herself in Nainai's room, taking care not to disturb her grandmother. Nainai liked to keep Ah Mei in sight, and she would often call out, "What are you doing, Ah Mei?" to check up on her granddaughter. And Ah Mei would always respond promptly. When her eyes were tired, Nainai would take off her glasses and rub her eyes, then she'd walk over to where Ah Mei was whispering with her doll, pick her up and take her for a walk around the garden. If she had time to spare, she'd take Ah Mei out. Just down the road, after the turning, there was a tiny patisserie. Ah Mei knew whenever they went out for a walk that they would be going there, and that Nainai would buy her a tiny cream cake. Ah Mei loved it at the little cake shop. She would raise her arm and offer Nainai some of her cake. Nainai would pretend to take a bite, and say, "Mmm, what a lovely buttery flavour!" Then, with a grin so big that it squeezed her eyes shut, she would watch as Ah Mei ate the cake. When she saw the look of satisfaction on Ah Mei's face, she'd say, "I'll have to bring you here again." And Ah Mei, licking the cream from her lips with her little red tongue, would nod enthusiastically.

Ah Mei had noticed that their visits to the patisserie had become fewer and fewer, that the gaps between visits had grown longer and longer. She mentioned it a few times, and each time, Nainai put on a surprised face. "Now, how could I forget something as important as that!" After a while, Ah Mei stopped mentioning the patisserie, but she still thought about it. She missed the little cakes, but mainly she missed the joy of going there with Nainai, and the warm feeling she had as Nainai watched her eating her cake.

One morning when they were out walking, Nainai said she wanted to take Ah Mei to the patisserie.

"Nainai, I don't want to eat cake any more," said Ah Mei.

"Why ever not? I thought you liked going to the patisserie," said Nainai, pointing up ahead.

Ah Mei leaned against a tree. "I don't like cake any more."

It seemed that Nainai could read Ah Mei's mind. She went over to the litte girl, crouched down and patted her cheeks, before picking her up and carrying her into the patisserie. Nainai's heart was aching.

This time, Ah Mei ate her cake very slowly.

As she ate, she thought about what she had seen two days earlier, when Nainai had gone to make a cup of coffee after lunch. She had taken the coffee beans out of the tin and stared at them as though in a trance. She spent a long time looking at them, and eventually scooped up half the beans with the coffee scoop, and poured them back into the tin, which sounded as if it was almost empty.

Ah Mei finally finished her cake, but this time her

expression was not one of contentment as it had been before. Instead, it was wooden.

Although Ah Mei was only five, she understood a lot of things. She knew this would be her last visit to the patisserie. She didn't want to go there ever again. If they were going out and she knew they'd have to walk past it, she would suggest a different route.

A few hours after Nainai and Ah Mei had visited the patisserie for the last time, Yeye discovered that Nainai was going to the pawn shop.

He had realized that Nainai wasn't at home, and had asked Mrs Hu where she'd gone.

"Madam was heading east, I think," she answered.

As he was free that day, Yeye thought he'd go and meet her. He'd always loved walking with Nainai. Many years had passed, and there'd been children, and now grandchildren, but just like in Marseilles and Lyons all those years ago, as soon as they stepped outside together, off they'd walk, arm in arm. The only difference now was that they were getting slower, and it looked more like they were supporting each other.

That afternoon, there was an autumn wind blowing in Shanghai. Yeye looked forward to walking with Nainai, letting the wind catch their hair and their clothes. He thought about all the times they'd walked together in the wind: along the edge of the blue sea in Marseilles, on Nanjing Road heading towards the river, on the banks of the Huangpu…

Finally, Yeye spotted her in the distance, but when he

saw her, he froze. Nainai was coming out of a pawn shop, keeping her eyes down as she negotiated the steps, one at a time, her legs and feet much stiffer than he'd just been remembering.

Yeye went to help her down the last step. He didn't say anything, just put his hand on his waist, allowing Nainai to slip her hand through the crook in his arm, as naturally as ever. They didn't go straight home, but followed the road east for a while, towards the Huangpu.

The wind gradually grew stronger.

Yeye held Nainai's arm tightly. They walked side by side, and when the wind blew hard, he turned his body to shield her, moving back to her side when the wind subsided.

In the distance they could hear the ships' whistles blasting. The sound seemed to quiver in the strong wind.

They walked as far as the Bund, and sat down on the steps.

Nainai leaned her head against Yeye's shoulder.

They didn't speak, just gazed at the smoky haze that hung over the river in the distance.

That night, Yeye waited until Nainai was asleep, then he crept out of bed. He selected a dozen or more items from around the house: antiques, calligraphy, paintings, the woollen coat he'd worn as a seaman, and some of his late father's things. He gathered them together and put them in the wardrobe. The next day, he opened the wardrobe door and told Nainai, "I won't let you pawn any more of your things. Your fur coat is missing from the wardrobe, the ring your mother gave you is missing from your finger, and now I know why. From today, if we have to pawn something, we can use these. Don't feel bad about taking them. They used to mean something to me, but they don't any more. They're just things we happen to have in the house."

Mrs Hu had known for a while that Nainai had been going to the pawn shop. One evening about six months earlier, she had told Nainai that she'd been thinking for some time about leaving the Blue House. She said her son had a new baby, and the family wanted her to look after her grandson.

Nainai shook her head. "That's not the real reason, is it." Then she said to Mrs Hu, "I hear that life in the countryside is very hard. I couldn't send you to hardship, after all you have done for us." She reassured Mrs Hu, "I know life here isn't like it was, but we can manage. As long as you're here, you'll be able to earn some money. It may not be much, but for your family in the countryside it will make a difference. Please don't think about leaving, I'm sure we can find a way. What's more, Ah Mei is still very young, and you've looked after her since she was born. She can't live without you." Eventually Mrs Hu agreed to stay.

But now, after hesitating for several days, Nainai had to speak to Mrs Hu and Mrs Song and tell them that she had no choice but to let one of them go. Dagu was seriously ill in hospital, and Nainai, having pawned everything in the wardrobe, was now using the little that was left of her savings. She was having sleepless nights worrying about the future. They simply couldn't afford to keep both Mrs Hu and Mrs Song, but she couldn't bring herself to tell them. She kept putting it off.

"How can I tell them?" she asked Yeye.

"I don't know, it just feels so unfair," Yeye sighed. "They've both been with us for so many years they're like family now. But we have no choice. Perhaps I should do it."

Nainai shook her head. She would do it.

That afternoon, Nainai finally called Mrs Hu and Mrs Song into the lounge downstairs, and told them of the decision she had to make. Nainai was clearly very uncomfortable, the difficulty of the task showing in her face. She could barely bring herself to meet their eyes.

Mrs Hu and Mrs Song listened. It didn't come as a shock; the thought of leaving had been preying on their minds for a while now. The pressure on the Blue House was growing by the day; they could see it with their own eyes. But the pressure was growing in the countryside, too, and the money they received every month was more vital than ever. They appreciated that Nainai had continued to pay their wages on the same day each month, but the money wasn't the only reason they had stayed – they simply couldn't bear to leave the Blue House, to leave Nainai and her family. They knew every chopstick and every spoon in this house, they knew the family inside out. They liked this home, they loved this home. All year round, their hands and feet never stopped moving, as they worked to keep the Blue House neat and tidy, clean and fresh.

As money became tighter, they had found ingenious ways of minimizing the family expenses. Mrs Hu went to the market several times a day, walking around, comparing prices so she could buy from the cheapest trader, and even then she haggled. The sellers knew she was a servant. "It's not even your money! Do you have to be so tight?" And Mrs Hu would laugh, "Every little helps." At these times, she didn't seem like a servant, but more like the head of the family – she was a meticulous housekeeper. Yeye and Ah Mei both liked to eat green soya beans, and you could buy them ready-shelled, but Mrs Hu worked out that if she bought them still in the pods and shelled them herself at home, she could save five *fen* per *jin* of beans. When Nainai asked why she didn't buy them ready-shelled, Mrs Hu said, "It's fun shelling beans together." She glanced round at Ah Mei. "Ah Mei thinks it's fun, don't you?" And Nainai had found she enjoyed shelling beans too, chatting and laughing with Mrs Hu and Mrs Song, and praising Ah Mei: "You do it so fast and so well!"

Nainai had never thought of Mrs Hu and Mrs Song as servants; they were more like sisters. And they didn't think of themselves as servants either. It felt as though they had been there as long as the Blue House had stood on this street, and that they and the Blue House had come into this world together.

The atmosphere in the lounge was strained.

Ah Mei, who was naturally sensitive, felt it straight away. She was sitting on the floor, playing with her doll, but she stopped to peer up at the three adults, her long eyelashes fluttering as she blinked, her eyes scanning their faces. She looked at Nainai, Mrs Hu, Mrs Song, then at Nainai again.

Mrs Hu broke the silence. "Madam," she said, smiling,

"there's no need to feel uncomfortable. You've kept me on all these years, and I cannot thank you enough. Life at the Blue House is harder than before, and Mrs Song and I are well aware of this. We think about it all the time, every day, every night, worrying and fretting about it. Madam, you smile all day long, but we know how painful it must be for you. Every day we are here is a burden on you. Please don't worry about us. I'm from the countryside and I've been through hard times before. I'll return home and work on the land. I won't starve. I'll count my blessings and look after my grandson, keep chickens and ducks and pigs! But I'll miss you – this place, Sir, Madam, Ah Mei…" Mrs Hu turned to Ah Mei and clapped her hands, beckoning, and when Ah Mei ran over, she scooped her up in her arms, pressing her face against Ah Mei's – one face covered in lines, the other soft and smooth. "I've never known such an adorable child…"

A moment or two later, Ah Mei felt something wet on her face – Mrs Hu's silent tears.

Then it was Mrs Song's turn to speak. She said a lot, much of it to reassure Nainai. She didn't want Nainai to feel bad, or for her to worry about them in the future. Heaven would provide. But the Blue House held a place deep in her heart, and she would miss the house, and Yeye, Nainai, Ah Mei and everyone here. "Your family are such good people, the best in the world," she said, over and over again.

Mrs Hu and Mrs Song expressed their appreciation of Nainai with total sincerity. They were from the countryside, and their language reflected this. They loved her blue eyes, the high bridge of her nose, her hair the colour of wheat, her tall, elegant figure, her beautiful pale skin. From the moment they first saw her, she had taken root in their hearts. She looked so different, and yet there was no barrier between them, no sense of being strangers. When the two women were chatting, and Nainai came up in the conversation, Mrs Hu had always said, "I feel we know each other from a previous life." And Mrs Song agreed. She felt the same.

Nainai smiled throughout, the same smile that Mrs Hu and Mrs Song knew so well – a smile that was calm, warm, pure and understanding. At the same time, there was a slight awkwardness in that smile – a girlish awkwardness that she still had, despite her age, despite the visible slackening of the skin on her neck and arms.

They talked about the past, the present and the future, about many, many things, with tears streaming down their faces.

Seeing the three of them in tears, Ah Mei started to cry too. She didn't really understand what their tears were about, but it upset her to see them like this.

Mrs Hu quickly wiped away Ah Mei's tears with her sleeve. "What have you got to cry about, child!"

It made Ah Mei cry even more.

The three women started to laugh – big, booming laughs, which sent their tears rolling into their wrinkles.

It turned out to be a very wet afternoon indeed.

CHAPTER 7

Qipao

"You stay," said Mrs Hu.

"No, you stay," said Mrs Song.

"Your family needs it more than mine," said Mrs Hu. "My family is south of the Yangtze, in Jiangnan. Yours is north of the Yangtze, in Jiangbei. Life's harder north of the river."

"Your husband is asthmatic and is confined to his bed six months of the year," said Mrs Song.

Mrs Hu and Mrs Song each came up with countless reasons why the other should stay at the Blue House. Neither of them was prepared to give in. "In that case…" said Mrs Song, and she called for Ah Mei. She led her into another room, and took two of Ah Mei's favourite tops out of the wardrobe. One was bright pink, the other was pale green. "Ah Mei, in a moment, I'm going to leave the room. I want you to choose one of these tops and put it on. When you've done that, I want you to call out, 'Ready!'"

Ah Mei looked quizzically at Mrs Song.

Mrs Song sighed. "It's the only way. Ah Mei, I want you to

stay there until I tell you to come out, do you understand?"

Ah Mei nodded.

Mrs Song walked out of the room, closing the door behind her, and went back to Mrs Hu. "We have to come to a decision," she said, and told Mrs Hu her plan. "In a few minutes, when Ah Mei comes out, if she is wearing the pink top, then you'll stay, and if she is wearing the green top, then I'll stay. Would you agree to this?"

Mrs Hu thought about it and nodded.

"I'm ready!" Ah Mei called from the other room.

"Give us another minute, Ah Mei," said Mrs Song. She looked at Mrs Hu. "Do you give your word? There's no going back."

Mrs Hu nodded.

Mrs Song repeated to Mrs Hu what they had agreed: "If Ah Mei is wearing the pink top, then you'll stay. If she is wearing the green top, then I'll stay." Then she went to the door and called out, "Ah Mei, I gave you two tops and asked you to choose one of them. Did you choose it all by yourself with no help from me?"

"Yes!" said the voice behind the door.

"And are you wearing the one you chose?" asked Mrs Song.

"Yes," said the voice behind the door.

Ah Mei wondered what kind of game Mrs Song and Mrs Hu were playing with her.

"And did I see which top you chose before I left the room?" asked Mrs Song.

"No!" said the voice behind the door. "Can I come out now?"

"Yes, you can come out now," said Mrs Song.

The door opened. Ah Mei was wearing the pink top. She looked at Mrs Hu, then at Mrs Song, and wondered what would happen next in this game. Then Mrs Song said, "Ah Mei, run along and play. Mrs Hu and I need to have a little chat."

Ah Mei walked away, pulling a face. It wasn't much of a game after all.

The two women watched as Ah Mei toddled off, and laughed. But as they laughed, the tears started to flow again.

"We gave our word, and there's no going back," said Mrs Song. "Let's go and tell Madam our answer."

Mrs Hu had to be dragged by the arm all the way to the study on the first floor, where Nainai was usually to be found, proofreading translations.

Mrs Song spoke first. "We've discussed it and agreed that Mrs Hu will stay."

Mrs Hu wanted to speak, but Mrs Song pushed her back.

"You pay our wages at the beginning of the month. It's the beginning of the month now, and I've already been paid, so I'll work to the end of the month and then leave."

Nainai nodded. "But please, stay as long as you can."

From that day on, Mrs Song spent most of the time in her room. When Nainai asked what she was doing, she answered vaguely, "A few sewing jobs."

Mrs Hu and Mrs Song had different responsibilities in the house. Mrs Hu looked after the food shopping and the cooking. Mrs Song looked after the family's clothes – she did the washing and starching, the sewing and the mending. Mrs Song was a dab hand with a needle and thread. From the oldest to the youngest, everyone in the family wore clothes made by Mrs Song. She had nimble fingers.

"It's never-ending with sewing. Once you start, the jobs keep on coming," said Nainai. "Do what you can, but don't work all night."

The skin around Mrs Song's eyes grew darker by the day. You could tell at a glance that she was working through the night.

One day, Ah Mei went into Mrs Song's room. She saw what Mrs Song was working on, and said, "You're making a qipao for Nainai."

Mrs Song was surprised. "Well I never. How on earth did you guess?"

"I just knew," said Ah Mei smugly. "Nainai loves wearing qipao. She says that I can wear one when I grow up, and that I'll look lovely."

"I'll remember that, Ah Mei. When you're grown up, I'll make you lots of qipao, so you can wear them all year round." Mrs Song rested her sewing on her lap, and said to Ah Mei, "Ah Mei, promise me you won't say anything to Nainai?"

Ah Mei nodded.

Mrs Song continued, "There isn't a woman in this world who looks as beautiful in a qipao as your nainai. It's as though she was born to wear them. I want to make her a few before I go."

Ah Mei knew that Mrs Song would be leaving them soon. She wanted to stay in Mrs Song's room. "I'll be quiet," she said.

"Of course you can stay. I don't know when I'll see you again." Mrs Song's nose started tingling, and she became red around the eyes.

"Nainai said she'll take me to the countryside to visit you," Ah Mei comforted Mrs Song.

Mrs Song chatted with Ah Mei as she sewed. "You can come to my place in the summer holidays. There are lots of rivers – big ones and little ones – and there are so many bridges – high bridges, low bridges, long bridges, short bridges. You have to cross at least five bridges if you want to go anywhere! As soon as you step outside, you see water, and boats and sails, and big fish leaping up and then splashing back into the water. At night, when you lie in bed, you can hear the river flowing, and the sound of oars pulling through the water, as people row their boats through the night. There are reeds growing everywhere, and when they flower in the autumn, they look so beautiful. Then the wind blows them all over the place, and the feathery bits land on your clothes and in your hair. Ah Mei, will you promise to come and see me?"

"Yes."

"I'll remember your promise. Will you promise me something else?" She raised her head and looked straight at Ah Mei.

Tell me, Ah Mei answered with her eyes.

"Promise me, Ah Mei, that when you grow up, you will look after Nainai."

Ah Mei nodded, again and again.

Mrs Song laughed. "There's no need to keep nodding! Once is enough. I believe you. You won't find a nainai as good as yours anywhere else in this world."

Mrs Song stopped sewing, and looked at Ah Mei. She blinked a few times: all those months and years she'd spent with Nainai passed before her eyes.

"I feel blessed to know your nainai," she said. "I'm going to miss her when I leave. I'll miss her very much."

Ah Mei nodded.

"Of all her children and grandchildren, do you know which one she likes best?"

"Me," said Ah Mei.

"How do you know?"

"I just do."

"It's true, you're her favourite. Mrs Hu and I could see that from the beginning. You look like her, and you have exactly the same spirit."

Mrs Song kept talking – about this and that – her needle and thread moving in and out of the qipao.

The day Mrs Song left, she slipped her hands under three carefully folded qipao, walked into Nainai's study and stood in front of her. Nainai was at her table proofreading texts. When she heard footsteps, she looked up and peered over the top of her glasses at the qipao in Mrs Song's hands. She took off her glasses and placed them gently on the table. But she did not take her eyes off the qipao.

"Madam."

"What's that in your hands?"

"Take a look."

"Qipao?"

"Yes, qipao."

Nainai stood up, walked towards Mrs Song and held out her hands.

Mrs Song gently moved the qipao into Nainai's hands.

"All that time when you said you were doing sewing jobs in your room, were you making these?"

"I'm leaving," said Mrs Song, "so I thought I'd make a few for you. Do you know how beautiful you look in a qipao? When you step out of the house, the entire street looks at you. Nothing can hold their attention like you do."

Nainai smiled.

"Put them away for now. There are three of them. You won't need to try them on; I know your size, and I guarantee they'll fit nicely. You have such a lovely figure – you were made to wear qipao."

"Where did you get the material?"

"You gave it to me a while ago. But I'm from the country-side. I grew up wearing rough cotton clothes. I can't wear fine material like this. So I kept it, in case you could use it one day. And here it is. It's first-class material, and it will suit you perfectly."

Nainai's hands were trembling, as though the three qipao were weighing her down.

After Mrs Song left the room, Nainai unfolded the qipao. One by one, she put each qipao onto a coathanger, holding it up and admiring it. She loved all of them.

The first time Nainai had worn a qipao, she had seen a new version of herself in the mirror. It had been such a surprise. Caught up in the moment, she had stared at her reflection for a long time, then turned to face Yeye, who was looking on from the side. "Could it be that I have travelled a thousand miles across oceans and seas because a qipao was waiting for me?"

Yeye looked at her. His words of appreciation were exactly the same as Ah Mei's: "You look beautiful!"

"Is that all you can say?" asked Nainai.

"No words can express how beautiful you look."

Mrs Song had made her many beautiful qipao over the years. Mrs Song was from the countryside. She didn't wear this style of dress, or know its origins – "It must have floated down from heaven," she told Mrs Hu – but she had a gift for making them. When she took out her needle and thread, everyone knew the result would be stunning. She made one after another for Nainai. Nainai would take her to the draper's to choose the material, and they would often travel all over Shanghai to get exactly what they needed.

When Nainai went out in a qipao, people would stop her in the street and ask who made such beautiful clothes. And to their surprise and envy, she would answer, "Mrs Song, at home."

But now Mrs Song was about to leave. Nainai gazed at the qipao. She was so sorry to lose Mrs Song. She couldn't bear it.

Ah Mei had been playing in the garden. She ran into Nainai's study. Nainai wrapped her arms around her granddaughter, and rested her elegant chin gently on Ah Mei's head. She still hadn't taken her eyes off the qipao.

"Oh, they're beautiful!" said Ah Mei.

Nainai nodded gently. "Mrs Song's leaving tomorrow…"

Ah Mei felt hot wet tears fall into her hair. She tried to look up at Nainai, but Nainai's chin was still resting on her head. Her gaze fell where Nainai's gaze was, on the beautiful qipao.

CHAPTER 8

Red Oil-Paper Umbrellas

Life was getting harder. It was becoming more and more difficult to keep up the old lifestyle at the Blue House. The entire family had cut back on clothes and food. By the time Ah Mei started school, famine was creeping across China; there was suffering in cities and villages. Shanghai was no exception: like flowers after the storm, the once vibrant Shanghai was withering and dying. In the past, when children saw soft clouds in the sky, they thought of candyfloss; now they stared blankly, and watched them drift by.

One day, Nainai and Ah Mei bought five oranges at the fruit store, and were on their way home when they saw a boy, filthy from head to toe, rummaging through the bins for something to eat. When he heard their footsteps, he looked up at them with big, hungry eyes, and spotted the orange in Ah Mei's hand. She hid it behind her back, as though his gaze might scoop it away. They continued walking, but kept glancing back at the boy. He was standing by the bin, watching them. Nainai and Ah Mei walked more and more slowly, and eventually came to a stop. "Let's give him your orange," said Nainai, and before she had finished speaking, Ah Mei was running back towards the boy, holding the orange up in the air. It glistened in the sunlight. When Ah Mei was back by her grandmother's side, Nainai took her hand, and gave a long sigh.

Although times were hard, Nainai put on a brave face … and smiled.

Nainai refused to let life at the Blue House deteriorate overnight. She took a few items to the pawn shop every so often, and was very careful with the housekeeping. Like two of a kind, she and Mrs Hu kept track of every penny they spent, and made every penny count. If daily life could no longer be like before, at least they could ensure that everyone enjoyed a little elegance and style now and again. In Nainai's mind, one's quality of life depended on one's attitude. She would not let the Blue House become dark and miserable. The night lights would continue to shine in the garden. The children would have presents at Chinese New Year. And no matter how poor they were, they would wake up to find sweets in their stockings at Christmas. Ah Mei would go to school looking immaculate. Nainai could not bear the thought of Ah Mei turning up at school in clothes with patches on them. Ah Mei was growing, but they couldn't keep buying new clothes for her, so Nainai took some of the clothes she had brought with her from France out of the wardrobe. Together with Mrs Hu, she worked out how to restyle the clothes, and then Mrs Hu adapted them for Ah Mei. As a result, Ah Mei always had a "foreign" air about her.

And they would drink coffee. It was important to Nainai, even if it was only once a week. Yeye, Baba and Mama would go to great lengths to source coffee beans. They still used the coffee pot they had brought with them from France. It was old and shabby now, but Nainai was still very fond of it. She thought it was the best of its kind, both in design and in the quality of material it was made from. She had never seen another coffee pot that touched her heart quite like this one. As far as Nainai was concerned, if it wasn't made in this pot, it wasn't coffee.

Yeye and Nainai drank coffee on Sundays, either before breakfast or after lunch. Sometimes Baba and Mama joined them, but usually it was just the two of them. When the weather was warm, they'd have their coffee on the verandah, or in the garden. They'd take it outside on an exquisite tray with a matching set of exquisite cups. And they used exquisite spoons to stir their coffee, slowly and gently. They drank the coffee leisurely, as though the passing of time was irrelevant to them.

Ah Mei liked the smell of coffee. "Mmm, that smells good," she would say, sniffing the air. But when Nainai gave her a spoonful to taste, she screwed up her nose, and cried, "Ugh, that's bitter!" Yeye and Nainai laughed. They took their coffee-drinking seriously, and found great pleasure in it. And it touched Ah Mei that they did. Later, when Ah Mei was grown up, she would find that these memories of Yeye and Nainai had infused something into her blood. She couldn't articulate what, but it felt very special.

As Yeye and Nainai drank their coffee, they would recall

again and again the tiny café on the corner of the street in Marseilles. They would describe its appearance, its colour and its warmth. They couldn't always remember everything precisely, and when they argued over some detail or another, Ah Mei would drop the homework she was doing upstairs, and, leaning her head on her hand, she would call out from the window, "Nainai's right."

Yeye would look up, and say, "You weren't even there!"

"But Nainai's told me this story countless times."

It was as though Ah Mei had been to Marseilles, and had visited the little café on the corner.

"What Nainai says is right." She knew that when they argued, it always ended with Yeye acknowledging that Nainai's memory was more accurate.

Sometimes Yeye and Nainai would sit for a long time without talking, just quietly stirring their coffee, dreaming about the little café.

Eventually, one of them would sigh and say, "We don't even know if the café's still there."

Nainai's eyes would glisten with tears.

Then Yeye would change the subject: "Whose pigeon is that up there? It makes such a lovely cooing sound!" or "Look at Ah Mei sticking her bottom up in the air, just like you do!" which made Nainai blush, and glance around at Ah Mei to check if she'd heard.

In those difficult times, Nainai paid attention to her Sunday coffee, and to her appearance. She made sure she looked smart when she went out. Her clothes might be a little shabby, but Mrs Hu would iron them well. All year round, whatever the season, whatever the weather, whenever Nainai left the house, she was impeccably dressed. She would not let standards slip.

Nainai liked rainy days best of all because on rainy days she could put up her red oil-paper umbrella. Nainai had loved these umbrellas since the first time she'd seen one – she had not been able to take her eyes off the tall, slim young woman with a red oil-paper umbrella that miserable drizzly afternoon. The scene was like a painting, a scene that could only appear under a Chinese sky. It had never occurred to Nainai that an umbrella could be so beautiful. The young woman seemed to know how beautiful it was, and to know that its beauty was enhanced by the elegant way she held it, and the elegant way she walked with it. As she passed Nainai, the umbrella tilted slightly behind her, and Nainai caught a glimpse of her face in the rosy glow, which was like the glow of a gorgeous sunset, or a beautiful flower. And when the young woman walked on, Nainai turned and watched the umbrella slowly disappear into the distance.

That very same day, Nainai had asked Yeye to go shopping with her. They went to a few umbrella shops and selected an oil-paper umbrella in a perfect shade of red. After that, Nainai had always used a red oil-paper umbrella when it rained. She had gone through more of them than she could remember. Once, when Mrs Hu saw Nainai coming home in the rain, her umbrella blown to shreds by the wind, she had said, "Why not use an oil-cloth umbrella instead? They last longer." But Nainai had shaken her head. "I love my red oil-paper one."

When Ah Mei started school, Nainai could indulge her childlike love of the rain, because on wet days she could use her red umbrella when she went to collect Ah Mei from school. She would take a red oil-paper umbrella for Ah Mei too, a very small one, with a matching red handle.

She would arrive at the school gates early, and stand in the rain, waiting for Ah Mei. There would be water splashing all around her. The rain would bounce off her umbrella, then fall again, and roll across the oiled paper before splashing on the ground. When there was rain but no wind, the raindrops would fall like a curtain of flowing beads that swayed at the slightest breeze. Sometimes, while Nainai was watching, the curtain of raindrops would start to blur, or appear to stop in mid-air. It was an illusion, of course; the rain was still falling. At such times, there would be an inexplicable sadness in Nainai's eyes.

Old Mr Jin, the caretaker, had stopped offering her shelter in his office and opening the door to let her into the school corridor. He had asked her a few times before, but Nainai had smiled and refused politely. And after that, when Nainai appeared at the school gate holding her red oil-paper umbrella, old Mr Jin would simply watch her quietly through the window. He didn't think she was strange – if anything, she was like one of the trees, and there was nothing wrong with trees, was there? But it was a big, empty space, and she looked rather forlorn, and sometimes he'd sigh, and feel like opening the window and calling, "It's cold out there in the rain, come and wait inside till the children come out." But he didn't open the window, and just watched her instead.

Nainai's red umbrella looked particularly bright and shiny from having been washed by the rain so many times.

The children would finally pour out of school, and run higgledy-piggledy to the gate, like ducks leaving their pen.

Nainai never had any trouble spotting Ah Mei. She didn't go up to greet her, but waited under her umbrella, watching Ah Mei flinch at the threads of rain in the sky. Nainai would feel a rush of joy and love, in anticipation of what would come next.

It was always the same. As soon as Ah Mei saw the red umbrella, she leaped through the rain like a little frog, with her school bag on her back. Every now and then, she gave a little wave to Nainai. She loved the rain even more than her grandmother did, because she knew Nainai would be there waiting for her by the school gate. She knew that when it rained, Nainai would arrive early and stand by the entrance. Ah Mei loved to see Nainai waiting for her with her red oil-paper umbrella. She would picture the scene while she was still in class.

The other children loved to see Nainai and her red umbrella too. When it rained, they didn't think about their own families waiting outside, only about the red oil-paper umbrella. And even when they were standing under their own umbrellas, they still turned and looked enviously at the red umbrella with Ah Mei's grandmother standing beneath it. They were intrigued that she was always smiling.

When Ah Mei was about seven or eight steps from Nainai, a second little red umbrella always popped open.

Ah Mei rushed over and took the umbrella from Nainai's

hand. She looked back, glanced around, and when she was sure none of the children would hear, whispered, "Océane."

Nainai leaned forward, pressed her cheek gently against Ah Mei's moist little face and replied, "Aina."

Nainai and Ah Mei had a pact: when it was just the two of them, Ah Mei called Nainai by her French name, "Océane". And Nainai called Ah Mei "Aina", the French name that she had chosen for her. She had wanted her granddaughter to have a French name as well as a Chinese one. Ah Mei liked this name, and kept it a secret. She used it to refer to herself whenever she could: "Aina, it's time to do your homework", "Aina, it's time to go to bed now", "Aina, look how dirty your hands are!" No one else in the house, not even Yeye, Baba or Mama, knew that Ah Mei had a French name. It was a secret that she and Nainai shared.

It felt so special when Nainai called her Aina, with a twinkle in her eye.

Gradually, the school playground emptied, and Nainai and Ah Mei set off for home too, each holding her red oil-paper umbrella. They didn't hurry. As though going for a stroll, they walked down the main roads, the buildings towering on one side of them, the trams clanging on the other, and the ships' whistles blasting on the river and sending tremors through the curtains of rain.

"Océane," Ah Mei said, for no particular reason.

"Aina," Nainai answered, knowing that was all that was wanted.

They repeated this exchange a few times, Ah Mei looking up, and Nainai looking down. When a tram passed them, the faces looking out saw two red oil-paper umbrellas, one large, one small, one short, one tall.

Although it was raining, it was still afternoon, and the sky was not dark. Against the grey and sandy-coloured walls, the two red oil-paper umbrellas seemed brighter than ever. The little red umbrella darted in front of the large red umbrella, and behind it, but mostly they were side by side, the little one tucked under the big one.

Most people avoided the rain, and those that couldn't were rushing about purposefully. Nainai would pull Ah Mei out of their way, or Ah Mei would duck behind Nainai's back, and when they dodged people like that, one or other of the red umbrellas would swerve, and wobble in the air for a moment, like a kite about to fall.

In the past they might have stopped at the little patisserie – it was a shame those visits had stopped. When the patisserie came into view, Ah Mei would say, "Océane!"

"Yes?" Nainai would ask, pretending not to know.

Ah Mei would lick her lips and smile at Nainai.

And Nainai would say, "Greedy puss!" and move her umbrella from one hand to the other, and pat Ah Mei on the head with her newly freed hand.

As they approached the patisserie, the little red umbrella would fly ahead, and by the time the big red umbrella reached the door, the woman in the shop would have collapsed the little one and put it in a tall porcelain vase.

Nainai would buy Ah Mei a tiny cake. They were never in a hurry, and would choose seats by the window. Nainai would watch Ah Mei eat. And, as usual, Ah Mei would offer her a forkful of cake. "Thank you, Aina," she would say quietly. Ah Mei would watch Nainai eat, her mouth moving and twisting, and smiling so sweetly – she looked more like a girl eating honey than a grandmother eating cake. They would stay in the warm little patisserie on the corner of the street until the rain stopped.

Nainai remembered with sadness that one afternoon, when the whole of Shanghai was shrouded in mist and mizzle and the two of them were walking home from school, Ah Mei started to slow down as they approached the patisserie. She didn't call out "Oceane!" like she used to, but trailed behind. When Nainai glanced back and called, "Aina!" the little red umbrella glinted as she ran to catch up, but soon slowed down again.

As soon as she saw the patisserie, Ah Mei held her umbrella upright, and ran as fast as she could, straight past the shop. And as soon as it was out of sight, she stopped under a wutong tree and waited for Nainai, tilting her umbrella, perhaps to gain a better view of Nainai, or perhaps to feel the raindrops on her face. There was an autumn wind. The chill rain ran across her face and trickled down her neck, sending shivers down her spine. By the time Nainai reached the wutong tree, Ah Mei's hair was wet through.

Nainai straightened Ah Mei's umbrella. "You silly thing."

She didn't ask Ah Mei why she had run on ahead. She knew Ah Mei was saying goodbye to the patisserie. Nainai's heart stung with regret. All the way she had been clasping a few coins in her hand, deep in her pocket, intending to buy a cake for Ah Mei today. As her hands let go of the coins, she felt a tightening around her heart. She reached for Ah Mei's umbrella, collapsed it, put her arm around Ah Mei, drawing her granddaughter close, and held the big umbrella over them both.

They walked on, Nainai's arm around Ah Mei's shoulder.

Nainai felt that her granddaughter – Ah Mei, Aina – was just like her.

Afterwards, it was as though the patisserie no longer existed, except as a memory that Ah Mei would cherish for the rest of her life.

But Ah Mei and Nainai still had their red oil-paper umbrellas, and on wet days they held them up in the rain as they walked through the main streets and the little alleys, through the hustle and bustle, and the peace and quiet. And Ah Mei wondered if in years to come, when she was grown up, and as old as Nainai – perhaps even older – she would still use a red oil-paper umbrella on rainy days?

Thunder rumbled through the sky over Shanghai. The low sonorous moan rolled over the Huangpu, and over the city. Lightning flashed like a sword splitting the sky. Dark clouds surged, rolled and twisted across the sky. The wind began to pick up, and turned violent. Pedestrians walked fast, or ran, keen to get home before the storm broke, or at least find somewhere to shelter from the rain.

Nainai took the two red umbrellas, and hurried to Ah Mei's school.

She didn't have to wait long. By the time they met, it had started to rain, though not too heavily at first. As they hurried on their way, the sky grew dark and heavy. It was terrifying. At this time, on a bright day, they were used to seeing the tall buildings stained red. But now they were darker than the sky, as heavy and black as can be.

"Océane!" Ah Mei kept as close as she could to Nainai.

"Aina, let's get home as fast as we can."

The bright red oil-paper umbrellas looked black too.

The downpour started. Raindrops clattered on the umbrellas like transparent pebbles.

"Océane!"

"I'm here!" said Nainai. "Don't be afraid, Aina. I'm right by your side."

Ah Mei nodded beneath her umbrella.

The pebbles of rain fell faster and faster, louder and louder, as if firecrackers were exploding all over Shanghai. You could hear nothing else. A few people pulled their jackets over their heads, or tried to protect themselves from the rain with an old tin lid or whatever they could find, and began to run through the storm.

Nainai held herself and her red oil-paper umbrella upright.

Ah Mei did the same.

Rainwater flowed down the roads, and poured into drains. At times there was too much water, and with nowhere to go, it swirled round and round.

There was a pigeon that hadn't been able to get home in time. Its wings and body sodden, it was now too heavy to fly. It had fallen to the ground, and after a flurry of wing-flapping, had found a place to shelter from the rain, unperturbed by all the people running past.

Suddenly, the wind swept in from the east, and snatched the umbrella from Ah Mei's hand.

"Océane!" Ah Mei cried out in shock.

She watched it somersault down the street, too absorbed to think of the rain.

Nainai quickly passed her umbrella to Ah Mei. "Aina, child, hold it tight with both hands!" Then she ran through the rain, chasing after Ah Mei's umbrella.

"Océane!" Ah Mei shouted after Nainai, her hands gripping the handle of the big umbrella.

Nainai chased after Ah Mei's little umbrella. She almost caught it a few times, but it was like a living creature rolling out of reach whenever she came close.

Still gripping the big umbrella, Ah Mei ran after Nainai. The wind blew the umbrella inside out and filled the newly formed sail, which swept her westwards at such speed that Ah Mei worried it might sweep her up to the sky. Then she relaxed and let the wind carry her, and somehow managed to keep her feet on the ground.

As Nainai caught hold of Ah Mei's umbrella, a sudden gust of wind snatched both umbrellas away.

This time Ah Mei didn't hesitate.

"Aina!" shouted Nainai.

Ah Mei wiped the rainwater from her eyes with the back of her hand and, without glancing back, ran after Nainai's umbrella. She didn't take her eyes off it for a second. She slipped a few times, but picked herself up straight away.

Finally, Ah Mei caught it. She struggled to hold it upright. Nainai started to giggle at the comical sight of this pale, thin little girl trying to hold up a big red umbrella. With her wet clothes clinging to her body, she looked like a drenched chicken.

"Aina!" Nainai pointed at her granddaughter. She couldn't stop laughing.

Ah Mei looked at Nainai and started to laugh too. Tall, slim Nainai was soaked to the skin, which made her look even taller and slimmer. And there she was, holding a little red umbrella.

"Océane!" Ah Mei was doubled over with laughter, completely obscured by Nainai's umbrella, and as she slowly straightened up, rainwater fell into her mouth, making her splutter and choke.

Nainai quickly crouched down beside her and patted her on the back.

They swapped umbrellas and continued walking. They didn't need the umbrellas; they were already soaked to the skin. But they were determined to walk home, through the rain, holding the umbrellas upright, which they did, laughing and calling each other's name on the way.

The two umbrellas had been soaked and blown about in the storm. Both had been damaged, not once, but several times, and it was not long before they were completely wrecked. Their skeletal frames were broken, and the oil-paper, ripped to shreds, flapped noisily in the wind.

But Ah Mei and Nainai didn't discard the umbrellas. When they looked up, they no longer saw the inside of an umbrella, they saw the sky and threads of rain. They twirled the umbrellas, and spun around, and laughed and laughed.

They were a sight to behold! As they walked home, the windows on both sides of the street filled with faces eager to catch a glimpse of these two figures, one tall, one short, holding up their broken umbrellas so seriously, so properly.

Then, Nainai and Ah Mei started to run. They ran to the house, threw open the door, stepped inside and let the two umbrellas fall to the floor. They couldn't stop laughing.

Mrs Hu hurried over. She took one look at the broken umbrellas, and at Nainai and Ah Mei, standing there, dripping onto the floorboards, and quickly went to fetch a couple of towels.

Nainai and Ah Mei wiped the water from their faces and clothes. They were still laughing.

Mrs Hu got down on her knees. "Two crazy people! One big and one little!" she said, mopping the floor with a dry cloth.

A week later, Nainai took one of her beloved gramophone records to the pawn shop and bought two new red oil-paper umbrellas.

CHAPTER 9

The Little Leather Suitcase

When the family had moved to Shanghai, they had brought a lot of luggage with them, leather suitcases large and small. Apart from the one that Xiaogu had taken, the rest were still at the Blue House. Most of them were full of clothes. Every summer, concerned that they might go mouldy in the humid weather, Mrs Hu would choose a bright sunny day, and take the clothes out of the cases and air them on the verandah and in the garden. The bright colours made a beautiful scene at the Blue House, one that Ah Mei and Nainai both loved. Nainai would look up from her manuscripts to take in the sight. She enjoyed seeing the colours of the clothes as much as Ah Mei did, but she would also go and look at the open suitcases that were airing in the sunshine. The suitcases triggered all kinds of memories for her.

Ah Mei would weave in and out of the clothes. Now and then, she'd hide, and call for Nainai to come and find her.

And Nainai would say, "I can see you!" even when she couldn't see her at all. But Ah Mei didn't know that, and her little face would peep out from between the clothes. Sometimes, Nainai could see exactly where Ah Mei was, and would put down her work, and say, "I wonder where Ah Mei could be?" then deliberately walk past her, at which point Ah Mei would take great pleasure in calling out, "Nainai!" then hold her breath and keep as still as possible, hidden behind the clothes.

Eventually, Nainai would say, "I have to stop now – I've got manuscripts to check." Then Ah Mei would head upstairs and play the piano, and when she'd had enough of that, she might weave in and out of the clothes again, and when tired of that, she might climb into one of the big leather suitcases and lie down inside. She'd stay there until she felt that Nainai could take another break, then she'd call out, "Nainai!" and carefully pull the lid down on the suitcase. Nainai would search everywhere, and when she eventually found her, she would pretend to be so worried. "You silly thing, you could have suffocated in there." And Mrs Hu's voice would come from the balcony, "Don't worry, I was keeping an eye on her."

In the late afternoon, when the temperature began to drop, Mrs Hu would fold all the clothes and put them back in the leather suitcases.

They were good quality suitcases, and Nainai treasured them – they had come all that way by sea, from France to China. Nainai's favourite was a little leather suitcase. All year round, it stayed in Nainai's bedroom, on top of the cabinet closest to her bed, and there was never so much as a speck of dust on it.

Everything about the little suitcase was handcrafted, and the workmanship was superb. Although it was old now, the leather didn't seem to have hardened at all, and there was no sign of cracking or splitting. In fact, the reverse was true: it seemed to give off a dark sheen even at night.

The little leather suitcase was kept locked.

Ah Mei was allowed to touch anything of Nainai's except for that little leather suitcase. Ah Mei was as interested in the suitcase itself as she was in its contents. She longed to pick it up and walk about the room. There was something special about the little leather suitcase that captured her imagination. What if Nainai were to give it to her one day! She could put all her favourite things inside, close the lid and click the locks.

As soon as Ah Mei stepped inside Nainai's bedroom, her eyes would land on the suitcase, in the same way a dragonfly always lands on the same reed tip.

But if Nainai caught her looking, she would warn her off. "Aina, don't go getting ideas about the little suitcase!"

For Nainai, the little suitcase and its contents were treasured possessions. Inside the suitcase were some old gramophone records, a few faded photographs, a silk scarf, school graduation certificates, Christmas cards from her parents and sisters, and a few little things from her childhood: a hairclip, a tiny cloth doll. Sometimes, when she was alone, Nainai would open the suitcase and randomly take something out. Her thoughts would wander from the room to a place far, far away...

The suitcase was Nainai's connection to the past, to her

life in France. And while she was happy in Shanghai, she still dusted the little leather suitcase almost every day.

Ah Mei had been looking forward to summer camp at the end of the school year.

Nainai would have helped her to pack but she had to leave the house early to return a manuscript to the publisher's. She had found a lot of mistakes in it, and needed to go through them one by one with the editor, which would take at least a day. So she had asked Mrs Hu to help Ah Mei get ready for camp. Ah Mei wanted to take this, and then that, and Mrs Hu, who was trying to help, said, "You're just like your nainai, wanting everything to be perfect. And you're only eight! You're only going for three nights. You'd take the whole room with you if you could!" Ignoring her, Ah Mei picked out a rag doll that Nainai had given her at New Year, and handed it to Mrs Hu to put in the case.

"Aiya, what are you taking that for?" said Mrs Hu, tossing the doll back where it had come from, beside Ah Mei's pillow.

But Ah Mei rushed over, picked up the rag doll, and stuffed it back into Mrs Hu's hands. "I can't sleep without it."

They were still packing when Ah Mei's friend Qiu Qiu arrived.

Qiu Qiu was carrying a small leather suitcase. She told Ah Mei that she'd packed everything she needed for summer camp. Ah Mei was struck by how beautiful Qiu Qiu looked when she appeared in the doorway, holding the suitcase with both hands in front of her knees. She'd never seen her friend looking so lovely. She kept staring at her, and it took a while for her to realize that the reason Qiu Qiu looked so beautiful was because she was holding a little leather suitcase.

Qiu Qiu thought she looked good with the little suitcase too.

Ah Mei was so busy looking Qiu Qiu up and down that she forgot about packing.

Then, all of a sudden, she ran to Nainai's room.

As always, Nainai's little leather suitcase was sitting quietly on top of the cabinet by the bed. It was much nicer than the one Qiu Qiu had, more stylish, and Western. Ah Mei stepped gingerly towards it. Nainai had forgotten to lock it. Ah Mei's heart was pounding. The lure of the little leather suitcase was stronger than ever, pulling her closer, step by step.

Qiu Qiu and Mrs Hu called to her from the other room.

"Ah Mei, hurry up! We need to go and join the group."

"Ah Mei! Are you going to finish this packing or not?"

Ah Mei stood in front of the little leather suitcase, and looked at it. She stroked it, then after a while, she opened the lid very slowly. She glanced hastily at the things inside, but it wasn't the contents she was interested in. It was the suitcase itself.

Qiu Qiu and Mrs Hu called out again, urging her to hurry up.

Ah Mei hesitated, then began to walk towards the door. After only a few steps, she turned around, rushed back to the little suitcase, lifted it up with both hands and tipped the contents onto Nainai's bed. There was a *whoosh* as everything fell out, but Ah Mei wasn't interested in what was inside. Filled with excitement, she ran back to her own room.

"Ooh!" Qiu Qiu gasped, wide-eyed, when she saw the little leather suitcase in Ah Mei's hand.

Mrs Hu was busy tidying up, and was facing the other way.

Ah Mei paraded in front of Qiu Qiu holding the little suitcase. She put one foot in front of the other, heel to toe, which made her body sway as she walked. It was something Nainai had taught her. She had told Ah Mei it was how the fashion models in Paris walked, when they sashayed down the catwalk.

"Lovely!" said Qiu Qiu.

Mrs Hu glanced round to see what was going on. She was aghast. "Ah ... Ah Mei, what's that ... you're holding?"

"A suitcase, a little leather suitcase."

"What are you doing with it?"

"Packing my things."

"Stop this nonsense! That's your nainai's suitcase, the one nobody's allowed to touch."

"I didn't touch anything inside it, not a thing, not even with the tip of my finger. I'm just borrowing the case for a while."

"You can't do that!"

"Why not?"

"Nainai will be furious."

"No, she won't." Ah Mei could not recall a single occasion when Nainai had been furious with her.

Neither could Mrs Hu. She hesitated. "And you honestly didn't touch anything inside the suitcase?"

"Nothing. That would be asking for trouble."

Mrs Hu was of the same mind. Like Ah Mei, she thought that it was the contents of the suitcase that were important, and that the case was just a container. Even so, there was concern written all over her face.

"Ah Mei, you need to hurry up and finish packing. If we're late, they'll go without us." Qiu Qiu was getting anxious.

"Don't worry," Ah Mei said to Mrs Hu. Then she scooped up everything they had packed in the canvas bag, and put it all into the little leather suitcase.

Mrs Hu helped her, saying, "You're a cheeky little thing, bold as brass, scared of nothing. You've got it coming to you this time."

"Nainai never tells me off," said Ah Mei, smugly.

"Let's hope she doesn't," said Mrs Hu.

In no time at all, two little girls were sashaying down the road, each holding a little leather suitcase.

That evening, when Nainai came home and discovered the little suitcase gone, and its contents scattered across the bed – covered with a cloth because Mrs Hu hadn't dared to touch them – she hurried out of her room.

"Mrs Hu!"

Mrs Hu answered immediately.

"Where is my little leather suitcase?" Nainai's face was tense, like dark clouds gathering before a storm, a storm that could break at any moment.

When Mrs Hu saw Nainai's face, she lowered her head.

"Where is my little leather suitcase?" Nainai repeated.

Mrs Hu had never heard Nainai speak as sharply as this. She didn't dare raise her head.

"Why don't you answer me?"

Mrs Hu stuttered, "M-madam, the little leather suitcase … Ah Mei … Ah Mei took it."

"Ah Mei? Why would she take it?"

"To go … to summer camp, to … put her things … in it."

"*WHAT?* How could you let her have my suitcase? And pack it with her things? And take it out of the house?"

Mrs Hu hung her head even lower. She felt very uneasy.

"Children need watching and guiding! How could you, Mrs Hu? How could you let her do this?" Nainai's face was terrifying.

Mrs Hu raised her head, glanced at Nainai's face, then quickly lowered it again. "I'm sorry, Madam!"

Nainai shook her head, sighed and went back to her room. "It's inexcusable!" she said, adding a few more words in French.

Mrs Hu couldn't understand what Nainai was saying, but she could tell from the tone of her voice how angry she was.

Mrs Hu had the evening meal on the table as quickly as she could, then fetched the canvas bag that Ah Mei had cast aside, grabbed an umbrella and slipped out of the house. It was drizzling outside.

Very soon, Mrs Hu was on the bus to Chongming. Ah Mei had told her that the summer camp was in the countryside near there, and she'd remembered the name of the small town. It was ten o'clock by the time she managed to find the summer camp. Mrs Hu went to find one of the leaders, and explained why she had come. The camp leader listened, laughed, and went to wake Ah Mei.

Ah Mei was still half asleep when she saw Mrs Hu. She blinked several times, thinking it might be a dream. "Mrs Hu? What...? What are you doing here?"

Mrs Hu shook her finger at Ah Mei. "As if you don't know!" She took the little leather suitcase, opened it, pulled everything out and transferred it all to the canvas bag. "You're a cheeky thing, but at least now you'll be allowed back home."

It took Ah Mei a while to catch on. And then, when she had realized the severity of the situation, she stood there blankly, not making a sound.

Back at the Blue House, Nainai had discovered that Mrs Hu had vanished. "Mrs Hu! Mrs Hu!" she shouted anxiously.

There was no response.

Yeye heard the urgency in Nainai's voice and rushed over. "What's the matter?"

"Mrs Hu's not here." Nainai was wracked with worry.

"Perhaps she's gone for a walk," suggested Yeye.

"She never goes out unless there's a specific reason," said Nainai. "I hope she hasn't left because I was angry with her."

Yeye pushed open the door to Mrs Hu's room and peeked inside. "It doesn't look like it. Her things are still here."

Ah Mei's parents were working late, and by the time they got home it was already nine o'clock. They could see how upset and worried Nainai was, and once they understood the situation, they tried to reassure her.

"Don't worry, Ma."

"I shouldn't have taken it out on her," said Nainai. "How could I have done something like that? It was just Ah Mei borrowing the little leather suitcase, nothing to lose one's temper over."

"Ah Mei shouldn't have taken it," said Ah Mei's mother. "And when she comes back, we'll make sure she apologizes to you."

Nainai shook her head. "I know how much she likes that little suitcase."

"She has you wrapped around her little finger," said Baba.

Yeye, who was standing near by, laughed.

Nainai bared her palms, as if to say, *What can I do?* "The little devil knows my weak spots, and gets away with everything. But this time, I'm going to put her in her place."

"We'll believe that when we see it!" Mama laughed.

"But, please, could you try and find Mrs Hu first?" said Nainai.

Baba and Mama each took an umbrella, and hurried off to look for Mrs Hu.

After they'd gone, Nainai stood on the verandah, watching the rain.

"What are you thinking?" asked Yeye.

Nainai smiled. "I'm picturing Ah Mei walking down the road, with the suitcase in her hand."

Yeye, who had just put his pipe in his mouth, burst out laughing. There was a splutter, and the force of his breath made the lit tobacco fly out of the pipe, like fireworks in the evening sky.

Mrs Hu did not return that night.

After getting the suitcase, and going over and over the situation with Ah Mei, Mrs Hu had missed the last bus back to Shanghai. She had spent the night, half awake, half asleep, on a bench at the bus station, clutching the little leather suitcase to her chest.

At first light, Nainai was standing at the front door, holding an umbrella.

Yeye, Baba and Mama urged her to go inside, but Nainai was determined. "I'm waiting for Mrs Hu," she said, refusing to move.

As they had to go to work, and as Nainai obviously couldn't be persuaded to come inside, they had no choice but to leave her standing on the doorstep.

The rain fell more and more heavily. At one point the water on the road could not drain away fast enough. All over the road, raindrops splashed into the flood, like hundreds and thousands of tiny fish leaping into the air.

When vehicles drove past, the water rushed to the sides of the road, creating liquid wings that rose and fell just above the ground, now and then splashing Nainai as she stood there on the verandah, holding her umbrella, looking east, looking west.

Just after nine, she finally spotted Mrs Hu.

Worried that the leather suitcase might get soaked in the rain, Mrs Hu had been carrying it on her back, supporting it carefully with one hand, and holding an umbrella over it with the other. The clothes on the lower half of her body were wet through, and left a trail of water as she walked.

When Nainai saw Mrs Hu like this, she told her again and

again how sorry she was. She didn't know what else to do.

"Madam had never been cross with me before," said Mrs Hu, "and you were very cross indeed. I know how much that suitcase means to you."

"It's not such a big deal," said Nainai, but as she thought about the history of that suitcase, she couldn't stop her eyes from watering.

It had been a going-away present from her mother when she left France.

"You'll need at least one small suitcase," Nainai's mother had said. "Somewhere to keep the things you'll need along the way, like lipstick and jewellery."

Her mother had bought the little leather suitcase at a well-known luggage store in Marseilles, and it had not left Nainai's side since. On board the ship, she had kept it by her pillow when she slept, and taken it with her to the restaurant at mealtimes. Occasionally, she had entrusted it to Yeye while she went to the bathroom. When she came back, she'd laugh when she saw him clutching the suitcase to his chest, afraid someone might snatch it away. When Yeye asked, "What are you laughing at?" she'd point to the suitcase and say, "It's not going to fly away, you know!" And Yeye would clutch it even tighter. Deep down, he knew that for Nainai – being so far from France and Marseilles, and her family – this little leather suitcase was extraordinarily meaningful.

Nainai had never imagined, when she said goodbye to her mother that day, just how long they would be apart.

Nainai looked at the little suitcase now and remembered

the scene as the ship had pulled away from the harbour. Her mother had been standing on the quay with her father behind, Nainai's two sisters on either side of her mother; her mother waving, her long hair blowing about in the sea breeze; her mother standing there as the ship slowly moved further away, her figure gradually diminishing, becoming less and less distinct, and then disappearing completely … until all that was left was the blue sky of Marseilles.

A tear fell from Nainai's face onto the little leather suitcase, the wet stain spreading slowly across its surface.

On Sunday afternoon Ah Mei came home from the camp.

Mrs Hu saw her first. "Ah Mei's back!"

Yeye, Baba and Mama rushed out to greet her – everyone except Nainai, who was pretending to be angry. But she didn't look like an adult who was cross with a child – she looked more like a child who'd been wronged by another child.

"Nainai's angry…" was the first thing Mama said when she saw Ah Mei.

"Nainai's angry…" was the first thing Baba said when he saw Ah Mei.

"Your nainai is so angry…" was the first thing Yeye said when he saw Ah Mei.

The three grown-ups smiled secretly at each other.

Ah Mei lowered her head, and went quietly to her room.

She did not see Nainai until supper that evening. She addressed her tentatively, "Nainai…"

Nainai acknowledged her, but her manner was cold.

There were tears in Ah Mei's eyes. She didn't lift her chopsticks from her bowl, just moved the food this way and that. Her tears dropped into the bowl: *plop, plop.*

Still Nainai held out.

Ah Mei looked at Nainai, her eyes brimming with tears.

"Nainai, Nainai...!" she started to wail.

Yeye was sitting next to Nainai. He nudged her with his arm. "Ah Mei's talking to you."

Nainai passed her handkerchief to Ah Mei.

Ah Mei refused to take it. She wiped the tears away with the back of her hands.

Yeye nudged Nainai again. "Ah Mei's crying. She knows what she did was wrong." Then he turned to face his granddaughter. "Ah Mei, you know it was wrong, don't you?"

Ah Mei nodded again and again. Tears were escaping between her fingers, like spring water seeping through cracks in the rock.

Nainai got up and walked over to her granddaughter. She hugged her, and patted her gently on the head. "It's all right. It's all right. Nainai forgives you."

After supper, Ah Mei lay down beside Nainai, just as they had always done.

Nainai told Ah Mei all about the little suitcase, and the things inside it. Ah Mei's eyes were full of tears the whole time. She didn't say a word, just listened quietly as Nainai poured her heart out. Every now and then she would reach out her hand to wipe away Nainai's tears, and Nainai would gently push it away.

That day, Ah Mei learned how much the little leather

suitcase meant to Nainai. The suitcase and its contents were living memories of Marseilles, Lyons, all of France. They were Nainai's childhood. They were her family in France. They were her bright and beautiful life in the past.

CHAPTER 10

The Apricot Tree

Nainai was like a white cloud from far away that had floated into the Shanghai sky and met a gentle breeze, and turned into crystal-like raindrops that had fallen into the Huangpu River. The raindrops had dissolved in the flow of that enormous Chinese river that coursed through the Chinese landscape, and through the city of Shanghai. Decades had passed, and Nainai was practically a Shanghainese now, and a very local one at that. Shanghai's charm and taste, its spirit and soul and its elegance flowed through every gesture of her hand, and through every step she took.

Nainai went to see a Shaoxing opera at the theatre almost every week. Occasionally Xiaogu went with her, or Mama, but usually it was Yeye who accompanied her, and later Ah Mei, when she was old enough.

Nainai had seen most of the operas many times before. The way the actors expressed themselves through the beautiful costumes, the soft mellow tones, the long mournful airs, the poignancy of the librettos – Nainai was entranced by them all. She would watch the stage intently, her eyes glistening with tears, her mouth curled into a smile. Yeye would pass his clean handkerchief to her. Like Nainai, he would be moved, sometimes more deeply than his wife, but there would always be a smile on his face when he sat beside her. When Ah Mei was old enough to go to the theatre with Nainai, he would always be sure to tuck a clean handkerchief into her pocket before they left, and say, "Pass it to Nainai when you see her tears falling." But as soon as Ah Mei was in the theatre, she would be moved to tears too. There was rarely anything earth-shatteringly distressing in Shaoxing opera, and Ah Mei couldn't follow all the intricacies of the libretto, but she could still feel the emotion, which touched her deeply. When Nainai sensed this, she would turn her head and look at Ah Mei. It warmed her heart to see another pair of teary eyes and, for a moment, she would forget that Ah Mei was her granddaughter, and see her as a kindred spirit, a friend for life. The handkerchief wiped Nainai's tears, and Ah Mei's tears too. And when Nainai remembered that Ah Mei was her granddaughter, she would tease her. "You're far too young to be able to understand any of this! What are you crying about?"

Over the years, Nainai learned to sing Shaoxing opera. She sang well, with all the exquisite gestures that were part of the performance, expressing emotion through a flick of her fan, the twist of her body, by walking around in a circle. And at exactly the right moment, Yeye would join in.

"Niangzi!" he would sing, addressing his wife, not in

that deep voice of his that came from the throat, but in an unrecognizably elegant, cultured and erudite voice, the broad-chested seaman completely transformed.

Nainai had grown to love Chinese paintings, too.

Ah Mei's other grandfather, Waigong, was an artist. He lived in Hangzhou, and every now and then he would come to Shanghai and stay at the Blue House. When he stayed for a few days, he would paint. He liked to paint at the house, and Nainai liked to watch him. There was something about Chinese paintings that fascinated her – a gentle grace, a lively charm, something spiritual that she couldn't quite explain.

Sometimes Nainai would prepare the ink for him. She'd grind the ink in the inkstone, then stand and watch him paint. It was a scene that surprised people, that touched something inside them, that made them feel the world was full of possibility, full of beauty. And at that moment, a calm would come over them, and they would stand there, watching quietly, the only sound being the gentle grind of the inkstick on the inkstone.

Waigong called Nainai "the old French lady", and she called him "the old Chinese man". When he arrived at the house, he'd pretend not to see her, and ask Ah Mei, "How's the old French lady that lives here?" And Ah Mei would run over to Nainai and say, "Nainai, you've got a visitor!" Nainai would glance at him and say to Ah Mei, "I wonder who it can be?" And Ah Mei would rise onto her tiptoes and whisper in her ear, "It's the old Chinese man." When he heard this, Waigong would harrumph, and pretend to be offended:

"You're Chinese too, you know!" And Nainai would hug Ah Mei tightly, pretending to protect her: "But don't you forget, she's a quarter French!" When Nainai poured him a cup of Dragon Well tea, and its fresh fragrance rose into the air, Waigong would sigh with genuine feeling. "The thing is, you are every inch an old Chinese lady."

When Ah Mei was a baby, Yeye would hold her in his arms and watch while Nainai ground the ink, and Waigong did his painting. When she was a little girl, she would stand on a chair and watch. She didn't say anything, just observed quietly as Nainai moved the ink slowly round and round in circles, and as the tip of Waigong's brush, heavy with ink, danced over the paper as though it were a cloud blown by the wind, the black ink seeping into the paper, at first wet and dark, later dry and pale.

These memories would stay with Ah Mei all her life.

Nainai could even make Chinese delicacies.

In fact, her salted ducks' eggs were as delicious as her bouillabaisse. From her first taste of this unusual delicacy, she had been intrigued. Salted ducks' eggs? Who would have thought it! It was beyond her imagination. And it tasted incredible! She decided that she would learn how to make these delicious eggs with her very own hands.

Mrs Hu, using her own family's secret and rather complicated recipe that had been passed down through the generations, spared no trouble showing Nainai how to make salted ducks' eggs. And once Nainai could make them, whatever the season, there were always some ready to eat at the Blue House, or for visitors to take home with them. Every time Waigong came to Shanghai, he would take a few dozen home with him.

"The salted ducks' eggs that my nainai makes have an orangey-red yolk, just like the sun rising in the morning," Ah Mei had once written in an essay.

When Nainai went to the local market she was just like an old Shanghainese lady, speaking the language she loved and had mastered. Occasionally, she said something that marked her out as a foreigner, but unless you were unusually attentive, you'd think she spoke perfect Shanghainese. Like countless other women in Shanghai, she went to the market early every morning, bamboo basket in hand. Everyone knew her, and waved to her as soon as she appeared. Then, there was the haggling. At first, Nainai wasn't used to arguing over the price, but after she'd been to market with Mrs Hu a few times, she soon got the hang of it, and even started to enjoy it. The haggling became fun, like a game. She took it seriously, but not so seriously that she was quibbling over the last penny or ten grams.

When Ah Mei was little, she would go to the market with Nainai. Nainai liked to hear people complimenting her granddaughter. She would make sure that Ah Mei looked nice, and would choose her clothes and plait her hair, combining French style and Chinese style in such a way that the two complemented each other naturally.

Nainai would walk from stall to stall, to give the impression she was comparing prices. The stallholders knew what she was doing, and played along, giving the impression they didn't want to talk. But the result was always the same: both sides would end up happily doing business together. And there would be another little event just as they were about to leave the market. If it had happened once, it had happened a thousand times. The tomato seller would select the best tomato on his stall, and call out, "Hey, little girl!" and then he'd place the tomato in Ah Mei's hand. Nainai would smile and nod her head. And so it was that Ah Mei would always leave the market clutching a tomato, or an apple, or something nice to eat.

Nainai was like a seed blown in from afar that had taken root in Shanghai and flourished. She seldom mentioned Marseilles and Lyons any more, and as the years and months slipped by, it might have seemed that her homeland was fading from her memory.

But it was clear to Yeye that Nainai never forgot where she was from, not for a moment. And he sensed that, as she grew older, as life became more difficult, and the situation in Shanghai more uncertain, she missed her homeland more and more, and found it harder and harder to adapt to the changes in their lives. Yeye could sense all of this from the sleepness nights, her blank stares and the way she would sigh for no apparent reason.

During their second year in Shanghai, she had had an opportunity to return to France, and they had bought her a ticket. But the day before she was due to set sail, the oldest of the six children was taken seriously ill and rushed to hospital. The doctors diagnosed meningitis. The boy's fever wouldn't subside, and while he was in a coma, Nainai stayed with him day and night. When he finally came round, he took one look at Nainai, who had aged so much in those few days, and closed his eyes again. Tears seeped from the corners of his eyes. Nainai's ticket to France was still valid, but she said, "When he's discharged and goes home, he'll still need someone to look after him for a while." By the time he was fully recovered, Nainai couldn't have gone back to France even if she'd wanted to. Because of the war, communications with Shanghai had stopped.

Later on, for one reason or another, any thoughts of returning to France were thwarted, and eventually Nainai lost all hope of returning and stopped thinking about it. Yeye tried as hard as he could to find a way. When he finally acknowledged that there was nothing he could do, he told Ah Mei's parents, "I would swap this whole house if your mama could have one journey back to France, one chance to go home." As soon as he'd finished speaking, his head was in his hands, and tears were streaming down his face.

More and more often, Nainai would run her fingers over the little leather suitcase and open it up. And once it was open, it would be hours before she closed it again, as though there was no end to the marvels inside. She looked at every single object, not once or twice, but over and over. Sometimes she wouldn't even look; she would just pick something up and walk over to the window. She'd gaze out, not at the vehicles and the people on the street, but at the sky. She'd stand there, leaning against the window frame, until her legs started to go to sleep. Then she'd hobble back to the little leather suitcase, and put whatever was in her hands back inside. When the lid was closed, she'd stare at the suitcase, and run her hand gently over it again.

On Sundays and during school holidays, Nainai would often take Ah Mei to the Bund. Sometimes they went by bus, and sometimes she'd take Ah Mei's hand and they'd walk all the way there.

When they arrived, they would choose a step and sit down side by side, an old lady and a little girl.

And there they'd sit, watching the river, its water surging or calm. Then they'd raise their heads and gaze far into the distance at the line of ships on the boundless sea. They never moved – they seemed to have been there for years, and would probably be there for years to come. As they gazed at the ships, seagulls, in twos and threes, would keep darting into their line of vision, though never breaking it completely. Their eyes would be drawn to the seagulls, but only for a while, and they would soon be staring into the distance again.

Far away, on the horizon, sky and water met.

Ah Mei was looking because that was what Nainai was doing. She understood some things, but not everything. She didn't need to. She understood enough to know that for Nainai sitting here gazing into the distance was very important. She loved being with Nainai, and she felt that she was doing something important too. She was helping Nainai to see. After all, Nainai was quite old now, and her eyes weren't as sharp as a child's.

"I know what you're looking at, Nainai."

Nainai turned and smiled at Ah Mei.

"You can see Marseilles."

Nainai pointed into the distance. "That's where I came from all those years ago, when I arrived here with Yeye and the children."

A long slow sea route seemed to stretch before Nainai's eyes.

Nainai had done this countless times before, looking as far as the eye could see and describing Marseilles, the city and her family to Ah Mei. Ah Mei could describe Marseilles in as much detail as she could describe Shanghai, with the Bund, Nanjing Road, Beijing West Road and their Blue House. She could describe Marseilles with its harbour, the quays, the cobbled streets, the cafés, the blue sea, the vineyards, the fields of lavender, the *ateliers* that made soap, and the fierce sunshine. She could talk about Nainai's old house as though she'd been there many times herself: it was one of the old-style houses, built on different levels – sometimes one, two or three storeys high, but all part of the same house. There were dark red tiles with moss growing in the cracks. Shrubs grew by the house and creepers up the walls, their tiny leaves trembling, almost covering the house and windows. There were two gardens full of flowers, a smaller one at the front and a larger one at the back, with trees and a gazebo where you could sit in the shade.

It was the apricot tree in the back garden that made the deepest impression on Ah Mei.

Again and again Nainai would tell her about the apricot

tree, how she and her sisters used to sit beneath it, reading and playing games. This tree featured in so many of her memories.

When Nainai sat by the river and talked about the apricot tree, it was as though the river had vanished and she was looking out over the garden with the apricot tree standing right there in front of her, covered in lush green leaves, white blossom bursting into flower, branches laden with fruit.

Of course, the apricot tree was standing in front of Ah Mei as well. Nainai described the tree in such detail she seemed to describe every leaf and every flower.

One day, Ah Mei told Nainai, "Last night I dreamed about your family's apricot tree."

Nainai sighed. "I wish I could see it in my dreams. I never have – not even once. I don't know why. And yet you've seen it."

It was autumn and the sky over the Huangpu was surprisingly blue. Some clouds drifted in from the horizon, white clouds, like snow drifts in the sky.

Ah Mei would often ask childish questions, which Nainai found quite comforting: "Océane, do you think that cloud might have drifted all the way from Marseilles?"

"Maybe," Nainai would say, kissing Ah Mei's hair. "I believe the clouds over Marseilles are exactly like that." And, still craning her neck to look up at the cloud, "Aina, if it has drifted all the way from Marseilles, how long do you think it has taken?"

"Fifteen days? No, sixteen. No, no, a month."

Nainai nodded. "That's how long it takes, more or less."

The two of them would often play games like these, and, putting one sentence after another, they could carry on talking for hours, their conversation slipping further into fantasy.

One afternoon in early spring, a truck stopped outside the Blue House.

There was a tree in the back of the truck. It was a big tree, much longer than the back of the truck, and they'd had to put down the rear barrier to fit it in. Although the truck had already come to a standstill, the branches were still trembling. There were tender new shoots on the branches, but it was impossible to tell what kind of tree it was. The rootball was bound with rope, wrapped round several times, to preserve the roots and not lose any soil. It was a mature tree, large enough to stand four or five people around it.

The driver's door opened, and someone jumped down. It was Yeye.

Then, a dozen or more young men leaped down from the back of the truck.

When Yeye opened the big iron gate to the garden, this team of young men slowly lowered the tree onto a makeshift ramp. Then, using a rope, they secured the rootball to three long poles, and lifted the poles onto the shoulders of six of the men. In their half-crouching positions, they felt the weight of the poles, and when the head of the team gave the word, they slowly straightened up. The rootball rose from the ground. There was a rhythm to the instructions, and the men followed it, moving forward in neat, strong steps.

Yeye led the way, walking backwards, facing the men and beckoning with hand gestures.

Finally, the tree was in the garden.

The young men took a moment or two to catch their breath, then went back to the truck to fetch the shovels and hoes. When Yeye had chosen the ideal spot in the garden, they started to dig. The hole grew deeper and deeper, then two of the men jumped into it. The others darted to the side, dodging the earth that kept flying up out of the hole and landing on the ground around it.

Nainai, Baba and Mama had all gone out; only Mrs Hu and Ah Mei were at home.

Mrs Hu did not know what to make of the scene in the garden. "What are you doing out there, Sir?" she asked Yeye.

"Planting a tree!" Yeye replied.

"What kind of tree?"

Yeye smiled. He wasn't telling.

"I know what kind of tree it is," Ah Mei called out, trying to avoid the flying earth.

Everyone turned to look at Ah Mei.

Ah Mei stared into Yeye's eyes. "I know."

"You know?" asked Yeye. "How could you know? What kind of tree is it, then?"

"An apricot tree!" said Ah Mei.

The digging stopped, and all the men looked at Ah Mei again.

Yeye was stunned. "What did you say?"

Ah Mei climbed onto the mound of earth, the air around her smelling of fresh mud, and pointed to the tree that was lying on the ground. "It's an apricot tree!"

Everyone froze. How did this little girl know?

By the time the chill breath of the late winter wind was coursing through Shanghai's streets and alleys, the apricot tree had been planted in a deep hole and was standing securely. The branches looked bare, but there were plenty of new shoots, a sure indication that as long as the tree could survive the spring winds and spring rains, there would soon be fresh young leaves, and it would not be long before the tree was covered in green.

The men were thorough and considerate. They made sure the garden was neat and tidy, then picked up their tools, slung them over their shoulders, and, one by one, said goodbye to Yeye.

Nainai came through the front door.

Ah Mei had been by the door for ages, waiting for her to come home. Yeye was on the verandah, standing and admiring the tree.

As soon as Ah Mei saw Nainai, she led her straight out to the garden.

A dozen steps from the apricot tree, Nainai stopped.

Ah Mei was already standing under the tree. "Nainai, come over here!" she cried out excitedly.

Nainai walked slowly to the apricot tree. She looked it up and down. The trunk was the colour of old bronze, and was gleaming. It didn't look like wood. It looked more like metal, as though it would clang if you knocked something against it. The new shoots on the branches were tiny, so tiny that you would miss them unless you looked closely, but these pale hints of green signalled that life was flowing through the branches, and that although the weather was still bitterly cold, the tree was stirring, preparing for spring.

Nainai stroked the tree trunk, over and over. When she realized Yeye was watching, she turned around and walked towards him.

"It's like the apricot tree in your back garden at home, isn't it?" he asked.

Nainai nodded. There was a thin veil of tears in her eyes.

"It's from a garden in Suzhou. It wasn't easy to find such a big one The moment I saw it, it was like being back in Marseilles, as though I was looking at the apricot tree in your family's back garden. It's almost identical!"

Nainai threw her arms around Yeye's neck, and kissed him on the cheek.

"Ah Mei's watching," whispered Yeye.

Nainai glanced back at Ah Mei.

Ah Mei closed her eyes.

Nainai kissed him again.

She didn't ask Yeye where he had found the money to buy the apricot tree. Later, she noticed that he had stopped wearing the Rolex watch that he loved – and that he hadn't been wearing it since the tree arrived. She didn't ask what had happened to the watch.

The apricot tree soon adapted to its new environment. Like someone recovering from a shock, it slumped for a few days, and then very quickly rallied in the warmth of the spring breeze and the moistness of the spring rain.

It took only a few days of late spring sunshine for the leaves to unfurl, for the tree to be covered in a lush green, and to stand like a huge green parasol in the garden. It took only a few days of light rain for the tree to burst into bloom. The blossoms jostled for space and snow-like clusters formed against the green leaves. When the wind picked up, it blew the petals away and they danced like snowflakes in the air.

Then the fruit started to grow, and the branches began to bend wearily under the weight.

Nainai loved to spend time under the apricot tree. It was her favourite place. She liked to sit there on a rattan chair, either proofreading manuscripts or doing nothing at all.

Ah Mei often played under the apricot tree. She loved it too.

CHAPTER 11

The Piano

Ah Mei was only three years old when Nainai first lifted her onto the raised piano stool so she could learn how to play the piano. To begin with, Nainai let her press whichever keys she liked, and Ah Mei thought the piano was a very big toy: especially as when she pressed the keys, she saw the insides of the piano going up and down, apparently with a life of their own. The more she played, the more she liked the sound of the piano. It was a sound unlike any other – a sound no other instrument could make. It was clearly mechanical, the piano being a machine made by humans, but also somehow divine, the notes sounding at the point where heaven and earth meet. Of course Ah Mei could not fully understand the wonderful sounds, she just loved them, as though they had lain dormant within her, and were now coming to life.

Nainai arranged for a piano teacher to come to the house and teach Ah Mei how to to play.

Xiaogu could have taught her, but Nainai wouldn't hear of it: "It won't work. You are aunt and niece, not teacher and student. You've spoiled her, not given her boundaries, and she has you wrapped around her little finger. She'll never learn to play the piano like that."

The piano teacher was a tutor from the Conservatory of Music, a thin woman in her forties, who wore a long skirt. When she sat down, her skirt would spread and almost cover the piano stool. The first time she came, she grasped Ah Mei's hand and examined it, then told Nainai, "She has very long fingers, it would be a shame for her not to learn the piano."

Ah Mei was a quick learner. More often than not, the teacher only had to show her once. Although her little hands weren't all that fast yet, and she had trouble with the rhythm, she threw herself into it, and gave the appearance of someone who was playing from the heart. The teacher told Nainai, "This young girl of yours has a very rare gift for music."

Ah Mei hadn't been playing the piano for long when she said, "I want to wear a long skirt too." Nainai nodded, and immediately bought two long skirts for Ah Mei. After that, Ah Mei would only sit down at the piano when she was wearing a long skirt. She was very particular, and it made people smile.

"Excellent!" the piano teacher said to Nainai, when she saw Ah Mei in her long skirt.

The more Ah Mei played the piano, the more of a pianist she became. By the time she was nine, she was performing solo on stage. She sailed to first place in a local children's piano contest. Nainai, who had gone to watch her play, felt that the judging panel had awarded her first place from the moment she sat down at the piano.

They had seen a very young girl in a long skirt walk out of the wings, her shoes click-clacking across the stage into bright lights. If she appeared a little shy, she was also natural and gracious. Her appearance captured everyone's attention. As she walked onto the stage, it was though a giant curtain had come loose and fallen to the floor, revealing a bright crescent moon. The audience was enraptured. Before Ah Mei had reached the piano, the sound of applause rose all around.

That evening, Ah Mei commanded the stage. The lights were on her, the audience was rooting for her. She played as though she had been transported into another world, playing a difficult piece seamlessly, catching every intricate moment. As soon as she finished, while she was still on the piano stool, the otherwise reserved judges rose spontaneously to their feet and applauded.

After Ah Mei came first in the competition, the family started to take her piano-playing seriously, especially Nainai, who promised, "I am going to make sure Ah Mei develops into an outstanding pianist!" Nainai seemed to have it all planned out, more or less. Except there was no more or less about it – Nainai's heart was set on it. She dedicated some time to it every morning and evening. Nainai had learned to play the piano as a child, and although she hadn't played for years, now, for Ah Mei's benefit, she started to play again. She went to the bookshop and bought lots of books about playing the piano, and some piano scores too, and went through them herself before giving them to her granddaughter. She read them, and when Ah Mei was not at home, she would sit at the piano and slowly try to play the pieces she had learned as a child. She was feeling her way, trying to keep a step ahead of Ah Mei. Nainai knew that a few lessons a week with a piano teacher was nowhere near enough. She had to make sure that Ah Mei spent at least as many hours again practising, and that when she practised, it was more than mechanical repetition – otherwise Ah Mei would never be able to make progress, and might come to hate the piano. With her help and guidance, she would make sure that it always felt fresh and interesting for Ah Mei, so that she would constantly improve, and feel encouraged. Nainai carefully went through every piece, checking the correct fingering, and familiarizing herself with the rhythm of the melody, and then, when the time came, she would magically help Ah Mei to understand.

The piano teacher was astonished by Ah Mei's progress.

"The girl's a genius!" she told Nainai.

Nainai smiled and said nothing.

"If we're not careful, we'll end up with two pianists in the family," said Yeye.

"I'm doing it for Ah Mei," said Nainai.

And Ah Mei was for a large part doing it for the glory it brought to her school. There were often inter-school performing arts competitions, both local and city-wide. Ah Mei's school did well in them, especially now Ah Mei was winning first place. As long as there was a piano on the stage, and Ah Mei was sitting in front of it wearing her long skirt, when her nimble fingers started to dance over the keys, it was difficult to imagine her school not doing well. The walls of the school hall were covered with certificates, and the large cabinet was filled with all kinds of trophies and medals. Many of these were prizes from performing arts competitions, and when the teachers and pupils saw them, they couldn't help thinking about Ah Mei.

Ah Mei was the pride of the school. There were always clusters of children around her, and she loved the attention, although she always felt a bit shy. She'd inherited this shyness from Nainai, and it was something she would never grow out of. The girls wanted exclusive rights to appreciate and adore her, and would often shoo the boys away. "Don't play with them," they'd say bluntly to Ah Mei, "they're dirty." Ah Mei just smiled. Although she went with the girls, she'd look round from time to time at the filthy boys.

Ah Mei's piano-playing got better and better. But life at the Blue House grew harder and harder.

Shanghai had been so vibrant, but there was famine across the entire region now. The situation was serious.

In the sky above China, the sun, like a huge ball of fire, blazed furiously all day: trees were dying, crops were wilting, rivers were running dry. A parched smell spread from the outskirts into the city centre, searing into the hearts of all who smelled it, generating anxiety. The sparrows that used to be everywhere disappeared, perhaps starved to death, or left with no choice but to fly off to the villages to look for food; food like vegetables, fruit, oil and meat were in ever shorter supply. People looked thinner by the day. Their clothes, whether bought from shops or made to measure by tailors, seemed too big for them; when the wind blew off the river and down the streets, it set their clothes flapping so much that it seemed they might fly away. There were fewer and fewer boats on the river, and a lot of the activity had stopped. They bobbed about on the water, coming to the bank when the tide was high, and drifting away when the tide went down, until they were just black dots in the distance. The whistles of the enormous steamers were rarer too. The river seemed so empty. On the odd occasion that a ship's whistle blasted, it sounded hollow. There weren't as many seagulls either; they had flown away, because no one was feeding them any more.

Shanghai was a compact city, perhaps a little too crowded, but now it seemed to be getting emptier by the day. The streets looked so much longer and wider than before. One day, Yeye and Nainai went to Nanjing Road, and after walking for what seemed like ages, Nainai stopped, and asked Yeye, "Meixi, why does the Bund seem further away than usual?" Yeye stopped too. He was looking at two buildings in the distance, and said, "I was just thinking the same thing. I was wondering why those buildings seem further apart than before!" The two of them pondered for a while, then continued walking. They were still puzzled, though.

A few minutes later Yeye said, "Perhaps it's because there are fewer people walking about."

"Or perhaps because we don't have as much energy as before? Perhaps that's why the road feels so long," Nainai suggested.

One day, when Ah Mei was at school, she noticed that Qiu Qiu, who sat right in front of her, was, for no obvious reason, finding it difficult to sit up straight. She kept leaning to one side. All of a sudden, she fell to the floor with a thud, her limp arms sweeping her textbook and homework book and a bottle of blue ink from the desk. The bottle smashed as it hit the ground, spattering Qiu Qiu's face and body with blue ink. Ah Mei gasped in shock. Then everyone else gasped and leaped to their feet. The teacher dropped her textbook, and ran over. "Qiu Qiu!" she called her name and tried in vain to pull her up. All the colour had drained from Qiu Qiu's face, her lips had gone blue and her hands and feet were limp. When the teacher put her arms round Qiu Qiu, the girl's head rolled, her thin hair trailing after. She looked gaunt.

"Qiu Qiu!" shouted the teacher again.

"Qiu Qiu!" cried Ah Mei, her voice trembling with shock.

"Qiu Qiu!" All of the children called out her name.

Qiu Qiu opened her mouth and gave a long sigh. Then, slowly, she opened her eyes.

The teacher suddenly realized why Qiu Qiu had fainted, and told Ah Mei, "Go and get some water from the office! Take the cup from my desk, and fill it from the tap. Be quick!"

Ah Mei ran out of the classroom, a few other children behind her.

By the time Ah Mei came back with the water, two desks had been pushed together and Qiu Qiu was lying on a makeshift bed.

Ah Mei had run so fast that the water kept sloshing over

the top of the cup, and when she handed it to the teacher the cup was only half full.

Supporting Qiu Qiu's head with one hand and holding the cup in the other, the teacher slowly let the water run into the girl's dry mouth.

When Qiu Qiu felt a bit stronger, she looked at the teacher. "I'm hungry," she said.

The children looked this way and that, as though there might be some food in the classroom. They knew there wasn't, but still looked inside their desks, or checked in their pockets. Some of the boys turned their pockets inside out. No one had anything to eat.

No one except Ah Mei. Holding a toffee in the palm of her hand, she used her other hand to push her way gently through the children who had gathered around Qiu Qiu.

The children's eyes lit up when they saw the toffee.

Ah Mei held it up to Qiu Qiu's mouth.

Qiu Qiu looked into Ah Mei's eyes, as if to say, *What about you?*

"I have more at home," said Ah Mei. "Nainai bought half a *jin* of them for me."

In fact, Nainai had bought the sweets three months earlier, and they had been making them last. There were only a few left now.

More and more children in Ah Mei's class were going hungry. In the past, after school, the children would charge out of the classroom and tear around the playground. The playground had been like a duck pen, so loud that you couldn't hear what anyone was saying. But now all the children were quiet: they had to save their energy for the walk home and for their schoolwork. The teachers, who were used to the playground being noisy, found it rather desolate. It didn't feel right somehow.

There were more and more children wandering the streets, too. They were constantly rummaging through bins, competing with cats and dogs, hoping to find some food to put in their mouths. They were filthy and thin, with eyes round as bells. At night, they wandered like ghosts from one bin to another, dropping by the roadside when their energy was spent. The whole city was getting weaker and weaker. There was no way of providing accommodation for these orphans, or of looking after them. There was nowhere for them but the street, though it was sickening and distressing to see them like that.

One morning, Ah Mei was just leaving the house to go to school, her school bag on her back, when she saw a child sitting on the doorstep. She had big, black, shiny eyes, brilliant white teeth, and a dirty but beautiful face. Her neck was thin, and so were the arms and legs that poked out of her clothes. Ah Mei stood there with a slice of bread in her hand – she'd taken a couple of bites already. She could have finished it very quickly, but she had wanted to take her time and eat it slowly, and make it last all the way to school. The little girl stared, entranced by the slice of bread in Ah Mei's hand. She was staring so intently that Ah Mei could hardly hide it behind her back.

Nainai was watching Ah Mei from the window. When she saw her stop, she came out to see why. She soon realized what was happening. It broke her heart to see that wretched little girl.

Ah Mei walked over to Nainai. She nudged her with her shoulder and waved the bread that was in her hand as if to say, *I'd like to give it to her.*

Nainai nodded.

Ah Mei walked slowly back towards the girl.

The little girl tried to stand up but was too weak.

Ah Mei bent down and held the bread out to the girl.

The girl's hand slowly reached for the bread, then snatched it from Ah Mei as though she was going to run off with it. But then, as though feeling ashamed, she lowered her head and took some big bites. The bread must have caught in her dry throat, because she started to cough, and a mouthful of crumbs sprayed out and landed on the ground.

Ah Mei hurried back inside the house, and fetched a bowl of warm water from the kettle. She handed it to the girl.

The little girl downed it in one. She was in such a hurry that some water spilled from the corner of her mouth and ran down her neck.

When Ah Mei left for school, Nainai kept an eye on the girl.

Eventually, the girl gathered enough strength to stand up, and slowly walk back along the main road. She stayed close to the wall the whole time, as though she might fall at any moment, and would need its support.

As Nainai watched the little figure heading into the distance, she closed her eyes and made the sign of the cross.

* * *

Ah Mei's family was in a better situation than most, but they were by no means well off. There had been money at the Blue House in the past, and life there had been the envy of all Shanghai, or so it had seemed. But one morning they had woken up to find that none of it belonged to Ah Mei's family any more. Fortunately, they still had the Blue House, and it was full of beautiful furniture, wardrobes full of clothes, and all kinds of valuable items around the house. So, for a few years before Ah Mei was born, every now and then Nainai would take something from the Blue House to the pawn shop. This way, the family could maintain a certain standard of living, although it took some effort. But after Ah Mei was born, the worry of not being able to make ends meet fell like a dark shroud over Nainai's heart. Nainai did not want any of this to affect Ah Mei, so she steeled herself, and took some of their treasured pieces to the pawn shop. The harder life became, the more inadequate Nainai felt. She would get flustered and start pacing up and down inside the house, as though she was lost in the desert, all on her own. They were down to one cup of coffee a week now, and even that was difficult to maintain. And the coffee itself was no longer rich and strong, but thin and weak.

From the mahogany furniture to the grandfather clock, from the fur coats to the English porcelain … piece by piece, the Blue House was gradually emptied until it was just a shell. There had once been a wardrobe and some ornaments in the room with the piano, but these had all gone now, leaving only the piano and the piano stool looking all forlorn in the middle of the room.

"If this carries on, we'll have to let the house go too." Nainai sighed a lot more than before. The constant worry had caused the lines on her face to deepen, and the skin on her neck to slacken. When she felt particularly anxious, she would ask Ah Mei to "play a tune for your nainai".

Ah Mei, appearing to understand how Nainai was feeling, would immediately come and sit on the piano stool, lift the lid and play.

Nainai would pull up a rattan chair and sit there, listening to her granddaughter. She was exhausted, and would sometimes fall asleep while she was listening. But Ah Mei didn't stop playing; she knew from experience that as soon as she stopped, Nainai would wake up. She would continue playing, but switch to some calm, gentle music that suggested a stream flowing in the moonlight, or the forest stirring in the early morning breeze.

Then Nainai fell ill. At least, the family said she was ill, but that wasn't exactly true. Nainai had collapsed. She was taken to hospital, and examined, but the hospital couldn't find anything wrong with her. Still, she was too weak to get out of bed, and had to stay in hospital for observation.

Members of the family went back and forth to the hospital, and there were always people gathered around Nainai's bed. The doctors and nurses were amused to see this foreign lady with her blue eyes and her foreign nose being called Mama and Nainai by all these people who were clearly Chinese. They often came over to see what was happening.

Nainai just smiled.

"Don't keep rushing to the hospital," Nainai told Dabo and the others. "You've all got work to do. Go and get on with it. I'll stay here a few days, but I'll be home soon." She glanced at Ah Mei and joked, "As long as I've got Ah Mei here to look after me, I don't need anyone else, do I, Ah Mei?"

Ah Mei shook her head.

Everyone laughed.

Instead of going home after school, Ah Mei would head straight to the hospital to see Nainai.

There was a chair by the bed. Ah Mei would sit there and tell Nainai about her day at school – what she had seen on the way, how the leaves on the apricot tree were starting to fall; everything. Nainai felt as though she had been away for a long time, and was very happy to listen to Ah Mei chattering about things that were happening in the world beyond the hospital.

During the day, when her children and grandchildren were at work or at school, Nainai felt time passed very slowly indeed. Although Yeye was retired now, in order to earn some money he had been to see the factory boss and suggested he could guard the factory gate. The boss had agreed. He was a decent man, and he knew that the silk mill had once belonged to Yeye's family. But this meant that, like the other members of the family, Yeye couldn't keep rushing to the hospital. He felt bad about it. "Never mind, I'll pack the job in," he said to Nainai. She reminded him that life was probably going to get harder. She had an alternative idea that would stave off the loneliness and earn some money at the same time. "Could you bring me that pile of manuscripts?" she asked Yeye.

"But you're not well," he said.

"The publishing house needs them."

"Then I'll take them back."

Nainai was against that idea. She didn't say anything about wanting to earn money, only that it would stop her feeling lonely.

"It will be so much easier being here if I have something to do."

After that, every day Nainai would prop herself up in bed and proofread the texts from the publisher, in between being seen by the doctors and nurses. But, she wasn't recovering – Nainai could only walk a few steps before she felt the world spinning around her.

"Surely I'm not going to have to spend the rest of my life in one of your beds?" she asked the doctors. They laughed and told her to stop worrying and rest.

Mrs Hu came to the hospital every day with food for Nainai: either chicken soup or soft-shelled turtle soup. Nainai thought these were unnecessary luxuries in such lean times. She told Mrs Hu that she didn't want to eat that kind of thing; she just wanted some rice porridge and dried radish. Mrs Hu knew that Nainai was only saying this to save money: Nainai might have been living in China for all these years, but she still couldn't stand rice porridge and dried radish.

"A big family like yours can always find a bit of cash," said Mrs Hu. "You've brought them all up, and now it's their turn to look after you."

Nainai knew her children's situations like the back of her hand.

"None of them has it easy right now," she sighed. She knew that her condition impacted all of them, and it made her feel uncomfortable.

There was a charge for every day spent in hospital. As Nainai wasn't employed on a formal basis, she had to pay all the costs herself. She became more and more anxious about spending all day in bed, unable to get up. Yeye and the others gathered at the Blue House almost daily, racking their brains over how to pay Nainai's hospital bill. "We'll smash the wok and sell the iron if we have to," Dabo said to the others. "We'll do whatever is needed to make Nainai better." They shared the costs, giving the money to Yeye, who took it to the hospital to pay the bills.

One evening, after visiting Nainai, and walking home with Yeye, Ah Mei had gone into her bedroom and picked up her piggy bank – a cute porcelain pig with a slit in its back. Yeye was just about to ask what she was doing when Ah Mei let go of the porcelain pig. It shattered as it hit the ground, sending coins rolling across the floor.

"Ah Mei!"

Ah Mei crouched down and started picking up the coins, one by one.

When Mrs Hu came in, and saw bits of porcelain and coins all over the floor, she bent down to help Ah Mei. When her hand brushed against Ah Mei's, she grasped it. She held it tight and sighed.

Yeye's cupped hands were filled with coins. He jiggled

them as though trying to weigh up how many there were.

"Ah Mei's nainai has no reason not to get better now," he said to Mrs Hu.

Mrs Hu took some money out of her pocket and placed it on top of the coins. "Sir, this is from my wages last month. I didn't send it all home."

Yeye nodded. "Now she has even less reason not to recover quickly!"

"I've been praying to Guanyin," said Mrs Hu, "asking for her protection and blessing."

"Thank you," said Yeye. It didn't feel right to tell her that Nainai believed in God, not in Guanyin.

Slowly, Nainai started to recover, and the whole family, who had been so anxious and unsettled, gradually began to relax. She would have one more set of tests the next day, then, all being well, Nainai could go home.

But the latest tests unexpectedly revealed that Nainai had a tumour.

The doctor called Yeye to one side. As Yeye listened to what had been found, his legs turned to jelly, and his body started to sway. His brain went numb, and he felt the world turning upside down. By the time he had been helped to a seat, his forehead was covered in cold sweat.

"Don't imagine the worst," said the doctor. "We hope it's benign but we need to operate." He told Yeye, in no uncertain terms, "The sooner, the better."

Yeye summoned the family to the Blue House, and told them the news. In that moment, they felt as though they had fallen into a bottomless pit. Xiaogu couldn't help bursting into tears, and Mama rushed over and hugged her.

Before leaving for school that morning, Ah Mei had heard Yeye say that Nainai was ready to come home. Ah Mei thought she would welcome her back with a new piece on the piano. So instead of going to the hospital after school, she had come straight home, put down her school bag and headed for the piano room. She practised non-stop for over an hour. When she finally finished, she realized that the whole house was quiet. It seemed strange not hearing any activity at all. She went into the lounge, where more or less the entire family was sitting with long, solemn faces. Something major must have happened. She stood there, rooted to the spot, her eyes scanning the adults' faces.

Then Yeye spoke. "Mrs Hu, perhaps you could take Ah Mei for a walk?"

Mrs Hu came over and took Ah Mei's hand. Ah Mei didn't resist, she simply followed Mrs Hu out of the Blue House. Mrs Hu's rough hand felt icy cold.

They walked and walked, and then Ah Mei started to cry.

Mrs Hu crouched down, and wiped away Ah Mei's tears with her hand. "What are you crying about? You silly thing!" But Ah Mei's tears flooded out, uncontrollably, and Mrs Hu couldn't wipe them away fast enough.

"Please, Ah Mei. Please don't cry… Your nainai's going to be all right. She's a good person. Nothing will happen to her."

Mrs Hu and Ah Mei carried on walking, hand in hand, with no particular destination in mind.

There was a chill wind blowing that evening. Wutong

leaves swirled in the pale light of the street lamps. It hadn't rained for a long time, and the dry leaves rustled as they landed on the dry ground. Every time a gust of wind rushed through them, it sent them scurrying away like mice, as far as the eye could see.

Mrs Hu and Ah Mei walked for a long time and when they couldn't walk any more, they sat down by the roadside. They stayed like that for what seemed an eternity, Mrs Hu looking up at the sky, watching the moon appear and disappear in the clouds. The moon had definitely moved to the west, and the wind was colder now. Passing cyclists hunched their shoulders to keep warm, and the ring of bicycle bells sounded dull and desolate. The old woman and the little girl sat in silence for a while longer, then finally headed home.

Once they were through the gate, Mrs Hu urged Ah Mei, "Tomorrow, when you see Nainai, you mustn't cry."

Ah Mei nodded in the dark. A tear rolled down the side of her nose to the corner of her mouth. It felt so cold.

Dabo and the others had already gone home. There were only three people left: Yeye, Baba and Mama. None of them said a word. They looked as though they might sit there in the lounge for ever.

They were all thinking about the money needed for Nainai's operation.

No matter how hard they tried, they couldn't get the money together. It was a major operation, and even if they could find the money to pay for the surgery, it still wouldn't be enough – they would need more for the post-operative treatment. Yeye, Baba and Mama were all wondering if there was anything else of value in the house that they could pawn. They thought and thought, but came up with nothing.

"It's getting late," Mama said to Yeye. "You should get some sleep. There's always a way."

Baba also tried to comfort Yeye. "And whatever it is, we'll find it."

Yeye put his hands on the armrests of his chair and pushed himself up. It was quite an effort. He seemed to have aged so much in the last few hours. The skin under his eyes hung thin and loose, and it quivered as he made his way to the bedroom.

As he walked past Ah Mei, he reached out and stroked her head. "Don't stay up too late, Ah Mei." He took another couple of steps, then, putting his hand on the wall to steady himself, turned around and added, "Your nainai told me to tell you to come straight home after school and practise the piano, and not to rush off to the hospital all the time." As he moved towards the bedroom, he asked, "Did you hear that, Ah Mei?"

"Yes, Yeye," she answered.

When Mrs Hu led Ah Mei to her bedroom, those three syllables rang in Baba's ear: *pi–a–no*!

Mama seemed to have heard them too. She glanced at Ah Mei, then at Baba, and then followed Baba's gaze into the dark room. The door was open, and from where they were sitting, they could see the vague outline of the piano that

Yeye had bought from a German man a long time ago. It was an old German piano that had improved with age; they didn't see it as as something made of metal and wood, but rather as a living creature with a soul.

Mrs Hu stayed with Ah Mei until she fell asleep, then finished her work, turned off the lights and went to her room.

The standard lamp in the lounge was still on. Baba and Mama were sitting on the worn old sofa. Neither of them said a word.

They could hear a bell ringing in the distance, from the direction of the Bund.

"Bed?" said Baba.

"Bed," said Mama.

The two of them went to their room. They lay in bed in the dark with their eyes open.

Finally, Baba said, "The only thing in the house that's worth any money is the piano."

Mama said nothing.

"Ah Mei would be upset," said Baba.

"She'd be even more upset if Nainai wasn't here any more," said Mama.

"Should we tell her?" Baba asked.

"We could, but we don't have to."

"What would we say?"

"She's old enough to understand. But maybe it's better to say nothing."

"If there was any other way, then we wouldn't be doing this. That child's so attached to the piano." There wasn't even a plan in place, and already Baba felt terrible.

Mama tried to comfort him. "Save her nainai first, then later, when we have enough money, we'll get it back. Ah Mei loves the piano, but it's not necessarily the best choice for a career. What's more, with all the practice she has to put in, who's to say that she won't suddenly lose interest one day? You know what children are like."

"Nainai is her favourite person in the world."

"And she's Nainai's favourite too."

"Do you know why my ma loves her so much?"

"Because she's the only girl?"

"And...?"

"Because she looks like her."

"They're mirror images of each other."

Baba and Mama came up with as many different reasons as they could think of why they should pawn the piano. It was a way of reassuring each other. By the time morning came, they had barely slept at all.

Around three o'clock the following afternoon, a truck pulled up in front of the Blue House. Baba had arranged for a dozen strong friends to help. They leaped down from the truck, and Baba led them straight to the piano room.

Mama was out. They had agreed it would be better if she wasn't there when the piano was being removed.

And, of course, they didn't want the piano to be removed in front of Ah Mei.

Baba had also timed the removal to take place when Yeye was visiting Nainai.

But that part of the plan hadn't worked. Half an hour before the men were due to arrive, Yeye had come back to the Blue House. Nainai had asked him to fetch the first few pages of the text she was working on. She'd checked those pages before she had fallen ill, and had left them on the table, but she needed to see them again and put the whole thing together, so that Yeye could deliver it to the publisher the following day.

Yeye was looking for the papers when he heard a noise upstairs. He went into the hallway, and saw a team of people lifting the piano and very carefully bringing it down the stairs. He raised his hands, but only so far, and he didn't say a word.

He watched as the piano was moved out of the house.

Yeye went back into the room, walked over to the window, and saw the men start to lift the piano even more carefully onto the back of the truck.

There was a blanket covering the floor of the truck, and another blanket over the piano.

"Slowly, slowly…" Baba kept repeating.

Mrs Hu was on her way back from the market. The scene in the distance stopped her in her tracks.

Yeye didn't stay to watch the piano being lifted into the back of the truck, or see the care that the team of men took. He moved away from the window, sat down heavily on a chair and buried his head in his hands. All you could see was his thick, grizzled hair.

After school Ah Mei went straight home, as Nainai had told her to. She put down her school bag, and hurried to the piano room. It was empty. She blinked several times, but the room was still empty. She stood there for a while, perplexed, then ran out into the hall.

"Mrs Hu!" she called.

Mrs Hu was in the kitchen. She heard Ah Mei calling for her, but didn't go to her immediately. She had no idea how to face her.

Ah Mei called for her again and again.

Eventually, Mrs Hu came hurrying out of the kitchen.

By this time, Ah Mei had stopped calling for her. She seemed to have realized where the piano had gone. When Mrs Hu appeared in front of Ah Mei, she was sitting on the stairs. She didn't cry.

Mrs Hu sat down beside her. Gently, she pulled the child towards her.

"Ah Mei, you mustn't blame your baba and mama," said Mrs Hu.

Ah Mei nodded.

"This way, your nainai can have the operation as soon as possible. The sooner she has the operation, the sooner she can come home." Mrs Hu looked all around her, left and right, up and down, and continued talking: "Since your nainai's been in hospital, this house has felt so empty, you know. In the daytime, there's just me on my own, and even though I know you're at school, for some reason, I keep calling for you."

Ah Mei put her head in Mrs Hu's lap, and lay very still.

"I know that you'd give anything to save your nainai. And I know how precious that piano is to you, and how badly you'll miss it. But you mustn't be upset, really, you mustn't. It was so hard for your baba and mama to let the piano go, and as soon as they have enough money, they'll go and get it back. It's just that you won't be able to play for a few days."

As they ate together that evening, Baba, Mama and Yeye did not say a word. They avoided looking at each other, and particularly avoided looking at Ah Mei.

But Ah Mei did not show even a hint of being upset. "Ma, our class teacher got married and gave each of us a wedding sweet," she said to Mama. To Baba she said, "Ba, my writing was chosen to be read out in class." Then she went to her room, fetched her writing book and held it in front of him. It was covered in red coils. A red coil under a sentence was a commendation, and there were so many of them! Baba took the book, and as he looked at it, the red coils started to spin, faster and faster, until everything was a blur.

Ah Mei returned to her food. As she was eating, she pointed to Yeye's face: "Yeye, you have such bushy eyebrows!" There was a smile on her face. Yeye stroked his eyebrows: "They didn't use to be so bushy. Somehow they've grown in the last few years."

"They're old-age eyebrows," Baba commented.

The atmosphere in the room lightened. They chatted as they ate, as though nothing of any importance had happened that day at the Blue House.

Nainai had the operation.

When she was in the operating theatre, the whole family waited in the hospital corridor, young and old, sitting and standing, no one saying a word, just quietly watching the theatre door.

Xiaogu held Ah Mei's hand the entire time.

The operation took seven hours. When the door opened and Nainai was wheeled out, the family swarmed towards her. The nurse put her arms out to stop them coming too close.

Nainai looked so peaceful on the hospital bed.

The surgeon, still in his scrubs, came to the theatre door, and asked, "Could I speak to someone from Océane's family?"

Yeye stepped forward.

"The operation went very smoothly. You can relax. And it looks as though the tumour's benign."

The family were overjoyed at the news.

"We'll have the final results in a week," said the doctor. "Then, all being well, she can go home."

Everyone in the family was thinking about Nainai, wishing and praying for her in their own way. Xiaogu kept looking up, closing her eyes and patting her hands together in front of her chest. Ah Mei desperately wanted to play a tune on the piano for Nainai, right there and then. She knew it was impossible, and for a moment she felt lost without the piano. Then, the thought of Nainai being out of danger gave her such boundless joy that she could think of nothing else.

It was early morning when Nainai came round from the anaesthetic. The pure light of the autumn dawn shone through the hospital window, and a few sparrows hopped about on the window ledge, chirping away. She wondered if she had woken up in another world. It was only a matter of hours since all her children and grandchildren had gathered round her bed, and she'd been wheeled slowly from the ward to the operating theatre. She had felt no fear whatsoever. She had held Yeye's hand until the very last minute, until she passed through the theatre doors. Then, as the doors closed behind her, the faces of her children and grandchildren had flashed before her eyes. She was surprised at how many there were! If they stood side by side, they'd make a very long line. She had suddenly realized how lucky she was. While the doctors and nurses were getting everything ready, as the surgical instruments were clanging into white enamel bowls, she had calmly thought that if she were to lose her life on the operating table, then she would die with no regrets. And, at that moment, she felt very strongly the depth of her attachment to China, to Shanghai.

After the operation, the nurses allowed only one family member to stay with Nainai, and, naturally, that person was Yeye.

He sat in the chair by Nainai's bed, his hands clasping her right hand.

When Nainai opened her eyes, she looked at Yeye. "Meixi…" she said in a weak voice.

"Océane!"

"Have I come back?"

"Well, I hope so, because I haven't gone yet!"

"Do you know what the nurse said when she saw how many people came with me to theatre yesterday?"

"I do. She said you were a very lucky lady."

"How do you know?"

Yeye smiled.

After a while, Nainai remembered something. "I was quite surprised," she said.

"By what?"

There was uncertainty and regret in her eyes. "Yesterday, at that moment between life and death, I didn't think about Marseilles or Lyons or France, or about my family there…"

Yeye held Nainai's hand tightly. "That's understandable. They're a long way away, and it's been a long time. But they've always been in your heart. Maybe you can't see it, but I can."

She closed her eyes. Tears trickled down her face.

Yeye brushed them away lightly with his hand.

Nainai recovered very quickly. The nurses relaxed the visiting rules, so whenever Ah Mei was free, she would drop by the hospital.

"Ah, here's the person I most wanted to see!" said Nainai, the first time she saw Ah Mei after the operation. Ah Mei glanced at Yeye. Nainai took hold of Ah Mei's arm. "I didn't mean him."

Yeye smiled.

Whenever Ah Mei came to see Nainai, she would chatter away for the whole visit.

Nurses would come in to take Nainai's temperature, slip the thermometer out from under her arm, check the reading and say to Ah Mei, "Young lady, your nainai needs to rest."

But as soon as the nurse had gone, Nainai would say, "Keep talking." They never seemed to run out of things to say.

Mama remarked on this to Baba. "I have the feeling Ma knew Ah Mei a long time before October 1953."

"You mean, in a previous life?" said Baba.

"I don't know, it sometimes feels like that."

One day, after school, Ah Mei went straight to the hospital to see Nainai as usual. The two of them talked for a while, then Nainai said, "I'm looking forward to hearing my Aina play the piano."

Ah Mei froze.

"How about now?" Nainai asked.

"But there isn't a piano."

"You can use my bed as a piano!" said Nainai, shuffling to one side to make enough room for her granddaughter.

"I'm not sure how to play," said Ah Mei.

"Imagine the bed is the piano," said Nainai. "When I see your fingers moving, I'll hear the music."

"What shall I play?"

Nainai said, "How about *La Marseillaise*? I've been lying here for ages now. I should get up. I need something invigorating to help me. When I was a very little girl I used to sing it. There was something about it – whenever I sang it, I would lift my head up and stick my chest out, and feel the power rising inside me. Play it, so your nainai can think of Marseilles and her family."

"All right." Ah Mei nodded, pulled the chair closer to the bed and tried to play her fingers on the covers. It took a while to get the hang of it, but she soon forgot it was a bed rather than a piano. She could picture the black and white keys on the white sheet. It was a well-sprung bed with a lot of bounce, and Ah Mei's small hands played vigorously.

Nainai, who, as she said, had been in bed for a long time, gradually sat up, unsupported – like a fallen rice seedling righting itself in the sunshine and rain. As Ah Mei "played" unselfconsciously, Nainai began to hum along. As she hummed, it was as if she might suddenly get out of bed and, with a perfectly straight back, walk through the door, out of the hospital and down the road to the Blue House … or even all the way to Marseilles.

After banging out the final part of the song, Ah Mei's fingers stopped in mid-air, like a bird in the wind.

Nainai put her hands on Ah Mei's and gently brought them down. "I'll soon be out of hospital and back home again," she said, letting out a very long breath.

It was getting dark outside.

"It's time for you to go home, Aina," said Nainai.

As she was preparing to leave, Ah Mei shuffled her feet, and said, "Océane, I want to stop playing the piano."

"*What?*"

"I want to stop playing the piano."

Nainai was taken aback. It didn't make any sense. "Can you tell me why?"

"I don't enjoy it any more."

Nainai didn't say anything, but her eyes didn't leave Ah Mei's face.

Eventually Ah Mei made her way towards the door. At the last minute, she glanced back. "I don't enjoy it any more," she repeated firmly.

"Go home now. We can talk about it when I get back."

A few days later, the results of Nainai's tests came through: the tumour that had been removed was benign.

The whole family rejoiced.

*   *   *

Nainai finally came home from the hospital. The following day she discovered the piano had gone. It was a Sunday, and the whole family was there. When she asked Baba and Mama about the piano, they told her the truth. Nainai's face completely changed colour. "How could you, Tony!" Nainai only used Baba's French name in very exceptional circumstances. "And you too, Shuping!"

Baba and Mama stood in front of Nainai and hung their heads.

"I will be frank with you both. You may have thought you were doing the right thing, but I am not happy with what you have done." Nainai's voice suddenly grew louder. "I AM NOT HAPPY WITH IT AT ALL!"

Mrs Hu was on her way downstairs. When she heard the anger in Nainai's voice, she stopped where she was.

Baba and Mama were standing side by side.

Nainai glanced over at Yeye. "Did you know about this?"

Baba answered quickly, "It was our idea, mine and Shuping's. He didn't know anything about it."

"I did," said Yeye.

Baba and Mama looked at Yeye, wondering what he would say next.

"I did know," said Yeye, more quietly than before.

Nainai pointed her finger at Yeye. "Du Mei Xi!"

Nainai rarely called Yeye by his full name. She usually called him by his first name, and when she did, whether in a French accent or a Chinese one, those two syllables – Mei-xi – rolled from her mouth with great warmth and affection.

"DU MEI-XI!"

Yeye shuddered at each syllable. They were like bullets to the chest.

Nainai turned around and stormed upstairs. Mrs Hu darted out of her way. A door slammed, and everyone else shuddered too.

Nainai's door stayed shut all day. Baba, Mama, Yeye and Mrs Hu all tried knocking, but Nainai ignored them. None of them knew what to do.

Eventually, Ah Mei went up to Nainai's door. She knocked gently. Nainai could tell immediately that it was her granddaughter, and when Ah Mei had knocked a few times, she opened the door.

"Nainai, it's dinner time."

"I don't want anything," said Nainai, then she lay down on the bed.

Ah Mei climbed onto the bed too, intending to lie down beside her, but Nainai's hands gently pushed her away – she was too angry. Ah Mei was persistent, though, and, like a kitten wanting to snuggle up, she moved closer.

"What do you want?" Nainai wouldn't even look at Ah Mei.

Ah Mei moved closer to Nainai.

Baba, Mama, Yeye and Mrs Hu were all listening out for sounds from Nainai's room.

Ah Mei and Nainai lay on the bed, in silence.

Then, finally, Nainai said, "You told me you didn't enjoy playing the piano any more."

Ah Mei nodded.

"But that's not how you really feel, is it?" As she spoke, Nainai turned to face Ah Mei.

Ah Mei snuggled closer.

When Nainai had said a lot of angry things, Ah Mei suddenly started crying. "We didn't want you to die!"

Nainai cried too.

Deep down, they had all wanted the same thing. Ah Mei sobbed in Nainai's arms until she had no tears left, and Nainai's mood lifted, like a wisp of smoke vanishing into thin air.

"They didn't ask you first, did they?"

Ah Mei didn't answer.

"That's men for you. Especially your baba, and Yeye, too. They're birds of a feather, those two. We girls would never do something like that."

Ah Mei wanted to laugh and remind Nainai that Mama had been in on it too.

"But we can forgive them. They did it behind your back because they wouldn't have been able to bear it otherwise." As Nainai spoke, she thought of the piano and of Ah Mei in full flow. She could hear the music now and couldn't help pulling Ah Mei closer.

Over the next few days, Ah Mei went to school happily and came back happily, as though the piano had faded from her mind. But it continued to bother Nainai. Surely Ah Mei couldn't have forgotten it so easily? The child was showing great maturity, and the more Nainai realized this, the more upset she felt. She wished it had not come to this.

The piano room was empty and the door was kept shut.

For years, the sound of the piano had flowed through the Blue House, filling it with life. But now the house felt empty and bleak, like a building in a desert – unlived in.

Every day when Ah Mei came home from school, before she was through the door, her cheerful voice would ring out: "Nai–nai… I'm ho–ome…"

And Nainai would appear and reply just as cheerfully, "Ah Me–ei!"

There'd be the usual happy hustle and bustle, and chattering, and then Ah Mei would go to her room to do her homework. And every day, at this time, a feeling of desolation would creep over Nainai, like the thin mist that lingers over the fields in early spring.

Nainai had seen Ah Mei walking past the piano room a few times. She had noticed how Ah Mei would look away and quicken her step, as though walking past something that was painful, that she was trying to avoid. Nainai had also discovered that Ah Mei had put away the sheet music: she had stuffed it all in a drawer and locked it. Mrs Hu told Nainai that, after locking the drawer, Ah Mei had thrown the key out of the window.

But the piano was already in Ah Mei's soul and couldn't be forgotten. It would suddenly appear in her mind when she was in class, or doing her homework, eating, walking, skipping with Qiu Qiu and the other girls. It would simply appear, and then, after a while, the music would start, and the black and white keys would begin to go up and down, as if they had a life and a soul of their own. Every now and then, Ah Mei had to clasp her hands over her eyes or her ears.

The old piano with the glossy finish you could see your face in appeared in Ah Mei's dreams several times. In her dreams it had magic powers. It arrived in different ways: sometimes drifting in on the mist; sometimes emerging from clear water. Sometimes there'd be a wilderness with tall grass, and when the wind blew, the grass would bend, revealing the piano, all shiny and bright… Ah Mei found these dreams strange and absurd. When she woke, she found it hard to go back to sleep. The same question would go round and round inside her head: if she had never seen these scenes before, then how could they appear in her dreams?

No one else in the family knew that Ah Mei had a piece of paper, on which was written the address of the piano. She had had it since Nainai was in hospital.

At first Ah Mei hadn't missed the piano, but after a week, she began to miss it terribly, and couldn't stop thinking about it. Then, one day, she had gone out to stretch her legs, and without realizing it, had started walking towards the pawn shop. It had changed its name – it was now a "credit store" – but the people inside were essentially the same people who had worked in the pawn shop. Nainai preferred to use the old name. Even though the characters for "credit store" were written clearly on the sign above the shop, and Nainai could read them perfectly well, she still called it the pawn shop. Ah Mei had come here with Nainai many times. It was a very big shop, and Ah Mei thought Baba must have brought the piano here. And she knew, from listening to the adults talking, that this was the fairest, most trustworthy pawn shop, that the staff were people you could talk to, who understood their customers.

Ah Mei shuffled her feet as she went in. The piano had gone. There were two pianos at the side, but neither of them was the one from the Blue House. The staff recognized Ah Mei, and greeted her with a nod – a combination of pity and awkwardness. They knew about this little girl and the piano, and they knew why her family had brought the instrument to them. They understood these things only too well. They had paid Baba quickly, and had paid the amount he asked, and hadn't tried to beat him down. On a personal level, they had hoped the piano would be a slow seller, and that Baba and the others would soon be able to raise the money to buy it back. But, someone had come along the very same day, seen the piano, fallen in love with it, offered the full asking price and taken it away then and there. As the shop had paid a significant sum of money to Baba, and they needed to keep the cash flowing, they couldn't turn business away, and without a second thought, they had let the piano go. And then Ah Mei herself had come to the shop. The man who had sold the piano told her what had happened. Ah Mei cried. She cried so hard and refused to leave the shop, as though it wasn't a case of the family having brought the piano to them, but of their having seized the piano and Ah Mei coming to demand that they return it. The staff tried to console her, but to no avail. Then she sat on the doorstep, silently weeping, as though her heart was broken. Finally, when it began to get dark, the man in the shop gave her a slip of paper. "This is the address of the man who bought the piano. Sitting here won't do you any good, you know. When your family can get the money together, you can ask them to go and see him. He looked a decent, reasonable kind of person. It's late, child. Go home."

Ah Mei looked towards the main street. The lamps were already lit. She took the piece of paper and slowly headed home.

Ah Mei kept the address under her mattress.

Then, one day, instead of going straight home after school, Ah Mei took the piece of paper and went to the house of the man who had bought the piano. The street, the lane, the door number were all written out clearly. The address wasn't close to her school, but it wasn't too far. Ah Mei took a half-hour bus ride, then walked for about ten minutes, asking people the way, and finally found the place she was looking for.

She didn't knock on the door, of course, because the piano didn't belong to her any more. The only reason she had come was because she missed the piano so much.

It was a small two-storey building, which looked very old. There were a lot of buildings like this in the neighbourhood – rows of houses, with a long flowerbed in front of each. Ah Mei was tired, and sat down by the flowerbed. She wished someone would start playing the piano. She didn't want to see it, she just wanted to hear it – to hear its notes would be enough.

It was rush hour and there were people everywhere coming and going. People with nylon string bags were buying small quantities of vegetables at the side of the road, as though these were the only vegetables that were available. The people walking up and down were so thin, their mouths seemed to gape, and after a hard day at work, their faces looked ashen. They barely had the strength to notice an unfamiliar young girl. Nobody even glanced at Ah Mei, although she looked quite different from other children. They weren't interested, and they didn't have the energy to look.

Ah Mei took her books out of her school bag. This was the time when she usually did her homework, so she did it while she waited to hear the sound of the piano.

Just as she'd hoped, eventually someone started playing. Ah Mei recognized the sound immediately. She could hear a thousand pianos at the same time, and be wearing a blindfold, and she would still be able to pick out the sound of that one piano.

When Ah Mei had started at middle school, she had written an essay about the piano, in which she'd said that it sounded old, like a sound from the past, from the forest, from the river, from the sea… It was the best way to explain how she felt about it. The teacher didn't seem to understand what she meant, but said she had a special sensitivity.

The piano music drifted out of the two-storey building and seeped into the dusk.

Ah Mei loved the piano, and she was a gifted player. She had earned spontaneous applause from so many people. But no matter how well she played, she was still a child. The person playing the piano now played well, exceptionally well. Ah Mei had a long way to go to reach that standard, and she knew it.

She knew for sure that the person playing the piano was not a child.

Ah Mei sat by the flowerbed and waited until the street lamps came on before dragging herself away and going home.

After that, every few days, she would take the same bus to the same street, and walk to the same lane. She arrived in time to hear the piano-playing, which started at about the same time every day.

Nainai noticed that Ah Mei was late home sometimes, and asked her why. When Ah Mei ummed and ahhed and failed to come up with a credible answer, Nainai grew suspicious, and decided to follow her. One evening, before the sun had completely set, there was a large moon shining over Shanghai. Ah Mei sat on the edge of the flowerbed, listening quietly in the moonlight. She had forgotten that her original reason for coming was because she missed the piano, and she had become so absorbed in the music that this in itself was now her reason for being there.

Nainai stood quite a long way behind her.

When Ah Mei finally got up and turned to go home, Nainai did not try to hide. Ah Mei had never expected to see her there.

"Nainai!"

Nainai came over and held out her hand.

Ah Mei slipped her hand into Nainai's.

Nainai held Ah Mei's hand all the way home. They didn't say much, and, of course, neither of them mentioned the piano.

Late that night when all was quiet, Nainai opened the little leather suitcase. There was a box inside, and inside the box were two necklaces, and a ring. The necklaces had been wedding presents, one from each of her sisters. The ring had been a gift from her mother, who had been given it by her own mother. Océane was the youngest of three sisters, and her mother's favourite, so when she got married, her mother had given her the ring as a gift, and as a dowry. It was a diamond ring, and the diamond wasn't a small one. Nainai didn't know how many carats it weighed or how valuable it was. What she did know was that the ring and the two necklaces would probably be enough to get the piano back. Nainai would willingly give them up for the piano.

The next day, Nainai took the jewellery box to the pawn shop. When she showed the salesmen the contents, their eyes lit up. "That diamond would fetch a small fortune overseas," said the old man, the one with the most experience. But what Nainai wanted to know was, "In China, in Shanghai, right now, how much can I get for it? Enough to get the piano back?" The old salesman was very careful. He looked at the diamond in the ring several times, and then said, "If the man who bought the piano doesn't try to take advantage of the situation and raise the price, then it's definitely enough."

"Do you think he'd be willing to let us have it back – I mean, now it belongs to him?" Nainai asked anxiously.

"He seemed a reasonable kind of person," said the old man.

"Should we offer the two necklaces as well?" asked Nainai.

"There's no need, the ring should be enough. The main thing is whether he's willing to part with the piano."

"I know him," said a young salesman. "He's a teacher at the music academy. He studied abroad, in Paris."

"Paris?" Nainai perked up immediately.

Nainai was ready to finalize the exchange at the pawn shop, but the old salesman tried to delay her.

"Take it home and think it over. I don't think it's a good deal for you. Here in Shanghai, there are still people who know a good piano when they see one, but as for a diamond like yours, there might be one or two who know its value, but I can't be sure. I don't feel comfortable about buying it from you."

But Nainai was sure. "I want to pawn it. As long as you can give me the money now, let's do it. My granddaughter loves that piano."

"We know," said the salesmen.

That evening Nainai knocked on the man's door.

She explained why she had come.

He had indeed been a teacher at the music academy. He was retired, and his name was Mr Ma. And just as the salesman in the pawn shop had predicted, Mr Ma was decent and reasonable, someone who would listen. When France and Paris were mentioned, Mr M's face brightened. In the blink of an eye, Mr Ma and Nainai became friends, as though they went back a very very long time. For over an hour, they didn't even mention the piano, but talked about France, Marseilles, Lyons, Paris, about Provence, lavender, vineyards, about the Alps, the Louvre, the Seine, the Sacré-Cœur. Eventually Nainai remembered why she had come to see this Mr Ma.

"That day, I was walking past the pawn shop, and just happened to see the piano. I knew immediately that whoever had taken it there wouldn't have parted with it unless they needed the money urgently. So I wrote down my address especially, in case one day its owners had money, and wanted it back."

He sighed. "I love this old piano. When I bought it, I never imagined it would have such a beautiful tone! This is no ordinary piano. And now that I know the story, I'm happy for it to go home. I won't take a penny more than I paid for it."

The piano returned to the Blue House the next morning.

It went back to its original position in the piano room. Nainai spent the entire afternoon polishing it with a soft cloth, although it hadn't seen a speck of dust while it had been at Mr Ma's.

That evening, when Ah Mei came home from school, Nainai was waiting for her. She led Ah Mei to the door of the piano room, and said, "Aina, push the door open."

Ah Mei looked at Nainai.

Open the door, said Nainai's eyes. *Open the door*.

Ah Mei pushed the door gently. When it was half open, she poked her head inside and saw the piano. She froze – she didn't let go of the door handle, or open the door any further. It was Nainai who pushed it the rest of the way, and when Ah Mei still didn't move, Nainai gave her a gentle nudge forward.

Ah Mei walked slowly up to the piano, and gently lifted the lid. It had been a while since she had played, and she let her hands touch a few random keys. "Océane," she said quietly. She didn't turn her head to look at Nainai, because her eyes were full of tears.

Her tears fell and landed on the keys. They were so big and so heavy that they were almost playing the piano themselves.

CHAPTER 12

The Interior

Long before Ah Mei started school, she and her parents had almost left Shanghai to go and live somewhere else.

Somewhere else didn't mean overseas, it meant in the "interior", the middle of the vast country of China. At that time, the political wind kept changing, and the situation was tense. From the way people were talking, there would be war soon: World War III. Things looked so tense that people felt they might wake up in the morning to see flocks of planes over Shanghai, dropping bombs that whistled as they fell. Yeye said, "It's only a few years since the end of the last World War, how can we be fighting again? What is wrong with this world? Is it so hard to live in peace?" This time, if there was war, they would be fighting different forces, because the Soviet Union, their past ally, was now their enemy. The fear of war was serious, and many important research institutes and factories were being moved to the interior where it would be hard for the enemy to find them, to places like Sichuan, and Henan. Shanghai was on the coast of China, and if the enemy came by sea, it would be the first place they reached.

Baba and Mama worked at a large factory that produced very important goods. But, it was cloaked in secrecy, and even when she was at middle school, Ah Mei still didn't know what the factory made. Baba never mentioned it at home, and nor did Mama. They never talked about work. There was no question of this mysterious factory not moving to the interior – the factory and all its staff. The family prepared to leave Shanghai, but when the time came for the factory to relocate to Yibin, in Sichuan, Baba stayed behind after all. He was an engineer in the research department, and it had been arranged that when the factory moved, the researchers could stay in Shanghai for the time being to continue their work. It was some kind of collaborative research with the universities, and as the universities could not move to the interior, it was agreed that the researchers could stay in Shanghai for a while. So, Baba and Mama didn't move straight away, but still had to go to Yibin from time to time. All Ah Mei knew was that their work involved lots of travelling to Yibin.

When Yeye and Nainai learned that Baba and Mama could stay in Shanghai, they gave a long sigh of relief.

However, during the next few years, the family was constantly on edge, and unable to relax. They knew that one day, they didn't know when, they would receive notification that the time had come to move to the interior. Nainai fretted about Baba and Mama leaving Shanghai. And she fretted even more about Ah Mei leaving her side. Without Ah Mei, her life would have no flavour. For now, though, Baba and Mama continued as always: they left home early in the morning, went to work in the research institute on Huating Road, and did not get home until after dark.

Meanwhile, Nainai continued proofreading manuscripts. Sometimes, while she was working, the term "the interior" would come to her mind. The thought of the interior distracted her, unsettling her so much that she couldn't focus on her work. She would rush off to a place with a public phone and call Baba and Mama. She needed to know they were still at work, and that everything was all right. Only then could she calm down.

This had been the situation for a few years now. Nainai compared it to being on a boat that was moored to the riverbank, knowing that one day the rope could suddenly break and the boat drift out to sea and never be moored again. Yeye had laughed at her many times, and tried to reassure her, but he couldn't entirely relieve her of her anxiety. Every so often she would ask him, "What's it like in the interior?"

Nainai's fears became reality when Ah Mei was twelve. That autumn, Baba and Mama were told that the factory, which had relocated successfully to the interior, urgently needed scientists at the frontline of production. They were to go to Yibin immediately.

Baba and Mama had been expecting this. They felt a sense of relief at not being left dangling in the air any longer. For the last few years, they had felt the uncertainty even more keenly than Nainai – they knew that sooner or later they would have to move to Yibin. It wasn't just a matter of moving to a new place far away from home, it meant leaving Shanghai for ever, as their residency papers would move with them.

For Nainai, hearing the news was like being struck by lightning. Although she'd been preparing herself for a long time, now that it was actually going to happen, she felt more unsettled than ever. Her mind raced all over the place, her thoughts wouldn't keep still. Her anxiety was boundless, she was unable to sleep at night.

"What about your *hukou*? Is there a way of keeping your Shanghai residency?" Nainai asked Baba and Mama.

"No," said Baba. "When we go, our residence permits go with us."

"Does that mean you won't ever be able to come back to Shanghai?" Nainai looked devastated.

Baba didn't answer.

Mama tried to reassure her. "Of course we'll be back. The world can't remain in this state of tension for ever. We'll be back in no time."

"What about Ah Mei's *hukou*?" Nainai asked.

Baba and Mama didn't answer.

"Will her *hukou* be sent to the interior too?" Nainai had been sitting down. At this point, she stood up.

"She's our daughter – she has to go with us," said Baba.

"Is this your decision?" Nainai continued her questioning.

"No," said Baba. "It's come from the top."

Nainai's hands started shaking. She was becoming a little unsteady. Yeye went to her, and helped her sit down again.

"Ah Mei can't leave Shanghai! She can't leave me!" Nainai was becoming distraught. "What are they doing making a child go to the interior too? Is she a factory worker or research staff? She's only a child! She's at primary school! What on earth do they want her to do there? She can't go."

Baba and Mama responded immediately. "We want her *hukou* to stay in Shanghai too. We'll go back to the office and try again."

"You have to let Ah Mei stay in Shanghai!" said Nainai. "How can they do something like this? How?"

While Baba and Mama were out, asking the relevant department about Ah Mei's *hukou*, Nainai tried to get on with her work. But her hands wouldn't stop shaking. She was too agitated to concentrate on the text. So she put it down, and walked around the house, upstairs and downstairs, inside and outside.

That evening, Baba and Mama came home with the news. The three *hukou* – for Baba, Mama and Ah Mei – had already been sent to Yibin, but Ah Mei could stay in Shanghai and go to school here.

There was nothing they could do about the *hukou*, but at least Ah Mei could stay in Shanghai for the time being.

"We mustn't tell Ah Mei that her *hukou* has been sent to Yibin," Nainai said.

Yeye, Baba and Mama all nodded.

"Let's keep her in the dark for as long as we can," said Nainai. "She would be so upset if she knew she wasn't a Shanghainese any more, and was only allowed to be here so she could go to school. Let her grow up first. Right now she has a lot on her mind. It's hard enough as it is, and this would crush her."

Nainai gradually calmed down, and tried to face this change bravely.

When Ah Mei saw Baba and Mama packing their bags, she seemed to know something unusual was happening. She didn't ask them where they were going, but went instead to Nainai. "Océane…" she said, pointing downstairs to her parents, who were busy packing.

Nainai didn't look at all worried. "Oh, your baba and mama are going to the interior, to give their support," she answered lightly.

Am I going too? Ah Mei wanted to ask. But she didn't.

Nainai could read Ah Mei's thoughts. "Aina, you can stay here with me. Would you like that?"

Ah Mei nodded.

"If you miss Baba and Mama, I'll take you to see them. And they can come and see you often."

Baba and Mama had only a week left in Shanghai. They were given time off work to spend with the family, to pack and to say goodbye to their nearest and dearest friends. After that, there would no longer be a place for them in Shanghai.

As each of those seven days passed, Baba and Mama became more and more emotional. They had grown up in this city, been to school here, they had worked here, got married here, and Ah Mei had been born here. They were accustomed to, and loved, the way of life in Shanghai. Life here was special. Shanghai was the largest city in China, the only city that could truly be described as "metropolitan". For so many years they had been a part of it, and they were proud of being a part of it. Like the rest of the city's residents, given the chance they would choose to speak the language of Shanghai, to show they were Shanghainese. But very soon – no, right now – they would stop being Shanghainese. They would be people of the interior, people of Yibin. From now on, when they came to Shanghai they would be visitors, people passing through, nothing more.

What upset them most of all – what they couldn't bear – was that Ah Mei was no longer part of Shanghai either. She would find out one day, and when she did, how would she react? She would be so upset, so hurt! They were more upset at the thought of how distressed Ah Mei would be than they were about themselves.

They did not want Yeye, Nainai and Ah Mei to see how upset they were, however, and they tried their best to appear relaxed and happy, so that to Yeye and Nainai, and especially Ah Mei, it would seem that they were just going on a trip – a very long trip.

Yeye spent almost the entire week sitting silently in a chair on the verandah. These past few years he had aged faster than any of them. He was a tall man, and had always had a good physique, but now that he was older he felt the burden of his body weighing him down. His movement was getting slower and slower. Going downstairs took him a long time, and left him out of breath. Even getting out of the chair felt like a huge effort, and seemed to take for ever.

Mama spent a large part of each day that week with Nainai.

Nainai loved her daughter-in-law, and was full of appreciation for her. She had taken to her the first time she came to the Blue House. Mama felt the same about Nainai: she loved her foreign mother-in-law, her second mother, and was full of appreciation for her too. They were always together, and always had plenty to talk about. So many years had gone by, and they had held the same opinions on almost everything. Mama liked Nainai's generosity of spirit, her tolerance and her elegance and grace in everything. And Nainai found Mama gentle, good at understanding others and kind in all ways. The two of them, one Western, one Eastern, couldn't have looked more different, and yet they came together under one roof as smoothly as water and milk. They were more like sisters than mother- and daughter-in-law.

They were so close that the thought of one being in Yibin and the other being in Shanghai was like them living at the other side of the world from each other.

On top of not wanting to leave, there was something else worrying Mama. Nainai was getting old, and now, when Nainai needed her most, she was going far away. On their last two days in Shanghai, after she and Baba had sent off the bulk of their luggage, Mama spent almost the entire time, from morning to night, either chatting with Nainai or doing jobs, as though she wanted to finish the next few years' worth of jobs before she left. Mrs Hu tried to stop her: "Leave that, I'll do it!" she said over and over again. But Mama was determined to sweep the floor that was already spotless, and to wash Nainai's clothes that Mrs Hu had just washed... Mama felt there was still so much more to be done, and she wouldn't be able to do it in future. Once she had gone to that faraway place, perhaps she could come back once a year, but she couldn't say for sure.

Mama took some comfort in knowing that Ah Mei would be staying with Nainai. Although she would have to leave eventually, for the time being she could stay. And although Ah Mei was only a child, and couldn't do very much for Nainai, at least if Ah Mei was by her side, Nainai wouldn't feel so deserted. Ah Mei was young and had so much to give her grandmother, things that Mama couldn't give her.

The night before Mama left Shanghai, she and Ah Mei slept in the same bed.

"When Baba and I have gone, you must look after Nainai," Mama told Ah Mei. She thought this was probably a ridiculous thing to say. After all, what could Ah Mei do? But she said it anyway. "Do what your yeye and nainai tell you. You're not a baby any more, you're a big girl now."

"I know," said Ah Mei.

"You can do things for yourself now," said Mama.

"I know," said Ah Mei.

"You must play the piano. You can't drop it. Nainai cares about this more than anything."

"I know," said Ah Mei.

Mama went on late into the night, telling Ah Mei what she should and shouldn't do. Then, noticing that Ah Mei had fallen asleep, she sighed and tucked the covers around her daughter.

The whole family came to the station to see Baba and Mama off the next day.

As they were saying their goodbyes and wishing one another well, everyone did their best to put on a happy face. Nainai, wearing a qipao and surrounded by her children and grandchildren, was smiling. When the train was ready to leave, Nainai lowered her head, and whispered to Ah Mei, "Go and give Baba and Mama a hug, but don't cry." Ah Mei nodded, and ran over to them. She hugged Mama first, then Baba, then the three of them hugged all together, as tightly as they could.

Baba and Mama were blurry-eyed, but Ah Mei didn't cry.

The train began to move.

People on and off it were waving.

Ah Mei wanted to run after the train, but Nainai gripped her hand firmly.

The train pulled out of the station, and gradually became, in Ah Mei's eyes, a stream of green, with fuzzy edges.

When Baba and Mama could no longer see Ah Mei and the others, they turned around and calmly sat down.

Mama said to Baba, "Your parents look so old."

Baba nodded.

CHAPTER 13

Ah Lang

1966. Ah Mei was thirteen.

The world seemed to be under some kind of magic spell. People did what people do – they ate, and slept, and walked, and talked, but there was a strange expression in their eyes now. Their mindset had changed. It was the same sun in the sky, the same Huangpu River, the same Shanghai, but none of these felt the same any more. The mood had changed: people had become angry, adamant, awkward. They went around with sticks, lashing out and smashing things. They looked excitedly for glass and fragile things, for the thrill of hearing them shatter and make a mess. One girl changed overnight: one evening she'd been sitting by the Huangpu, watching the moon rise and writing a poem, and the next morning she'd taken off her belt and started beating people, including her teacher, who had always liked her writing, especially when it was about the moon.

There were protests everywhere. There was shouting in the streets. Workers weren't going to work, farmers weren't going to farm, students weren't going to study – there were more interesting and more exciting things attracting their attention. Husband and wife no longer saw eye to eye. Father and son became sworn enemies. Students beat their teachers. Long hair was not allowed. High heels were not allowed. Lipstick was not allowed. Singing Shanghai love songs was not allowed. Kissing in the park was not allowed. Going to the temples to burn incense and touch your forehead to the ground was certainly not allowed. Girls with pale faces were no longer considered pretty. Bright clothes were no longer considered beautiful. Singing had to be vigorous, powerful, hot-blooded and passionate. Walking had to be loud; you had to pound the ground till it shook beneath your feet. Whispering was out. Talking had to be loud, you had to speak up and speak out, and make hand gestures when you spoke, and stick out your chest and punch the air with your fist.

There were events every day, things that made some people high with excitement, and others shudder with fear.

Mrs Hu often heard protests outside. She'd open the window or lean over the balcony, and watch the protesters as they marched down the street, shouting slogans. She noticed that they were shouting, "Down with …!" followed by people's names. She didn't know why they wanted to attack those individuals, or what those people had done to be attacked. She would stand there for a while, watching and listening, bewilderment written all over her face. Then, remembering where she was, she'd quickly close the window. She told Nainai, "Madam, it's not safe out there. Stay home if you can, stay away from the streets." And she told Ah Mei, "Come straight home after school. Don't stop on the way."

Nainai grew more and more uneasy. It might have been better if she had some proofreading to do, but there weren't any texts to check these days. The publishing houses appeared to have stopped publishing, and she didn't know if there'd ever be any more work like that. Ever since Ah Mei's parents had left Shanghai, Nainai had found the Blue House eerily empty. These days, it felt even emptier, disconcertingly empty. One day, she watched as a gust of wind blew through the apricot tree and sent a flurry of white blossom flying through the sky. It was a warm day, but Nainai felt a cold chill in the air around her, and instinctively hugged her shoulders.

Yeye gave up the gate-keeping job, and stayed at home.

He sensed that the Blue House could not escape the turbulence of the outside world. It was like a boat anchored at sea with the wind and waves raging all around. He had to come back, to return to the Blue House, to look after Nainai twenty-four hours a day. It seemed he had a very clear premonition: that his Océane would be caught up in the middle of the maelstrom. He couldn't say what this premonition was based on, only that he could sense what lay ahead. From then on, he would not leave Océane's side.

The children were also growing increasingly concerned about the Blue House. Baba and Mama, far away in Yibin, telephoned weekly to ask how things were.

The whole family felt weighed down with worry, unsettled and anxious, as though the raging winds and waves were heading straight towards them. And they were right to be worried – their fears were becoming reality.

The first to experience it personally was Ah Mei's cousin, Ah Lang.

Ah Lang's French name was Alain. Nainai had chosen it. And because Alain sounded like Ah Lang, that became his Chinese name. When Nainai called him, you could tell by the tone of her voice if she was using his French name or his Chinese name.

Ah Lang was Erbo's only child. He was fifteen, three years older than Ah Mei, and in the first year of senior high.

Ah Lang was a sensitive boy, the most sensitive child in the whole family.

Of all Nainai's grandchildren, Ah Lang's French heritage was the most apparent, the most persistent. One look at his slightly wavy, slightly fair hair and the high bridge of his nose was enough for people to judge that he was not fully Chinese. With his long legs, his tall height, broad shoulders and deep eyes, Ah Lang was a good-looking young man. Since he first started school, he had been admired for his looks. The boys envied him, the girls adored him, and none of them tried to disguise it. Ah Lang had grown up with countless eyes upon him. He might appear a little proud sometimes, but mostly his attitude was: *It's nothing. I'm just like everyone else*. He was a figure of modesty, like Nainai, and had inherited her diffidence, which made him even more attractive, even more lovable. He had always been popular, and surrounded by friends.

But he had recently begun to notice that the gaze in those eyes was changing. He was still the centre of attention, perhaps even more than before, but the envy and adoration were slipping away, replaced with doubt and scrutiny, as though his appearance aroused suspicion.

Before, when he had avoided people's eyes – the eyes of children and adults – it was out of bashfulness, because he felt the way he looked really wasn't anything special, and because, actually, he did look a little different from them. But now, when he avoided their eyes, it was because he felt a kind of isolation, a kind of terror. *Am I a monster?* he began to wonder.

Every morning before school, he would stand in front of the mirror for a long time. And when he returned from school, the first thing he did was come back to the mirror again and examine his face. He felt increasingly uneasy about his appearance, suspicious even. When he went outside, he would subconsciously lower his head, and look at the ground, whereas before, he always held his head high, like Ah Mei. Now, when he reached the school, he preferred to stand at a distance from his classmates, whereas before he had always enjoyed mixing with them.

Their probing eyes became more and more intense, more and more determined. They were conspicuously cold and hard, and it was not long before he began to feel their animosity towards him. Alarmed and tense, he would hurry to the side, where their eyes could not reach his face.

This continued until one day, after school, Ah Lang was walking towards the school gate, his school bag on his back, when a classroom window on the second floor opened, and two boys peered out. As Ah Lang hurried away, they yelled at him.

"Foreign devil!"

"Foreign devil boy!"

When Ah Lang looked up, he saw two mocking faces, their eyes full of malice. He lowered his head, quickened his pace and headed for the school gate. He felt as though the eyes of the entire school were on him, laughing, gleefully mocking the "foreign devil". Then he slowed down. He wanted to know exactly what that look in their eyes meant, to know whether or not he was imagining things. Feeling unsure of himself, he looked up and scanned the eyes of the children near by. Some turned away. Others continued to watch him – they were suspicious, probing, overtly hostile, their eyes piercing the high bridge of his nose, his deeply set eyes and the slight fairness of his hair.

Two girls walked past him.

"Do you think he's a German devil? Or an American devil?"

"I don't know, but he's some kind of devil!"

With all those eyes boring into him, Ah Lang looked down again. He wanted to run away as fast as he could. But he did his best to maintain a normal walking speed. He told himself that he was a boy, that boys should be strong and brave. At the same time, it felt as though his mind had gone blank, and everything was flashing before his eyes.

He felt no relief outside the school gate. He continued walking, his head down, keeping close to the wall, then crossing the street as timidly as a mouse. He had been looked at before – eyes turned to him whenever he appeared – but they had never been malicious, just curious, even appreciative, as though they were looking at a statue. The eyes on him now could not have been more different.

He caught sight of his classmate Shu Xiu. He began to feel flustered, his heart racing. He liked Shu Xiu, and he knew that she liked him … that she liked him a lot. When the two of them were together, Shu Xiu didn't talk much; she liked to listen to him talking, and when he talked, she narrowed her eyes and watched his face – his eyes, his nose, his mouth, his hair. He suspected she didn't listen, but he didn't mind; he liked the attention. So he talked, and she listened, until he got embarrassed and lowered his head, and she did the same, until he started talking again, and she went back to listening.

Their classmates all knew they were secretly in love.

The girls were rather jealous of Shu Xiu.

Shu Xiu didn't care. Often, during a lesson, her mind would start wandering – and she would gaze at Ah Lang's face. By chance, they sat in the same row. With a slight tilt of her head, she could see him out of the corner of her eye – she found his profile captivating. Ah Lang would sense that someone was watching him, and he would turn his face slowly, almost imperceptibly. Their eyes would meet, but only for a moment.

Shu Xiu was walking ahead of him now. Ah Lang wondered if he should try to catch up with her. Before, he would have quickened his pace until he was by her side. But now he hesitated. In the classroom, he no longer felt her silent eyes measuring him up. Whenever he turned to look at her now, she was always busy with her work, or staring out of the window. They had never arranged to meet before, but now they never seemed to meet by chance, either. Shu Xiu did not look at him any more – it was as though his face had dried up and no longer interested her.

Ah Lang walked along the main road, full of people coming and going, full of the noise of bus horns, bicycle bells and the cries of street sellers. He had never felt so alone.

Three large trucks drove down the road, one after the other, packed with workers squeezed into the back, shouting slogans at the tops of their voices.

As the large trucks sped past, Ah Lang felt a surge of air rushing towards him, pushing him against the wall. If the wall hadn't caught him, the air would have thrust him far, far away.

Gradually, the trucks disappeared into the distance.

Shu Xiu was still walking ahead of him, another lone figure.

Ah Lang stood and watched her for a while, and then, taking big steps, ran after her.

"Shu Xiu…" he called as he drew close, his breathing uneven from running.

Shu Xiu turned around, and when she saw it was Ah Lang, she flinched. The expression in her eyes was that of a stranger, startled and unnerved.

Ah Lang stood there. He didn't know what to say. There were so many people walking past, and they kept bumping into him, making it difficult for him to keep his balance.

Shu Xiu turned her head, looked for a while at the main road, then continued walking, noticeably quickening her pace.

Ah Lang was stunned for a moment, then hurried after her.

She seemed to sense he was following her, and turned into a side lane. It was one of those winding lanes that twists this way and that, like the character *gong* 弓 (an archer's bow), where you cannot see straight from one end to the other.

Ah Lang hurried to the entrance to the lane, then stood and watched as she disappeared.

He knew she didn't have to go down this lane on her way home.

Ah Lang wished she would look back, and give him one of those beckoning glances, as she used to do when they explored the lanes. But Shu Xiu carried on walking. She didn't look back. It was not long before she came to a turning, and then she was gone.

Ah Lang stood at the end of the lane for a long time. He was numb.

Then he dragged himself home – there was no strength in his legs – and locked himself in his bedroom. He stood for ages in front of the mirror, examining his face. The more he looked, the more useless he felt, and he began to loathe himself. He opened the window, and, leaning his hands on the windowsill, looked at the people walking up and down the road – men and women, young and old, long faces, round faces, big eyes, little eyes, all of them different, some with longer noses, some with flatter noses, but regardless of all these differences, still all of a kind. He went back to the mirror, and the more he looked, the clearer he saw it: he was different!

It was as though there was a flock of birds living in a forest, and all but one belonged to the same species. If there were a few more of that lone bird's species, then it would be fine, but there was only one. In fact, there were more – there was Ah Mei and the rest of the family – but at that moment, the bird felt isolated in the world, as if it didn't fit there.

The feeling of isolation lapped against Ah Lang's fragile mind, like the rising tide of the Huangpu lapping against the embankment.

He looked at his face in the mirror again. This time he grinned at himself, a cold, mocking grin. Then he got into bed and pulled the cover over his face, that weird, disgusting face that was so different from everyone else's.

The Blue House was on Beijing West Road. Although Ah Lang's family lived some distance away on Yan'an West Road, what happened at the Blue House also affected Ah Lang. After all, he was Océane's grandson, and a quarter of the blood running through him was Océane's, the same as for Ah Mei.

The atmosphere at the Blue House was growing tenser by the day. Nainai seldom left the house any more. She spent all day at home, occasionally standing by the window, watching what was happening outside. Shanghai had gone mad, like a giant wok bubbling furiously. Big trucks streamed past, filled, if not with students, then with workers, and sometimes even farmers from the outskirts of the city. Why were they coming into town and not looking after the land? Loudspeakers blasted constantly, near and far, the voices serious and angry. Fluttering everywhere were red flags of all sizes, a sea of red flags that created a red glow in the sky over Shanghai. Nainai couldn't make head nor tail of all this, but her anxiety, terror even, intensified by the day.

Her children came to the Blue House from time to time, but behind their relaxed appearances, they hid a similar anxiety and terror.

The situation in Yibin was the same, with red flags unfurling everywhere, and endless shouting, day and night.

Ah Mei's parents worried about Shanghai, about the Blue House and about Nainai. And Nainai worried about them, too. Whenever the phone rang, and Nainai heard their voices, she couldn't control her trembling excitement.

These days, it was Mrs Hu who went out most. She went out more than ever before. She would slip a basket over her arm, and walk through town, keeping her eyes and ears open. Adopting a casual manner, she'd make her way to busy places, and listen to what was being discussed and commented on. Then she'd piece it all together in her head. She began to realize just how bad the situation was. She was only a village woman, an old lady from the countryside, but she was like a spider guarding its web, catching any creature that happened to fly close. She wanted to tell Nainai, *It would be best if you could go back to France for a while,* but she knew she couldn't, as this would make Nainai even more anxious, because the truth was that Nainai couldn't go back even if she wanted to. In fact, Nainai had wanted to make a trip – she'd been wanting to do so for decades – but she had never been able to realize her dream, and now it was out of the question. Mrs Hu wanted to tell Yeye to take Nainai somewhere they could hide, but she knew this was impossible too. Where would they go? Where could they hide?

One day, when Mrs Hu was on her way home from the market, she saw people hanging around outside the Blue House. As they milled about, they'd pause now and then, and look up at the first-floor windows, exchange glances and whisper to one another. Mrs Hu tried to listen in, but couldn't hear what they said. She knew what they were talking about: the Blue House, and Yeye and Nainai. She stood to one side, and waited for them to leave, before going inside. Then she poked her head out, made sure the coast was clear and immediately bolted the door.

Nainai was coming downstairs as Mrs Hu was making her way to the kitchen. Mrs Hu looked up; Nainai looked down. When she saw the expression on Mrs Hu's face, Nainai's foot froze in mid-air.

"Mrs Hu?" she asked.

"Are you going somewhere, Madam?"

"It's so stuffy inside," said Nainai, "I thought I'd go and sit in the garden for a while."

Mrs Hu nodded and walked on, but after a couple of steps she looked back, and said, "It's wild out there."

"I know," said Nainai.

About a week later, Mrs Hu heard something in the market. She had just paid for two *jin* of radishes, said, "See you tomorrow morning," and started to walk away when Mrs Liu, the radish-seller, called after her. Mrs Hu often bought vegetables from her – they were women of a similar age, and got on well, so she called her *ah-sao*, Liu ah-sao.

"What is it?" asked Mrs Hu.

Liu ah-sao beckoned her to come back, all the while keeping her head down, and peering around to check it was safe to talk.

"The old lady from overseas at your house. I haven't seen her for ages. Is she all right?"

Mrs Hu nodded. "She's fine."

Liu ah-sao craned her neck and whispered in Mrs Hu's ear, "I heard them saying the old lady's a foreign spy, whatever that means."

Mrs Hu didn't know what that meant either, but it sounded serious. "Where did you … hear that?" she asked.

"I heard a couple of people from your lane talking about it," said Liu ah-sao. "It was their tone of voice, rather than anything they said. I tried to ask, but they wouldn't say anything more, just bought their veg and left. Tell the old lady to be careful. The world's changed; it's not like before…"

Mrs Hu hurried home. As she drew closer to the Blue House, she slowed down, on the lookout for any activity near by. She checked there were no suspicious-looking people around, then went inside. She started to make lunch, but she couldn't concentrate. After lunch, she tidied the kitchen, and went to check the lounge. Yeye was sitting in an armchair, on his own, lost in thought. He wouldn't mind her tidying up while he was there. In fact, the lounge was perfectly tidy, but she busied herself for a while, then finally asked, "Sir, what's a spy?"

Yeye gave a start, and looked at Mrs Hu. The last few days he had been in a high state of alert, and had become extremely sensitive.

Mrs Hu didn't dare to raise her head and look him in the eye.

"Mrs Hu!"

Mrs Hu had to look at him.

"Have you heard something outside?" Yeye asked.

Mrs Hu nodded. "There's people saying Madam is a foreign spy."

Yeye's huge frame swayed as he stood up. "Where did you hear this?"

"At the market. Liu ah-sao told me – she'd heard people talking." Then, seeing how tense Yeye was, she quickly added, "Liu ah-sao said they were guessing and didn't know for sure…"

They could hear Nainai moving about upstairs.

"Tell Madam to be careful," Mrs Hu added quietly.

But nothing untoward happened. At Yeye's insistence, Nainai stopped going to pick Ah Mei up from school. She waited for her at the gate to the Blue House instead, and wasn't outside for long, because recently Ah Mei had been coming straight home after school. Before, if Nainai didn't go to collect her, Ah Mei would lose track of time: she'd set off from school with her friends, maybe go to someone's house, and then at some point remember to go home. But now, it seemed no one wanted to play with her any more, or walk home with her. All she wanted to do after school was get home.

*　　*　　*

Although nothing had developed near the Blue House, there were skirmishes in Ah Lang's neighbourhood. A boy called Zhu Zi, who lived near the Blue House, had a cousin who was at the same school as Ah Lang, though in a different class. One day, when the two boys were walking past the Blue House, Zhu Zi repeated what he had heard the grownups saying: "A foreign old lady lives in this house, and she's a spy!" The cousin, Ming Zi, knew Ah Lang, and had been to the Blue House in the summer holidays the year before, and met Nainai. When the new term started and they were back at school, Ming Zi repeated the news to a friend, who repeated it to other classmates, and soon the news had spread round the playground: "Ah Lang's nainai is a foreign spy!"

From this point on, Ah Lang was regarded with overt suspicion and hostility. The older students at school seemed to have fallen under a spell: they were constantly rolling their eyes, sizing up the world around them, constantly on the alert, hot blood surging inside them, but cold and hard on the outside. One afternoon, the first dozen boys to leave the classroom positioned themselves on the road. When Ah Lang came along, they swaggered up to him.

"Stop there!" said the boys, who were all taller than Ah Lang.

Ah Lang froze. He looked at them. Did they mean him?

"Yes, you, Big Nose!" said a boy with a flat nose, pointing at Ah Lang's face. He kept pointing as he walked forward, until his finger was almost touching Ah Lang's nose.

Ah Lang's head tilted backwards.

Soon, a dozen boys surrounded Ah Lang, like a pack of dogs around their prey.

Not far away, a few girls were watching, silently.

The circle of boys started to move around Ah Lang, but each pair of eyes stayed fixed on his face. They had always thought he had a big nose, but now it looked huge, astonishing, excessive – there was no need for a nose as big as that; it was ugly, repulsive. They had always thought his eyes looked a bit sunken, but today they were more sunken then ever, as though they were lurking in the shadows, the eyes of a thief, sinister eyes that made the boys feel uncomfortable. How dare he look at them with eyes like that!

The way they saw it … this Ah Lang, he was different from them.

They started poking fun at him, laughing at his facial features, making exaggerated comparisons, using venomous words, some of them obscene.

Ah Lang's face went whiter and whiter. He threw his gaze beyond the circle around him, as though seeking help. But all he saw was more of the same kind of faces. He wanted to cry for help, but he abandoned that idea, knowing it would be futile. He was on his own. It was him against them.

After calling Ah Lang a monster, a freak and a long list of other derogatory names, finally, a tall boy said to Ah Lang, "Did you know your grandmother's a foreign spy?"

"A special agent," said the one with the flat nose.

"That's not true!" said Ah Lang, quietly at first, then immediately raising his voice, almost shouting at them, "THAT'S NOT TRUE! MY GRANDMOTHER IS NOT A SPY!"

It had never occurred to Ah Lang that people might say such a thing about Nainai. It was as if he'd been shot.

"She *is* a spy! I can't believe you didn't know?" said the tall boy. "But you would say that, wouldn't you. Even if you knew, you wouldn't admit it. A spy hidden for years!" he went on. In fact, this boy had never seen Nainai, he had only heard that she was a foreigner.

"Do not insult my grandmother," Ah Lang warned them.

"It looks as though you're not willing to draw a line between the two of you, right?" said the one with the flat nose. "I knew it. You've all got big noses." Then, suddenly thinking of an expression that had recently become popular: "You're raccoon dogs from the same hill!"

They launched another round of attack on Ah Lang's appearance, saying even ruder things about his face.

Slowly, Ah Lang put down his school bag. Then he charged at the boy with the flat nose.

Before the boy had time to react, Ah Lang had ripped the front off his shirt, exposing the boy's skinny chest to the world.

The boy pushed Ah Lang off, took a couple of steps back, then, raising his fist in the air, roared as he charged at Ah Lang, smashing his fist into his nose.

Ah Lang felt a searing pain, and feared his nose might be broken. He raised his hands to his face and slipped down into a crouch.

In the distance, the girls huddled together, apparently shocked, though no one had screamed or run to see if Ah Lang was hurt.

The boys linked arms and walked away, breaking into song.

Ah Lang was off school for a week. He shut himself away and refused to see anyone. When Yeye and Nainai heard what had happened, they went to see him, and had to knock on his door for ages before he would open it. When Nainai saw his ashen face, and how thin he had become, the life drained out of her eyes. Instinctively, she put her arms around her grandson and hugged him, stroking his head with one hand, and rubbing his back with the other.

Ah Lang wept silently in her arms.

Yeye and Nainai spent a long time with Ah Lang, eventually persuading him to go back to school.

But, from that day on, Ah Lang would not leave the house without a mask over his mouth. It covered most of his face.

He barely spoke any more. He kept as quiet as a block of wood or a piece of stone. On the way to and from school, in the classroom, wherever he went, no one could see the expression on his face, and no one could know what he was thinking deep inside. He was distant – distant from his classmates, distant from the world.

But there were still some children who wouldn't leave him alone. They felt the boy in the mask was either showing contempt or had something to hide. They didn't like him wearing a mask, covering up his peculiar face. They couldn't tolerate his hiding like that. They wanted to see his face.

One hot day, Ah Lang was wearing his mask. He wore it no matter what the weather.

Two boys in their final year at school mocked him. "Hey, have you seen that boy? Still wearing his mask on a hot day like this!" said the first boy, pushing his glasses into place. "Is he ill?"

"Hah! He's trying to hide. Does he really think it'll work?" said the other, with a toothy grin. "We can't allow that!"

They began to discuss how to expose Ah Lang's face. "Let's see how repulsive that face of his really is," said the boy with the toothy grin.

After school, when there were lots of people milling outside the classroom, the two suddenly cut through the crowd, and stood in front of Ah Lang. Standing side by side, without taking their eyes off him, they took a couple of steps backwards. Then they gave each other the eye, charged at Ah Lang, and, using one hand each, ripped the mask from his face.

Although it was only a mask, Ah Lang felt he'd been stripped of his clothes, and was standing there stark naked in front of everyone. Immediately, he crouched to the ground, as if in pain.

The two boys laughed and ran off.

The other children didn't laugh. They walked past Ah Lang in silence.

When he finally stood up, the school playground was empty.

He saw his mask, filthy and torn from being trodden on so many times.

He went back to the classroom, and packed everything that belonged to him in his school bag, everything down to the last slip of paper, and the last stub of pencil. Then he sat on the stool he had sat on so many times before. He sat there for ages, looking at the blackboard. It hadn't been cleaned properly. He thought about going over and cleaning it. He tilted his head – that was Shu Xiu's seat over there. He imagined her eyes, her smile. He smiled, and felt the heat rise on his face.

By the time Ah Lang left the school, it was getting dark.

He walked through the gate, then glanced back at the school one last time.

After that, Ah Lang shut himself in his bedroom. It was as though he wanted to spend the rest of his life locked up in that little space. His parents wept. What else could they do?

There was only one person who could get him to open his door – Ah Mei.

Of all his cousins, Ah Mei was his favourite. She was the only girl in that generation, and they all loved her, but no one more than Ah Lang. At family gatherings, Ah Lang and Ah Mei would spend the most time together. They never ran out of things to talk about. They usually saw each other every few days, and always on Sundays, when Ah Lang would visit the Blue House. Sometimes Ah Mei would say to Nainai, "It's been ages since we saw Ah Lang." And Nainai would say, "What do you mean? You saw each other only last week."

There was another, very important, reason why Ah Lang loved Ah Mei: they looked so similar. "Like brother and sister," the adults all said. "There must have been a mix-up somewhere because you'd think they had the same parents." "Not necessarily," said Xiaogu. "Think who they look like … They look like their nainai."

Whatever the reason, Ah Lang and Ah Mei were the closest of all the cousins, and they always had been.

Ah Mei was also facing similar experiences to Ah Lang, although not as bad. She felt very unsettled at times. The children at school were becoming more and more distant. They no longer tried to hide the suspicion and hostility in their eyes. It was there all the time; it was everywhere. Before, they had all wanted to play with her, be her partner, be in her group, but recently, when they'd had to form teams, no one had wanted her on their team, until Qiu Qiu stood up and let her join hers.

At some point, she couldn't remember when, she had started watching their eyes cautiously, at times even trying to win them over. What was she doing wrong? She didn't know. She was behaving perfectly, even better than before. But the situation wasn't like before. Back then, she was the full moon and they were the stars all around her. And now she knew the taste of disappointment and rejection. Like Ah Lang, she spent a lot of time in front of the mirror. Every day, she gazed at those eyes, that nose, that brown hair. She had been proud of them before, but now she looked with suspicion. She began to dislike the hints of colour in her hair, all the things that had been special, all the things she had loved about herself.

She felt she stood out in a crowd. She hadn't thought of wearing a mask to cover her face, but she had changed in other ways. Before, when she was walking, she would rise up on tiptoes, and scan the crowd with her little white face. But she had learned to keep her head down, to avoid other people's eyes.

Sometimes she felt so alone, as though a pack of wild animals was chasing after her.

Once full of life, she too had become taciturn, increasingly so.

You could see in Nainai's eyes that she felt knotted inside about her grandchildren's situation and experiences. She knew she was the cause of their discomfort.

She would soothe their little souls twenty-four hours a day if she could. But Ah Lang refused. She had been to his house several times, and stood outside his bedroom door, knocking and calling his name, but she could not get him to open up.

It seemed that door was shut for ever, never to be opened again.

Her only glimmer of hope was that he would open up for Ah Mei.

When Ah Mei went to see Ah Lang, Nainai would take her as far as the front door. Nainai didn't usually go inside, because she found it too painful to see all that worry on his parents' faces, and even more painful to see Ah Lang's closed door. She was battling her conscience; the guilt was wearing her down.

She would pat Ah Mei's head, her fingers gently saying, *Aina, I am so grateful to you!*

Ah Lang's parents welcomed Ah Mei like an angel.

As soon as Ah Mei said, "Ah Lang!" the door would open, as though he'd been waiting for her.

CHAPTER 14

In the Moonlight

Mrs Hu paid more and more attention to the outside world. She kept her bedroom window ajar day and night, and would stand there whenever she could, following what was happening outside. She felt the world was growing more and more chaotic, more and more difficult to understand. She could no longer conceal her worry for the Blue House. Often, when she was busy with housework, a thought would pop into her mind, and the wok-stirrer or whatever else she was using would slip from her hand and clatter to the floor. She'd turn around and, finding no one there, pick it up, and try to reassure herself. "What's the matter with you? Everything's fine. There's nothing to worry about."

Meanwhile, Nainai seemed to be rallying. She appeared less anxious and less fearful than before, as if everything was in hand. She told herself over and over that Yeye needed her, that Ah Mei needed her, that the Blue House needed her, that the whole family needed her. She had to be strong and put on a smile. The sky could fall down, but she would still be smiling.

There was only one person in the world who could smile like that – and that person was Nainai.

She resolved to be the same Nainai she had always been. Every day, she would pay the usual attention to her clothes and hair, as she had always done. She would not leave the house without applying a pale lipstick to her lips, and a drop or two of perfume, though that was extremely precious these days. Wherever she walked, she would leave a subtle, elegant scent in the air behind her.

Now that Nainai appeared calmer, the whole family felt reassured.

But Mrs Hu was more on edge than ever. There had been several occasions where she'd gone out and seen people walking past the Blue House, pointing to it and saying, "The person who lives there is a capitalist," or, "That Frenchwoman's been hiding as a spy for years!" More and more people kept stopping and staring at the house. She sensed that something was brewing. It was like seeing black clouds gathering in the sky, and knowing that at any moment the storm would break – the sudden flash of lightning and crack of thunder would come, the sky and earth would darken, a furious wind would sweep through Shanghai, and the heavens would open and threaten to submerge the city.

Daily, Mrs Hu would gently remind Yeye to look after Nainai.

But the days passed, and the sudden overthrow that Mrs

Hu had predicted did not materialize. On the contrary, Ah Mei came home with some exciting news. The headteacher had called her to the school office, and personally told her that the school had selected her to play the piano at an arts event for all the schools in the area, that would take place in two weeks' time. He said her performance would be the highlight of the event, and the success of the school would rest entirely on Ah Mei.

When Ah Mei came out of the headteacher's office, and saw no one around, she couldn't help jumping for joy. She wanted to bend over, take a deep breath, then straighten up, open her arms and scream with happiness, and if she hadn't put her hand over her mouth, she would indeed have screamed. Instead of going straight back to the classroom, she went over to the tree behind it, leaned against the tree trunk, and, with her face to the sky, wept silently.

The school hadn't forgotten her after all! She was still their treasure, like always!

That day, she ran most of the way home, and very soon the news had spread to all the members of the family. It was like a breath of fresh air, lifting the haze that had been hanging over them.

After dinner, Ah Mei and Nainai walked around the garden, hand in hand, Ah Mei's little face beaming. She was so happy that she wanted to leap in the air. She did leap a few times, and each time, Nainai almost lost her balance.

"Aina, let's go back inside."

"All right."

Ah Mei knew that Nainai would want to lie down on

her big bed, and that naturally she would join her. It was what they had always done every evening after dinner. Ah Mei loved spending time with Nainai, and Nainai loved it too. Sometimes they would lie there, each reading their own book. When Ah Mei came to an interesting part, she would chuckle, and Nainai would take the book from Ah Mei's hands, read it and chuckle too. Occasionally, she would toss the book back to Ah Mei, saying, "That's not funny!" They would talk, too, about anything and everything. They never set a topic, or boundaries. Sometimes Ah Mei would listen while Nainai talked, and sometimes Nainai would listen while Ah Mei talked. And sometimes they would just lie there, not doing or saying anything at all. And if they happened to be lying in the same position, and Mrs Hu or Mama came in, they'd say, "Look at those two, cast from the same mould."

That evening, Nainai lay down, grabbed a pillow and put it next to hers.

Ah Mei took a running jump, landed on the bed and stretched out next to Nainai.

Nainai turned towards her granddaughter. It was lovely to see colour in her cheeks again. Since coming out of the headteacher's office, Ah Mei had barely been able to contain her excitement. She'd gone a little mad in the garden, but now, lying down, she looked so relaxed, her face rosy and pink, her eyes sparkling. Nainai hadn't seen her like this for a long time. Ah Mei had seemed pale and thin, as though seriously ill, with a sorrow in her eyes that a child shouldn't have. Nainai kissed her tenderly on the forehead and whispered, "Aina." Ah Mei snuggled up to Nainai, and, after a while, began to cry. Nainai didn't say a word, just patted her gently on the back.

After a long time, when Ah Mei had uncurled herself and was lying flat on the bed again, and had remembered her excitement, Nainai said, "At the performance, you must play absolutely exquisitely."

Ah Mei nodded.

In the following days, apart from going to school, eating and sleeping, Ah Mei spent all her time in the piano room. She had to practise hard if she was to play absolutely exquisitely, as Nainai wished. Just like before, winning praise for her beloved school would be the highest honour.

When Mrs Hu heard the piano, she always said the same thing: "Beautiful!"

Nainai started to think about what Ah Mei should wear for the performance. Ah Mei had some very pretty dresses, but she had grown so fast over the last year that they were probably too small for her now. In any case, those dresses were for little girls. Nainai didn't want people to think of Ah Mei as a little girl any more – she wanted Ah Mei to dress more like the young woman she was. Nainai decided that her granddaughter needed a new dress. But when she calculated how much that would cost, she realized how far the Blue House had fallen into decline – they couldn't afford a new dress for Ah Mei, or the material to make one. Nainai realized that Ah Mei hadn't had any new clothes for over a year. An image of Ah Mei floated before her eyes: wearing a top that was too short, and trousers eight or ten centimetres above her ankles. Nainai felt a pang in her heart, and when she saw Mrs Hu, she said, "Why didn't I think about getting some new clothes for Ah Mei before now? I could see her clothes were getting too short!"

"You did think about it," said Mrs Hu. "It's just that circumstances have changed. It's not like before. They might be a bit short, but they're fine otherwise. They aren't patched, and they're always clean."

"Ah Mei was always asking for new clothes before," said Nainai. "She had new clothes every year when she was little. She wouldn't celebrate New Year unless she had a new outfit."

"She's grown up," said Mrs Hu. "She's not a little girl any more."

The more Mrs Hu talked like this, the worse Nainai felt. "This New Year, we must get her some new clothes."

Mrs Hu sighed. "Madam, I'll make a note of it, and remind you when the time comes. But we have more urgent things to buy first."

"Let me think about it," said Nainai. "There's always a way."

Nainai paced about, inside and outside, upstairs and downstairs, unable to keep still. Yeye knew that she was worrying about money again. Whenever he saw her trying to find a solution to an impossible situation, he felt overwhelmed with guilt. But there was nothing he could do, except watch her, or take her a cup of tea and encourage her to calm down.

In the garden, the apricot tree was flowering. Although there wasn't much blossom yet, there was a lovely scent.

Yeye moved a wicker chair under the apricot tree.

Nainai knew that Yeye had moved the chair specially for her, so she went to sit under the tree. It was just after ten. The morning sun shone down. She closed her eyes, and in an instant, her body relaxed. It was not long before she felt drowsy.

There was a breeze, so Yeye fetched a blanket from the house and softly placed it over her.

When Nainai woke up, she smiled. It was as though a light had come on and shown her a solution. She went back inside the house, straight to her wardrobe, and opened the door. There were only a few clothes hanging there. Seeing the wardrobe so sparse, she couldn't help feeling a twinge of regret. There had once been four wardrobes in this room, all those years ago, each of them filled with clothes. Now there was only one left, and in this one remaining wardrobe, there were just a few items of clothing, the rest having been sold, piece by piece. The wardrobe looked so big, and so empty. Nainai took out a long dress that she had worn when she was young. She held it up and examined it. It was a beautiful dress, and reminded Nainai of the times when she had worn it: walking in the garden in her home in France, walking along the street in Marseilles – the sunshine, the sea breeze, the gulls flying in the sky, the dress flapping in the wind, billowing like a cloud as she walked. For a moment, Nainai was carried away.

The sound of Mrs Hu's footsteps at the door brought

Nainai back into the present, the cash-strapped, threadbare present, where their clothes were so thin that there was some truth in the expression "Tug at your collar and your elbows will burst through your sleeves".

"Mrs Hu, come in!" called Nainai.

Mrs Hu entered, and the moment she saw Nainai holding up the dress, she knew what she was thinking.

"Beautiful, don't you think?" asked Nainai, holding the dress against her body.

Mrs Hu smiled. "Do you mean yourself, Madam, or the dress?"

Nainai sighed. "The dress, of course. I'm too old now to think about being beautiful."

"It's beautiful," said Mrs Hu. Then, glancing at Nainai's wrinkled face, she added, "And you're beautiful too, Madam."

Nainai shook her head, then said to Mrs Hu, "I'd like to turn it into a dress for Ah Mei. What do you think?"

"Don't you want to keep it? It would be a shame to alter it."

"No, I don't want to keep it. I'm never going to wear it again, am I? Not at my age."

"Think about it before getting the scissors out. Once it's cut, there's no going back." Mrs Hu knew very well that the few items of clothing still hanging in the wardrobe were very precious to Nainai, and held special meaning for her. For Nainai's sake, she couldn't bear to do it.

"I have thought about it," said Nainai. "Mrs Hu, over the next couple of days, let's work out how to turn this into a dress for Ah Mei's performance. It has to be done well; it has to be special. Ah Mei must have a special dress for the performance."

Mrs Hu nodded.

"It has to be absolutely perfect," added Nainai.

"I know," said Mrs Hu.

For the next few days, all Nainai's and Mrs Hu's attention went on designing and making Ah Mei's dress. It was a difficult task, much more difficult than making a new dress from a length of material. One tiny mistake and it would be ruined. First, they used an old newspaper to work out the pattern, and only when they were confident with the paper pattern did they lay the dress on the table. When the time came to use the scissors, Mrs Hu's hands were shaking. She passed them to Nainai, saying, "Better if you do it."

But Nainai hid her hands behind her back. "Better if you do it."

Yeye brought in a cup of tea. "You two! Which one of you will it be?"

"Perhaps it should be me," said Mrs Hu.

"Then this tea is for you," said Yeye. "Have a few sips, to settle your nerves."

Nainai took the cup from Yeye, and, holding it with both hands, presented it to Mrs Hu. *Please!* was the message in her eyes.

Mrs Hu sipped the tea slowly, down to the very last drop. In an instant, there was a *ss–nip*, *ss–nip* sound. The scissors cut with a measured rhythm. The three hearts in the room beat frantically. Nainai had only those few dresses left; there was no room for error. Mrs Hu held her breath, and focused on keeping the scissor blades on the chalk line they had drawn on Nainai's dress, moving along one centimetre at a time. When the cutting was finished, the three of them breathed a sigh of relief.

Then it was time to sew. Although Mrs Hu's needlework was not as good as Mrs Song's, it was still well above average. While Mrs Hu stitched the dress together, Nainai stayed by her side, watching as she worked.

Finally, the new dress was ready. It had two layers, an inner layer of cloth and an outer layer of gauze. It looked floaty and substantial at the same time. When Ah Mei came home from school that day, and put down her school bag, Nainai and Mrs Hu walked slowly towards her, holding up the dress by its shoulders.

"Turn around, Ah Mei!" called Mrs Hu.

Ah Mei turned around, and saw the dress hanging like a painting before her eyes.

"It's for you." said Nainai.

Nainai and Mrs Hu helped her into the dress, or rather, they dressed Ah Mei, who was as stiff as a plank of wood the entire time. She couldn't remember when she'd last had new clothes, and she was a girl who loved clothes and dressing up. But at that particular moment, she stood there frozen to the spot, feeling very unnatural, as though she'd grown used to wearing shabby old clothes that were too short, and was no longer used to pretty dresses like this.

Even when she was dressed, Ah Mei stood there, stiffly.

"What's happened to this girl? Has she lost her senses?" said Mrs Hu.

Nainai went up to Ah Mei, and carefully adjusted the dress. "Mrs Hu made it for you, to wear at the performance."

"We made it from one of your nainai's dresses."

Ah Mei looked down at the dress, then she raised her knee, and watched the material rise with it.

"Isn't it pretty?" Nainai asked.

Ah Mei didn't utter a sound.

"Nainai's asking you a question," said Mrs Hu.

Ah Mei nodded, a tear falling from her eye.

"This child … whatever is she crying about?" Mrs Hu hurried over, and wiped away Ah Mei's tears with her sleeve. "Don't let them fall on the dress – it wasn't easy to make, you know." Mrs Hu was annoyed – Ah Mei could see it in her eyes. Ah Mei responded immediately. She burst into a smile, and sparkled with life. She picked up the dress, made a few leaps, then started to walk backwards and forwards in front of Nainai and Mrs Hu, so that they could take a good look. Finally, she did a big twirl, and then came to a stop – the dress swirling on by itself.

"Thank you, Nainai!" said Ah Mei. "Thank you, Mrs Hu!"

At some point, Yeye had come in. "What about a thank you for me? I watched them doing the cutting, and even brought them tea. If I hadn't steadied their nerves, who knows what they would have done with those scissors!"

"Thank you, Yeye!" said Ah Mei.

They all smiled happily.

After dinner, Nainai said to Yeye, "I still feel there's something missing. I'm wondering if we should make a jacket for Ah Mei as well, like the ones the students have … you know, to wear over the dress. Then Ah Mei will look like a student as well as a young lady…"

Nainai looked at Yeye, as though she had more to say.

"What?" asked Yeye.

"Would you…?" Nainai was wondering about the blue seaman's uniform that Yeye had worn in the past. All these years, Yeye had kept it in his wardrobe, as a memento.

"I'll do whatever you ask."

"Would you let us have your seaman's uniform? I'm thinking we could make it into a jacket for Ah Mei, and then she'd look absolutely perfect."

Yeye was surprised by the request, but he responded quickly. "All right. And it's certainly top quality material!"

Ah Mei put tremendous effort into her piano practice, playing the chosen pieces over and over again. She could now play without looking at the keys, and without faltering at all. She played smoothly and her timing was spot on. In the evenings, she would ask Nainai to turn off the light, and let her play in the dark. Nainai would stay and listen, and when Ah Mei had finished playing, Nainai would turn the light back on and make only one comment on Ah Mei's playing – it was smooth.

Ah Mei had been counting down the days to the performance. At last the big day came. It was a Sunday.

After lunch, Ah Mei couldn't contain her excitement any longer. She wanted to put the dress on, but Nainai said it was too early, and she should go and practise some more. Ah Mei was holding the dress in her hands, but she put it down and went into the piano room. She played for a while, and then went back to Nainai. "Océane, I'd like to go to school early."

"The school told you to arrive at four o'clock, and then go for make-up, didn't they? It's only just gone one. Go and practise some more, or come and sit under the apricot tree for a while. Aina, what you need most of all right now is to calm down and relax."

Ah Mei chose to go and sit with Nainai in the garden.

Yeye and Mrs Hu helped them to move two chairs under the apricot tree. The tree was in full bloom.

Nainai asked Yeye, "Could you bring two cups of tea, please?"

Yeye seemed a little confused.

Nainai laughed. "Two cups of your special tea to calm the nerves: one for me and one for Ah Mei."

"Yes, yes, yes." Yeye nodded. "Mrs Hu, could you bring two cups of tea."

Yeye placed a small table in front of them, then turned around and went to fetch the tea-tray from Mrs Hu. As Yeye walked back towards them, he saw Ah Mei under Nainai's watchful eye, sitting as calmly as her grandmother. He placed the tea-tray on the table, and presented the first cup of tea to Nainai.

"The first one is for Ah Mei," said Nainai.

"Yes, yes, yes." Yeye turned around and, with two hands, offered the cup to Ah Mei.

Ah Mei accepted the cup of tea with both hands. She was smiling broadly.

"Be careful not to scald yourself," said Yeye.

After serving the tea, he left them in peace, smiling as he took the tea-tray back inside.

Nainai couldn't help taking the piano recital seriously. Recently, both she and her granddaughter had felt black clouds building up inside them. If only the clouds would part and the sun could shine through again – for both their sakes. She hoped that the recital would be a new beginning, that Ah Mei could be happy again, that the loneliness, rejection and uneasiness would disappear from her eyes, and she would come skipping home from school with rosy cheeks, rather than hanging her head in dejection, her school bag all but scraping the ground. She wanted Ah Mei to be calm, to be in the right frame of mind, so that she could throw herself completely into the performance that evening. It had to be perfect; it had to be a success. Nainai believed that Ah Mei could do it, but she needed to relax first.

"Aina, look at the blossom."

Ah Mei looked up. The blossom reminded her of the light dusting of snow they'd had that winter, except that it hung in mid-air, off the tip of the branch.

"The blossom's beautiful this year. So much better than last year!" said Nainai. "It's as good as the apricot blossom back home in Marseilles…"

As they talked about Marseilles, about Lyons, about France, about travelling across the sea, Ah Mei forgot about the piano, and about the recital that evening, and started to relax.

After a while, Nainai looked up at the sun. "Now you can go and put on your dress and go to school."

Nainai helped Ah Mei to get dressed, fastening every one of her buttons. And when Ah Mei was ready, Nainai took a few steps back, tilted her head to the left, and then to the right, and, after a thorough examination, nodded and said, "Aina, you are the most beautiful girl in the world. Of that there is no doubt!"

"Who's that girl?" asked Yeye in exaggerated surprise when Ah Mei appeared in front of him.

Nainai stood at the door and watched as Ah Mei left for school. "Ah Mei, you must relax. If you really can't relax, think of the apricot blossom in the garden, the pure white blossom."

Ah Mei arrived at school just as all the other children who were performing that evening were streaming into the playground. Their eyes widened when they saw her. But they didn't gasp in surprise, or come over and compliment her, they just stood there, watching from afar, and after a while, deliberately turned their heads and walked away. Two girls, who had wanted to go over to Ah Mei, hesitated for a while, then walked away too.

The children hadn't eaten yet. Usually, when there was an evening performance, the school would provide a packet of biscuits for each participant. Two boys carried a cardboard box full of biscuits to a clear space in the playground, then called out the names one by one.

Ah Mei was standing near by. Behind her was an enormous wutong tree. The day was drawing to a close, and the sun was glowing red in the sky. Everywhere Ah Mei looked was red. The children walking around were like black silhouettes against the red glow of the sky.

She waited for the two boys to call her name.

One name after another drifted past her ears.

She heard sparrows chirping in the wutong tree as they prepared for the night. Ah Mei looked up, hoping to spot them. But the tree was covered in leaves, and it was impossible to see anything beyond the green, though she didn't look too hard, because she was waiting for the boys to call her name.

"Gu Dawei…"

It seemed that Gu Dawei was the only child who had not gone up to collect a packet of biscuits. The two boys called Gu Dawei's name several times, and then crouched on the ground, guarding the almost empty cardboard box, waiting for him to turn up.

Ah Mei walked from the wutong tree towards the two boys.

When they heard footsteps, the boys looked up and saw Ah Mei. Then, with wide eyes, they clambered slowly to their feet.

What about me? Ah Mei wanted to ask. But she didn't. She stopped before she reached them.

The two boys finally came to their senses, and started once again to call out, "Gu Dawei!"

They continued calling his name for a while, then finally gave up, and walked off, one holding the box against his chest, the other following behind.

They must have missed my name off the list, Ah Mei

decided. She wanted to go after them, but she stayed where she was. "I won't be hungry," she told herself.

One of the classrooms was open, and was being used as a make-up room. Some children had already had their make-up done. They left the classroom and wandered down the corridor into the playground, eating their biscuits by the concrete table-tennis tables.

I should get my make-up done, thought Ah Mei, and headed for the make-up room.

A few more made-up children came out. They seemed surprised to see Ah Mei. They shot her a glance, then hurried past.

The two female teachers who were doing the make-up were focused on their task and didn't notice Ah Mei come into the room.

There were still lots of children in the queue, and it was a squash in the classroom. Ah Mei kept making way for them; when she didn't, she got knocked about. All she could do was lean against the wall and wait. She stood there for a while, but she couldn't bear the feeling that she was irrelevant, and so she walked out again.

I'll wait a while, and when everyone else has had their make-up done, I'll go back, she thought.

Ah Mei stood in the corridor, and every so often glanced through the window into the classroom.

One by one, the children went up to the two teachers. The teachers' nimble fingers powdered and painted, and dabbed rouge on the children's faces. Then they spread their arms wide to show they were finished, and by the time the newly made-up children had left the room, the next ones had already stepped into their places. After a few minutes in front of the teachers, their faces bloomed like flowers, like magic.

Ah Mei admired them as they passed her in the corridor: "Lovely!"

She knew it would soon be her turn to bloom. She was going to say, "Miss, please could you do it lightly?" Nainai had told her, "You're not in a show, you're playing the piano. What I mean is, you're not a little girl any more. Ask if the teacher can do your make-up lightly."

Whether the make-up was heavy or light, Ah Mei was confident that she would look beautiful.

Before, when the teachers had done her make-up, they had spent more time on her than any of her classmates, as though she was different from the others, a special work of art that needed care and precision. Sometimes the teachers had grouped together to discuss her make-up. There were always one or two girls who were jealous of her, who might give her the cold shoulder, but she didn't mind. In the eyes of the teachers and the children, Ah Mei was a girl who didn't get angry.

When there were only two more children waiting for make-up, Ah Mei returned to the classroom. By the time she was inside, the two children were standing in front of the teachers. Ah Mei stood to one side, waiting, without making a sound.

Ms Liu finished first. She sensed there was another child in the line, and without looking up, called out, "Next!"

Ah Mei hurried over. Ms Liu squeezed a dollop of

foundation into her hand. When she looked up and saw Ah Mei, she froze. "Ah Mei!"

Ms Jin, who was still busy with her child, turned to look. When she saw Ah Mei, she froze too. "Ah Mei!"

Both teachers looked shocked. Ms Jin stopped doing the last child's make-up. The child looked up at her. "You haven't finished me yet!" The two teachers glanced at each other and then stared again at Ah Mei. They looked awkward, as though unsure of what to do next.

Ms Jin quickly finished the final child's make-up. "You're done. Off you go."

Ms Liu wiped the foundation from the palm of her hand with a piece of waste paper, looked at Ms Jin, and then said to Ah Mei, "Ah Mei, you…" She kept rubbing her hands together, perhaps because of the foundation on her hand, or perhaps because she didn't know how to tell Ah Mei.

"Ah Mei, your recital has been cancelled."

Ah Mei started to sway. The teachers reached out their hands to support her.

"Did no one tell you?" asked Ms Jin.

Ah Mei shook her head.

"Wasn't Ms Su from the office supposed to tell Ah Mei this morning?" Ms Liu asked Ms Jin.

"Today's Sunday. Ah Mei wouldn't have been at school, so she couldn't have done," said Ms Jin.

"It was only decided this morning," Ms Liu told Ah Mei.

Ah Mei bent her head. "The headteacher … the day before yesterday … he told me, he said I had to play … to play the piano beautifully."

"Ah Mei, he's not the headteacher any more. As of yesterday," said Ms Liu.

Ah Mei started to cry. She tried her best not to make a sound, but her shoulders jerked visibly. The sobs rolled round and round in her throat, constantly and violently, as though a large hand was grasping her neck.

"Can I ... can I really not play?" Ah Mei asked through her tears.

Ms Jin put her arm around Ah Mei. Ms Liu patted her gently on the back.

"Go home, child." Ms Jin let go of Ah Mei, raised her hands to the girl's face and patted her cheeks gently. "Go home."

"Go home, Ah Mei," said Ms Liu. "Ms Jin and I both know how well you play the piano. You play absolutely exquisitely."

"That's such a beautiful dress," said Ms Jin. "Was it bought or made for you?"

"Made."

"Who made it?"

"Nainai, and Mrs Hu," said Ah Mei. "They used Yeye and Nainai's old clothes."

The two teachers said nothing.

They tried again to comfort her, but Ah Mei turned around and walked out. She walked slowly but without stopping.

The other children who had been in the make-up room were now running around and playing games. When they saw Ah Mei walk past with her head down, they stopped what they were doing, and followed her with their eyes.

Ah Mei didn't head for the school gate, but walked towards the little bamboo grove behind the classroom. She didn't want to go home. She didn't want to accept the truth, didn't want to believe the facts. If she went to the bamboo grove and waited there, perhaps someone might call her? Hadn't the headteacher himself told her to prepare for the recital?

Ah Mei sat down on the stone bench in the bamboo grove. She could hear the children chattering away. They would be going into the theatre very soon, and they were getting excited.

A black cat walked out of the bamboo grove.

It was a stray cat that lived in the school playground all year round. The children would feed it from time to time. Ah Mei fed it more than the others. She would often bring some food to school. When she called for it, the black cat would hear her voice and come running towards her. It would sit on its back legs, raise its head and look at Ah Mei. And she would crouch down, and place the food on a leaf or on the clean brick-tiled ground. Sometimes, on her way home from school, the cat would walk the first hundred metres or so with her, and then turn back.

The black cat sat facing Ah Mei.

Ah Mei felt guilty because she didn't have any food to give it.

But the cat's eyes seemed to be saying that it wasn't sitting there waiting to be fed, but because it wanted to look at her.

Ah Mei started to cry again.

The black cat sat in front of Ah Mei, keeping her company.

She was heartbroken. "They don't want me any more." The cat miaowed, and swept its tail over the ground.

Ah Mei looked at the cat through her tears. "Maybe I should stop coming to this school. If I go to Yibin, I can go to school near Baba and Mama. If Shanghai doesn't want me any more, and my residence papers are for Yibin…"

She reached forward with both hands to pick up the cat; it didn't resist. She held it against her chest, not caring whether it was dirty or not, and placed her cheek on its head.

Two girls were curious as to what Ah Mei was doing there. Wanting to avoid the school toilets, they relieved themselves in the bamboo grove, and when they had finished, they walked away, chatting to one another.

"Did you know? Ah Mei's yeye is a capitalist who exploits the poor!"

"I didn't know that!"

"And her nainai is a foreign spy, a special agent."

"I didn't know that!"

"She'll probably be arrested soon."

"How do you know?"

"The grown-ups are all talking about it, and the news was going around school yesterday."

The bamboo rustled as they walked past.

Now Ah Mei knew that her name would not be called out, and that her recital really had been cancelled. She stopped crying, and sat there, very still. The black cat stayed in her arms, not moving either. It slept for a while, breathing heavily. Ah Mei looked up at the sky, and although the bamboo was mostly blocking the view, she could see from the colour of the sky that it was getting late. But if she walked out of the bamboo grove now, she would bump into her classmates, and that was the last thing she wanted. So she decided to stay on the bench, and wait until they had all left the school playground before she came out.

The evening wind blew through the grove. As the bamboo swayed, there was a constant rustle as leaves brushed against leaves, branches against branches.

A bus drove into the school playground.

"It's time to go!"

"Come on, everyone, get on the bus!"

After the hustle and bustle came the sound of the engine starting up.

As the bus headed towards the school gate, all of the children on board, led by their teachers, began to sing together.

Slowly, Ah Mei stood up.

The school playground was quiet again.

Still holding the black cat, Ah Mei walked towards the school gate, taking very slow steps. She wanted to take a good look at the playground. It might be the last time she ever came inside the school gates. She wanted to leave. She wanted to leave so badly.

She had been at this school for nearly six years, and in another few months, she would be finishing here and starting middle school.

On her first day, the teacher had told them that the school had a history going back a hundred and twenty years. It was a Western-style building, with a small playground, but it was elegant and stylish. She thought of the colonnade with its tall, thick columns, the red-brick borders around the windows, the staircases, the long, wide corridors, the ginkgo trees in the distance, the geckos that covered the walls (the children called them "rock-climbing tigers"). When the school reopened after the summer holidays, the playground was always covered in leaves that were golden and fire-red.

During those six years, Ah Mei had come to know every corner of the school playground. Her shadow and her breath were part of it. She had listened to the teachers, she had read aloud in class, she had rehearsed for shows, and they'd had such fun in the playground, skipping, playing kicky-uppy with a shuttlecock, sneaking into the toilets to chat endlessly. She knew every inch of this place. She had so many memories, and as dusk fell over Shanghai, over the school playground, scenes from the past flashed before her eyes, one by one, sometimes fast, sometimes slow – a garden of memories bursting into flower. She didn't feel hurt or upset any more. She felt boundless joy and happiness.

She thought of break time and the noise of the playground, like a forest full of birds chattering and squabbling. They had chased around and had fun, and, like the little birds in the forest, Ah Mei and her friends had called out to each other. No one could hear what anyone was saying, but it was fun all the same. The bell would go, and in the blink of an eye, it was as though the little birds had flown away deep into the forest. Then the playground fell quiet again, so quiet that you could hear the ships' whistles on the Huangpu, and the wind in the tops of the trees. And when a real bird chirped from a branch, the playground seemed quieter than ever.

Ah Mei thought of the rain... She loved the rain. She'd sit at her desk, listening to the teacher and watching the fine threads of rain falling outside. She always hoped the rain wouldn't stop, that it would keep falling. Because then Nainai would come to collect her and bring her red oil-paper umbrella. Lots of parents would come to collect their children, but they only had plastic umbrellas, in muted colours. Nainai's red umbrella shone amongst the sea of umbrellas. She knew that Nainai would bring another smaller umbrella for her, and at the click of the button, the umbrella would open up like a flower, catching everyone's attention, adults and children alike. The pitter-patter of the rain on the umbrella was such a lovely, clear sound.

One scene after another flashed past. Ah Mei had spent almost six years of her life at this school, and she had so many dear memories. Her eyes seemed to mist over, as though she was seeing all of this in a dream. She walked slowly, turning at times to look around her. She loved this beautiful school, loved it with all her heart. But she had to leave it. And she would miss it so much. Ah Mei started to cry again.

The more she looked, the more she cried.

She approached the school gates.

Old Mr Jin, the gatekeeper, hadn't expected to see Ah Mei in the playground.

He had been the gatekeeper since Ah Mei's first day at the school. He had noticed straight away this child who looked different from all the other children. And Ah Mei had noticed him, because she had never seen such a kind and friendly old man. Every morning, they would catch each other's eye and smile, and no matter if it was freezing winter or scorching summer, they would both feel happy and content.

At first, Old Mr Jin watched Ah Mei from the window of his little room, then, after a while, he came outside. He didn't ask "What are you doing out here so late, all by yourself?" He just stood there watching her. He didn't smile – well, he did, but it was a sad smile.

Ah Mei stopped walking. Almost six years had gone past, and she suddenly realized that not once in all that time had she taken a close look at Old Mr Jin. She wanted to look at him now. Although there wasn't much light, she could see the wrinkles on his face, his grizzled hair, the slack skin on his neck. She thought he looked older, much older. Had he always been so stooped?

"That's a beautiful dress you're wearing, Ah Mei!" said Old Mr Jin.

"Mrs Hu made it, from one of Nainai's old dresses."

"You look beautiful! But then, you look beautiful whatever you wear."

"Thank you, Mr Jin." Ah Mei wanted to tell him that she wasn't going to come to this school any more, but then decided not to.

"It's getting late," said Old Mr Jin, dragging his feet towards the school gate. The gate was already closed, but he would open it for her. His legs seemed so heavy.

"I can open it by myself," said Ah Mei.

"I know," said Old Mr Jin. But he still walked the twenty

metres to the school gate by Ah Mei's side. His heavy feet slammed on the ground like a hammer. Ah Mei's steps were light, too light to be heard. They walked very slowly, as though neither of them wanted this short walk to end.

There were two iron gates, and they were heavy.

Old Mr Jin slowly opened the gates for Ah Mei. When there was a small gap, just enough to allow Ah Mei through, Old Mr Jin moved aside.

"Thank you, Mr Jin." Ah Mei stood beside him for a moment, then slipped through the gate like a fish. She took a few steps, then looked back and waved to him.

He raised his hand and waved back. It was a big hand, and his fingers were all crooked.

Ah Mei didn't go home. She walked aimlessly. She was beginning to feel hungry, and thought about buying some biscuits from the roadside shop, but she didn't have any money on her. She didn't want to go straight home, but to wait – to wait until the time the recital would have finished.

She wanted to go to Ah Lang's house, and see him. But, in the end, she somehow found herself by Suzhou Creek.

The street lamps on either side of the creek were already lit, their golden reflections rippling in the water. In the evening breeze, the ripples skittered, shattering the gold-leaf surface of the river. Soon, more lights would come on, in the buildings along the banks, buildings short and tall. They were almost all buildings from the olden days, each with its own style, each one as striking as a palace. Ah Mei had been for walks here many times with Nainai, sometimes on the south bank, sometimes on the north. Nainai had told her about every one of these buildings. She said they reminded her of Europe, of Lyons and Marseilles. But they had seldom come here at night. Ah Mei couldn't wait to tell Nainai how beautiful Suzhou Creek looked at night! But … no. She couldn't tell Nainai that she had spent the evening by Suzhou Creek when she was supposed to be at the recital, playing the piano.

The water in Suzhou Creek poured in from the west and poured out to the east. Ah Mei could see Waibaidu Bridge to the east. The water would flow under the bridge and into the much wider Huangpu River. She couldn't see where they joined, but she could picture it in her mind. Somehow the waters merged, they had to, or the creek wouldn't flow so freely, and the water in the creek was always moving, all day and all night.

Ah Mei turned to look west. She wanted to know where all this water came from, why the creek never emptied. She had asked Nainai, but Nainai wasn't sure. "It flows in from far away," she'd answered vaguely.

Ah Mei was lost in thought. When a fish leaped out of the water, Ah Mei heard a girl gasp in surprise. Half dreaming, she looked for her across the river, scanning the bank, before realizing that she was the girl.

Ah Mei forgot about being hungry and sad. She became a sightseer, exploring Suzhou Creek and the Bund by night. She was in a much better mood now.

In the distance, a steamer was leading a long line of boats to the east. As its searchlight lit up the creek, it revealed even more boats – so many small boats moving slowly. The water behind the steamer swelled, creating waves that surged towards the banks. Ah Mei worried that the small boats might capsize. She had been sitting for a while, watching the water, but now she stood up to check on the boats. She saw how they rose and fell with the waves – there was nothing to worry about.

The steamer led the long line of boats, too long to see the tail end, down the creek, passing slowly under Waibaidu Bridge towards the Huangpu.

Where were all these boats going?

Ah Mei couldn't guess. All she knew was that they would leave Shanghai and set out on a long voyage to a place far, far away.

Over on the Bund, the big bell of the Customs House rang out the hour. It was ten o'clock.

Ah Mei hurried towards Waibaidu Bridge. She had to cross the bridge, then cross the road that ran south, then follow the road that ran west towards home. She knew this area well.

On the bridge, two people were fishing with nets. A net flew up, opening in the lamplight like a golden umbrella.

As Ah Mei walked over the bridge, another net was being hauled up from the water. The catch hung in the net like a ball, dripping. At first glance it looked completely still, but as it reached mid-air, it suddenly started moving, like a baby kicking in the womb.

The people fishing hauled the net onto the bridge, and gathered round. As they changed position, Ah Mei could see, through their legs, that they were standing around a large fish that kept tensing and flipping, flashing silver through the net.

She was still thinking of this scene as she reached the other side of the bridge, crossed the road and turned onto the road leading west. Then it slipped from her mind. She remembered why she was walking this way, and her pace slowed. She felt terrible! She imagined the stage – although she didn't know what kind of stage it had been that night – and the lights, and the seats, and the audience in darkness, the stage curtain, the music, the black piano, the applause loud as a summer storm. Then she thought about tomorrow – what would she do? And the day after that? She began to feel scared. Although there were lights everywhere, and people were still out on the streets, she felt she was walking down an endless lane in the dark. She sped up until she was almost running. She could see people looking at her, and felt they were watching with suspicion. Then she really did start to run, as though they were coming after her.

As though all of Shanghai was pursuing her.

She wanted to shout out, *Nainai!* But she caught her foot on an exposed tree root, and tripped. As she fell, she remembered the beautiful dress she was wearing, and just as her knees were about to touch the ground, she lifted the skirt with both hands. The dress remained intact, neither dirty nor torn, but her knees were grazed and bleeding.

Ah Mei stood in front of Nainai with the biggest smile on her face.

"I'm back!" she said in a voice that was a little too loud and exaggerated.

Yeye and Mrs Hu heard her voice, and came to join them.

"How did it go, Ah Mei?" asked Yeye. "Did you play well?"

Mrs Hu wanted to know too. "Tell us all about it, Ah Mei! Tell us! Make me happy!"

"I played brilliantly!" said Ah Mei. "Do you know what kind of applause I got?" She clapped her hands together as hard as she could. "Applause like this!" She clapped until her hands were red and sore, almost bringing tears to her eyes.

Ah Mei's enthusiasm was infectious, and Yeye and Mrs Hu were completely caught up in her excitement. Yeye clapped away with his big, hard hands.

Nainai managed to force a smile.

Whenever Ah Mei came home after a recital, she was always hungry, as though she had used up all her energy in the performance.

"I'm starving!" she told Mrs Hu now.

"I've made something nice for you!" replied Mrs Hu.

Ah Mei followed her into the dining room and very soon Mrs Hu brought in a bowl of steaming wonton soup, and placed it on the table.

In the lamplight, the transparent wonton skins clung around the filling.

Ah Mei was genuinely hungry, but she also knew that she needed to really look it to appear convincing. She took her seat at the table, pulled the bowl towards her and gobbled away like a hungry monster.

"Slow down, slow down," urged Mrs Hu, who was standing close by. "You don't want to burn your mouth."

Usually, after a performance, Nainai would come and sit opposite Ah Mei. She took great pleasure in watching her eat, and hearing all about the recital. But this time, Nainai did not follow her into the dining room.

When Ah Mei had finished the soup, Nainai called her into her room.

Nainai was lying on her bed. She had left plenty of room beside her, and it was clear that she wanted Ah Mei to come and join her.

Ah Mei still appeared full of excitement at the great success of her performance and at being the star of the show.

Nainai smiled.

Ah Mei lay down beside her and patted her tummy. "Oh, I've eaten so much!"

Nainai didn't make a sound, just stroked Ah Mei's head.

Then, after a moment, Nainai asked, "Aina, why didn't you take part in the performance this evening? Can you tell me?"

Ah Mei sat bolt upright, and looked at Nainai's face.

Nainai put her arm around her granddaughter, and gently helped her lie down again.

"As soon as you came home, I knew that you hadn't. There was no make-up on your face."

After performances, Ah Mei always came home with her make-up on so that Nainai could see it. Nainai would gasp with delight – she loved to see Ah Mei all made up. And Ah Mei herself liked to see her face with make-up, and would spend ages in front of the mirror before washing it off. She always felt so sad when she had to remove it.

Now, Ah Mei covered her face with her hands.

"Why did they cancel your performance?" Nainai asked.

Ah Mei shook her head. "I don't know." There was a lump in her throat.

Nainai hugged her. "I'm sorry, Aina. I should be asking someone else, not you. I'm sorry."

Ah Mei didn't burst into tears, but, like a poor little kitten, snuggled up to Nainai.

Nainai could feel Ah Mei shivering, the kind of shiver you get when you can feel the wind in your bones. She could smell something in Ah Mei's hair. "Wherever have you been all this time?" Nainai knew how thoughtful the little girl in her arms could be, and it broke her heart to see her like this. As Nainai closed her eyes, tears rolled down her face.

Ah Mei described Suzhou Creek at night to Nainai – with words and tears, and, at times, even smiles and chuckles.

Then, pulling away from Nainai, she said, "I don't want to go to school any more."

Nainai was adamant: "There's already one person in this family who's stopped going to school. We can't have another one."

Nainai contacted all the rest of the family, and asked them to come to the Blue House on Sunday afternoon. She wanted to arrange a piano recital for Ah Mei at home, in the garden. It would be in front of the whole family, dozens of people – a major event.

It was impossible for Ah Mei's parents to get back from Yibin in time.

Over the phone, Baba asked Nainai with a heavy heart, "Given the circumstances, is it appropriate to arrange a piano recital for Ah Mei? In the garden?"

"There is no reason in the world to refuse music," said Nainai. "No reason whatsoever."

Nainai had the men move the piano into the garden, under the apricot tree.

"Couldn't we do it in the lounge, instead?" asked Xiaogu.

"No!" said Nainai. "It will be in the garden. I can't imagine the neighbours will be offended by the sound of Ah Mei at the piano. They can be the audience too! Doesn't our Ah Mei deserve a big audience?"

Nainai had suddenly become very determined.

The family was quiet.

Nainai looked at Yeye.

The rest of the family looked at Yeye.

He nodded silently at Nainai.

Yeye was Nainai's shady tree in the fierce summer sun, her flickering stove on cold winter nights; he was her rock. But, right now, his mood was dark. He could sense that a storm was brewing, a great black storm that was rolling straight towards the Blue House. Nainai felt exactly the same way – and it was for precisely this reason that she had organized the recital. She didn't want her children and grandchildren to see her fear, to see her hiding away. It might be her last chance to arrange such an event – and if that was the case, she was determined to make it happen.

Dabo tied an electricity cable to the apricot tree and fitted a 100-watt light bulb.

Mrs Hu and the children took all the chairs and stools from the house out onto the lawn.

Nainai dressed up for the occasion, changing into a qipao, and wearing the necklace with the dragonfly eyes.

When she emerged with Ah Mei on her arm, her children and grandchildren stood up and applauded.

Ah Mei was in her recital dress, and Nainai had done her make-up. They had spent almost the entire afternoon getting ready.

Nainai walked with Ah Mei, all the way to the piano.

The white blossom covering the apricot tree glowed in the lamplight, intensely white close to the light bulb, paling to more subtle shades as the light spread, in such a way that you could imagine the blossom you couldn't see in the dark.

Nainai took her seat next to Yeye.

Ah Mei sat on the piano stool. She could see the whole family. Even Ah Lang was there. He was wearing his mask, but it was hanging from one ear, revealing his face. He did not stop smiling at Ah Mei, the kind of smile that rarely touched his face these days.

Finally, Ah Mei's gaze stopped on Nainai's face.

As Nainai gave the nod, Ah Mei's hands rose a few centimetres above the piano, and hung in the air for a moment, like two little birds preparing to fly. Then they swooped down to the piano keys.

Nainai had chosen the music. There were some Chinese

pieces, and some foreign ones, some rousing and some plaintive.

Ah Mei played one piece after another. The old piano was like a kindly old friend, who, knowing that Ah Mei was still young, and still learning to play, backed her up, and carried her through the more difficult parts.

The applause went on and on.

Windows opened near and far. People stood by their windows, or leaned out, and listened. When the sound of clapping rose from the garden, they clapped too.

That evening, it seemed as though all of Shanghai was listening to Ah Mei as she played.

At some point, the wind began to pick up, and eventually to sigh. The apricot tree had been at its most stunning over the last day or two. And it is when a tree is at its most stunning that blossom falls most readily. Each gust of wind blew a shower of white from the tree. The petals fell on the piano, on Ah Mei's head and shoulders. After a moment, they were blown away, and more petals fell. The light bulb swung too, and the blossom twirled and whirled in the swaying light.

Ah Mei's eyes glistened with tears.

Then the wind calmed, and the blossom fell slowly and softly.

With a whisper, Nainai asked Dabo to turn out the light. She had seen the clear, bright moon in the sky.

Ah Mei played a very quiet piece of music.

The world around was silent, as though they had slipped into a dream. The soft, white apricot blossom twirled to

the sound of the piano, like snowflakes in the moonlight,
dancing into the darkness.

CHAPTER 15

The Other Side of the River

Nainai insisted that Ah Mei should stay in Shanghai, and continue going to school. Ah Mei burst into tears. Sobbing, she said she wanted to go to Yibin, where her parents were. "Océane, I know I'm not a Shanghainese any more."

Nainai froze. "What did you say?"

"My papers were sent to Yibin with Baba and Mama's papers," said Ah Mei. "Shanghai doesn't want me."

"How … how do you know this?"

"Qiu Qiu told me. Her aunt works at the police station."

"As long as no one tells you to leave, you are allowed to stay in Shanghai and go to school. And right now, there is no one telling you to leave."

Ah Mei was sitting on the floor, her head on Nainai's knees, her face streaming with tears. "I don't want to go to school here any more. I don't, I don't!"

Yeye tried to talk her round, but he couldn't change her mind either.

Mrs Hu wiped away her tears with the corner of her

apron. "Shanghai's such a big place, surely there's room for a little one?"

Nainai did not want Ah Mei to leave Shanghai; to leave her.

She asked Xiaogu to come over.

Ah Mei loved Xiaogu, and Xiaogu loved her. Ah Mei spent a lot of time with her aunt and loved everything about her: the way she looked, the way she dressed, her demeanour, even her voice. Xiaogu could also play the piano, and she played it very well. The piano at the Blue House had originally been for her, and when she was Ah Mei's age, she'd spent most of her time playing. When she'd moved out of the Blue House, Nainai and Yeye had said, "Take the piano with you." By then, Xiaogu was a music teacher. "Keep it here," she'd said. "There's a piano at school, and it's perfectly good for giving music lessons to the children. Keep it for Ah Mei." Ah Mei had only been very young then. When Ah Mei and Xiaogu were together, naturally they talked about the piano, and about music. Xiaogu wasn't Ah Mei's piano teacher, but that didn't mean she indulged Ah Mei and let her play what she liked, as Nainai had suggested. Instead, she shared her knowledge and experience diligently and carefully. She knew that Ah Mei understood everything she said, that she could grasp even the most abstract and mysterious-sounding concepts. In this way, Ah Mei had two piano teachers: the teacher from the music school, and Xiaogu.

Mostly, Xiaogu let Ah Mei take the lead, but at times, when a little more attention or consideration was needed, Ah Mei would let Xiaogu take over.

So Nainai asked Xiaogu to come to the house to try and persuade Ah Mei to drop the idea of leaving Shanghai.

But this resulted in another tearful outburst, and Ah Mei repeating over and over again: "I want to go to Yibin, I want to go to Yibin…!"

"Shanghai has broken her heart," Nainai sighed eventually.

That evening, Nainai made a phone call to Yibin, and spoke to Ah Mei's parents. "Could you arrange for Ah Mei to go to school there?"

The first raid at the Blue House happened on the day that Nainai started to prepare for Ah Mei's departure. And after that, there was no question of Ah Mei staying in Shanghai.

The night before the raid, as though foreshadowing the event, there had been thunder and lightning, and it had not stopped raining. Snakes of blue lightning hissed through the sky. Moans of thunder rolled over the Huangpu faster, bigger, louder, until they cracked above your head. The soft daylight sky had gone, replaced with the hardest substance in the world. Sparks flew when the night sky cracked, when it shattered over every corner of the city, startling everyone from their dreams, making them wonder what had been hit: a building, perhaps, or a tree.

Nainai gripped Yeye's hand. "It's been years since we had such frightening thunder."

"Indeed," said Yeye, feeling uneasy.

Lightning flashed through the room.

Then it was dark again. Nainai gripped Yeye's hand tightly. They waited for the thunder, the thunder that comes at the last moment, that tests your nerves, that pauses just long enough, until your heart is in your mouth, and then suddenly explodes … as though the sky is falling in.

As the thunder sounded, very faintly Nainai heard Ah Mei crying. In an instant, she let go of Yeye's hand, leaped out of bed, and was on her way to Ah Mei's room.

Ah Mei was already on the landing.

"Ah Mei!"

"Nainai!"

Nainai rushed to Ah Mei, and threw her arms around her. "Don't be scared, Nainai's here!"

Yeye had come out too. He and Nainai took Ah Mei back to their bed, and she squeezed in between them.

The flashes of lightning, like blue snakes and sharp claws, tore viciously at the sky. You could see the rain pouring down in their light. It was raining everywhere you looked. The heavens had opened, and it was terrifying.

"Nainai, will Shanghai drown?" asked Ah Mei.

"No, that won't happen," said Nainai.

"Is there thunder, lightning and rain where Baba and Mama are?"

"They'll be fine. You don't need to worry about them," said Nainai.

"They're upstream," said Yeye, "and we're downstream. If the river floods, it won't flood where they are."

There was another crash of thunder.

"Did the windows just shatter?" Ah Mei asked Nainai.

"No, that won't happen," said Nainai.

"I thought they just did," said Ah Mei.

"Stop all these silly thoughts, and go to sleep," said Nainai.

Ah Mei was soon fast asleep, in between Yeye and Nainai. She slept through the rest of the storm. The lightning didn't wake her; she merely trembled in her sleep at the peals of thunder.

"Shanghai could be under water, and she wouldn't know a thing about it," said Nainai.

Yeye smiled.

At about ten o'clock the next morning, when the thunder and lightning had stopped but it was still pouring with rain, a group of people in army raincoats stormed into the Blue House as though they couldn't wait any longer. They had been shouting slogans in the rain before they charged in – their voices were loud and serious, and hostile. Who were they? Yeye and Nainai didn't recognize any of them. They didn't ask, either, because they knew that these days there were groups forming everywhere, charging into people's homes and office blocks, and searching the premises, confiscating things and arresting people. Sometimes these groups joined forces, although not for long, as they'd soon start arguing, shouting and fighting among themselves. Even Ah Mei knew the term "armed struggle".

It was a group of young people that stormed the house: young Shanghainese, male and female, all with fine features, and clear, fair skin. Far from being robust, they had a perennial pallor. They didn't look at all fierce, and tried to make up for it in other ways.

There was another round of shouting.

This time they shouted the slogans at Yeye and Nainai from inside the house, so loudly that it hurt their ears. Nainai turned to one side, and put her hands over her ears, trying to block out the noise.

Ah Mei and Mrs Hu were upstairs. When Ah Mei ran to her for safety, Mrs Hu wrapped her arms around the girl and turned her back on the youths to shield her.

Ah Mei poked her head out of Mrs Hu's arms to look at the group, then pulled back and shut her eyes.

One of the girls spotted Ah Mei and smiled at her instinctively. Then, remembering what she had come to do, she immediately looked up, punched the air with her fist, and shouted again.

The slogans were very simple. They all began with "Down with…!" They were the two words that Ah Mei had seen and heard most during the last few days: "Down with…!"

When they had finished shouting their slogans, the raiders ordered Yeye and Nainai into the lounge for questioning. In an instant, it became an interrogation room.

Mrs Hu gripped Ah Mei's hand and did not let her go downstairs but made her wait upstairs with her. They could hear the interrogation from there, and listened anxiously.

The leader sat down in an armchair. It was soft, and as he sank into it, he couldn't quite summon the vigour he needed. He paused a while, then finally stood up, and went to sit on a hard chair. He crossed his legs and asked Yeye and Nainai, "Do you know why we're here?"

Yeye put out his hand and tried to sweep Nainai behind him. "No," he answered.

The leader raised his head and looked at Yeye. Yeye was taller than he'd expected, and he couldn't help feeling a little apprehensive. Then, with a flick of his hand, he barked, "You! Go and stand at the back. We're well aware of your history. You're a capitalist who's committed a long list of crimes!"

Yeye wanted to exonerate himself: *It's not like that! I gave my companies, factories, almost everything I owned to the state!* But he didn't say anything. They were so young, he thought, that they probably wouldn't understand if he told them.

"You!" The leader pointed to Nainai. "It's you we're interested in. Do you know why?"

"No," answered Nainai.

Nainai spoke in perfect Shanghainese. The leader, and all the others, were taken aback, and glanced at one other.

The leader nodded. "Well, it seems you've been hiding for a very long time."

Nainai didn't know what the young man was talking about.

"Are you going to hand it over to us, or are you going to put up a fight?" he asked.

"Leniency to those who confess, severity for those who resist!" the group shouted.

The leader flicked his hand, and the slogan chorus stopped.

It was like a stage act that had been performed many times before.

Upstairs, Ah Mei gripped Mrs Hu's hand tightly. *Be brave, Ah Mei.* Mrs Hu looked at her reassuringly. She wanted to take the girl into the bedroom, and lock the door behind them. But Ah Mei wouldn't go, and insisted they stayed where they were. She wanted to hear Yeye and Nainai.

"Where have you hidden the transceiver?" asked the leader.

"What do you mean, 'transceiver'?" Nainai didn't understand.

"What do you mean, 'transceiver'?" the leader repeated angrily. "Where have you hidden the transmitter?"

"What do you mean, 'transmitter'?" Nainai still didn't understand.

The leader laughed coldly, like they do in the movies: "Little old lady! Little foreign old lady! You're playing games with us!"

Nainai looked very serious. "I'm terribly sorry, but I really don't know what you're talking about."

"You really don't know?" asked the leader, adjusting his raincoat, and cocking his head to one side.

"I really don't know," Nainai repeated.

"Well, you'll know soon enough. But you do realize, don't you, how serious the situation will be when we find it? Are you going to hand it over voluntarily, or keep on resisting?"

Nainai didn't answer.

Yeye stood as close as he could to Nainai the whole time. His body blocked most of the light coming in through the window, which made the room dark, and annoyed the young people even more.

The leader, assuming the manner of an old soldier weary of the battlefield, rose slowly from the chair, turned around

225

and said to the group, "Looks like we'll have to find it ourselves." Then, as though summoning a sudden burst of energy, he shouted, "Search the house!" He pointed with his finger. "Start with the ground floor, then go all the way up to the second floor. And search the attic! My guess is that they're still here." Then he turned back to Nainai and gave her a gloating smile. "Ha! Just you wait – we'll find it! And then you'll get exactly what you deserve. Spy!"

"I am not a spy!" Nainai insisted.

Yeye quickly tugged at Nainai's dress. He didn't want to see her try to explain herself, it was only likely to antagonize these young people.

Mrs Hu and Ah Mei couldn't help but turn and watch as the group of young people ransacked each room in their search. Ah Mei kept glancing up at Mrs Hu.

"Do we have a transmitter?" Ah Mei whispered, when the group were out of earshot.

"They're idiots," Mrs Hu whispered back. "They haven't a brain between them!"

Ah Mei liked Mrs Hu's answer, and a smile spread across her face.

It didn't take long for the group to wreck the house. Eventually, Mrs Hu could hold her tongue no longer. "Please be careful," she said as they hurled things to the floor, but no one paid any attention.

Mrs Hu pulled Ah Mei into Nainai's bedroom, just as one of them was opening the little leather suitcase. They saw him lift it up and tip the entire contents onto the floor. Then he crouched down and flicked through the greetings cards.

But he found nothing of interest and tossed them back on the floor.

Mrs Hu's gaze fixed on the necklace with the dragonfly eyes. She wanted to dash over and pick it up, but was afraid to do so in case the youth saw her and took it away. So she kept very still, and deliberately looked elsewhere.

In fact, the youth did see the necklace. But he merely glanced at it, then kicked it aside as he walked off to search somewhere else.

Amituofu! Mrs Hu said a silent prayer of thanks.

As soon as the youth had left Nainai's bedroom, Mrs Hu dashed over, picked up the necklace, and, checking that no one was coming, hid it inside Ah Mei's shirt. "This is your nainai's most treasured possession!" she said, breathing a sigh of relief.

The group wasn't interested in money or treasures. All they wanted was the spy equipment they believed was hidden in the house.

The search lasted over five hours, after which the leader told Yeye and Nainai to move aside, and called in Mrs Hu and Ah Mei.

"Who are you?" the leader asked Mrs Hu.

"The servant," said Mrs Hu.

"And you, little girl?" The leader already knew that Ah Mei was the foreign old lady's granddaughter, but he asked anyway.

Mrs Hu answered for her. "The old lady's granddaughter."

The leader asked Mrs Hu, "Have you ever heard any beeping sounds in the house? Especially late at night, when everyone's gone to bed?"

Mrs Hu looked puzzled.

"A *beep, beep, beep* sound," repeated the leader.

"What makes a sound like that?" asked Mrs Hu.

"Are you pretending to be stupid?" The leader glared at her, then pointed his finger at Ah Mei. "Tell me, have you ever heard that kind of sound?"

Ah Mei hid behind Mrs Hu, shaking her head.

"How many years have you been a servant here?" The leader went back to questioning Mrs Hu.

"Several decades. I started working here when I was a girl," Mrs Hu said. "And I've never heard this *beep, beep* sound."

A light seemed to come on in the leader's head. "Several decades, you say? Then you've probably forgotten who you really are, and how to tell the truth!" He flicked his hand. "Go. Go."

Ah Mei clung to Mrs Hu.

The Blue House had been turned upside down. Even a few dodgy-looking floorboards had been taken up, but there was no trace of a transceiver or a transmitter.

The young people were furious. They felt frustrated, like thieves who have broken into a house and found nothing worth stealing. They started smashing things for the sake of it. A glass of water crashed to the ground. A thermos flask shattered on the floor. Each time something smashed, Ah Mei's eyes would widen in shock, and she'd put her hands over her ears.

"Stop!" Mrs Hu kept shouting.

Then someone lifted the lid of the piano and ran their fingers over the keys.

Nainai pulled her hand away from Yeye's and yelled at them, "You can't do that!"

She pointed at the young people. "Have you no shame, behaving like this in front of a child?"

This question pricked their consciences.

The leader looked around. Everywhere was a mess; you couldn't even see the floor. "We could have done a lot worse!"

"Down with…!" They could hear hoarse voices shouting outside.

Out on the main road, four or five trucks rolled past, blasting slogans through the loudspeakers. They sounded like thunder.

The rain was still falling.

As if encouraged by the chanting outside, the leader issued an order to his group: "Detain them."

Yeye and Nainai had not expected this, and instinctively took a step back.

"As long as you refuse to hand over the transceiver and transmitter and admit that you're a spy, you won't be coming back."

Yeye was outraged. "You wouldn't dare!"

The entire group froze, unsure how to respond.

When they came to their senses, they started singing one of those songs that boosted their morale, that made them burn with indignation and feel they could walk through fire and water without a moment's hesitation.

When the song was finished, they rushed for Yeye and Nainai.

Yeye did his best to protect his wife, but they were

outnumbered and pushed to the ground.

Ah Mei struggled free from Mrs Hu's hand, and ran downstairs. "Yeye! Nainai!" She slipped on the stairs, cutting her face as she tumbled down. Blood poured out. Mrs Hu rushed down. In her haste, she slipped on the stairs as well, and ended up next to Ah Mei, banging her face, arms and legs on the way down. She helped Ah Mei up from the floor.

By this time, Yeye had staggered to his feet, and was standing in front of Nainai with his arms spread out, cursing the group. "You're a pack of animals!"

Nainai darted out from behind Yeye and blocked his way. "All right," she told the group, "we'll go with you. But I ask you to let me do one thing first – let me go upstairs and fetch some clean clothes."

For a moment, there was silence.

"All right," the leader agreed.

Yeye and Nainai gave Ah Mei a goodbye hug.

"Aina," Nainai whispered in Ah Mei's ear. Then, a little louder, "Stay here with Mrs Hu, and wait for us to come home. Yeye and I will be back. You mustn't cry."

But as her grandparents walked out of the house, Ah Mei did cry out, a heart-rending, lung-splitting "YEYE! NAINAI!"

A few of the young people in the group moved closer together to block Ah Mei's way. And no matter how hard she rammed and butted against them, they did not move. They just stood there, a determined line of defence.

Mrs Hu rushed over and put her arms around Ah Mei, and did not let go. "Ah Mei, be a good girl. Yeye and Nainai will be back soon."

Shortly after Yeye and Nainai were taken away, thunder and lightning flashed in the sky.

Mrs Hu took Ah Mei out in the rain to a place with a public telephone. She called Xiaogu and told her what had happened.

Just before dark, all the adults in the family gathered at the Blue House. The men planned the search for Yeye and Nainai, and the women tidied up the terrible mess. They kept asking the same questions, for which there were no answers: "Has the world gone mad?" and, "What right do they have to do things like this?" and, "Is there no law any more?"

Ah Mei sat silently the whole time, leaning against the back of the chair.

Her aunts kept coming over to reassure her. "Ah Mei, don't cry. Yeye and Nainai will be back soon."

They stayed late into the night, the men talking, the women putting everything back in its place and sweeping the house. Then they all went back to their own homes.

Xiaogu stayed behind to keep Ah Mei company. That night, as they lay side by side in bed, Ah Mei said, "I'm not going to leave Shanghai any more. I'm going to wait for Yeye and Nainai, and stay here with them."

Xiaogu combed her fingers through Ah Mei's hair. "I know."

Three days later, Dabo found out where Nainai was. She and Yeye had been locked up together for the first day, then they'd been separated, and Nainai had been sent to labour at a brick field in rural Pudong.

Then Erbo found out where Yeye was. He was labouring at a pig farm in Chongming.

Baba and Mama had returned from Yibin.

The family formed two groups. The first – Xiaogu, Mama and Ah Mei – would cross the Huangpu River to see Nainai. The second – Dabo, Erbo and Baba – would go to Chongming to see Yeye. To avoid attracting suspicion, the rest of the family would stay at home and wait for news.

Xiaogu, Mama and Ah Mei set out early in the morning, and climbed aboard the river ferry at Shiliupu.

The strong wind and high waves rocked the boat hard. Ah Mei groaned and was sick, her face ghastly pale. Mama and Xiaogu ached for her. But the thought of seeing Nainai kept a smile on Ah Mei's face.

Pudong was a desolate place. Mama and Xiaogu were shocked by what they saw. They lived on the western side of the Huangpu, and could see Pudong, the eastern side, from the Bund, but they had never imagined the two sides of the river could be so different. They held Ah Mei's hands and asked everyone they met for directions, and at midday, after walking over ten *li*, they finally found the brick field.

The field was enormous. There were several brick kilns all being used at the same time.

Nainai was not the only person to have been detained and brought there to do manual labour. There were over a dozen such people, who had been labelled as "cow-ghosts and snake-spirits". They weren't guarded particularly closely, but had to move a certain number of bricks every day. Each of them had a personal quota they had to fulfil, even if it meant moving bricks deep into the night, otherwise they would not be allowed to sleep or eat.

The stacks of red bricks were like walls.

Ah Mei, Mama and Xiaogu searched for ages, and finally found Nainai in a long alley between two stacks.

She was carrying ten bricks, and struggling to walk the length of the alley to the river, where a line of boats were waiting to be loaded. As soon as a boat was loaded, it set off.

"Nainai!" shouted Ah Mei, as she ran towards her.

Nainai didn't know what to do with the ten bricks she was carrying. She longed to welcome Ah Mei with open arms, but she couldn't. All she could do was stand there awkwardly, and smile.

Mama and Xiaogu hurried over, and helped Nainai put the bricks down on the ground, one by one.

"Ma!" Mama and Xiaogu said at the same time, their tears raining down.

Ah Mei threw herself into Nainai's arms, and sobbed.

But Nainai carried on smiling. "What are you three crying about? I'm fine, aren't I? Just fine!"

Nainai's face was covered in sweat, and her hair was untidy. Some strands had drifted onto her face and were stuck there with sweat.

Her hair, which had once shone like gold, had lost its colour, and was now white and dry. The sweat didn't roll straight down her face, but ran into the deep lines on her forehead until they could hold no more. Her lips, which usually had the lightest touch of lipstick, were now drained of colour, cracked and peeling.

Mama and Xiaogu each took one of Nainai's hands. They were unrecognizable. Nainai's hands had always been clean as can be, free of marks and scars. But now they were rough and covered with cuts, some with scabs, others trickling blood. Mama and Xiaogu examined her hands, first one side, then the other. Nainai felt embarrassed. "Yes, they're my hands!" she said.

"Where's Yeye?" Nainai asked, anxiously. She was relieved to hear that Dabo and the others were on their way to see him.

The three of them helped Nainai to move her quota of bricks. The supervisor did not try to stop them. The scene just now had warmed his heart. *Let them help,* he thought. When the sun sets in the distance, the old lady's quota of bricks would have been moved.

Then a new person came on duty, a fiercer, colder type, who stormed at Mama, Xiaogu and Ah Mei, "That's not allowed!" And when they continued to help Nainai, "Then there'll be an extra thousand bricks tomorrow! And I mean it!"

The three of them had no choice but to put down the bricks they were holding.

"It's getting late, and you need to catch the ferry," said Nainai. "Go home."

The three of them refused to go. Unable to help, they watched Nainai moving her quota of bricks. They stayed by her side, talking to her, and from time to time, Mama and Xiaogu wiped the sweat from her face with a handkerchief.

Ah Mei saw a broken brick on the ground. Worried that Nainai might trip on it, she quickly picked it up and threw it into the distance.

"They wanted me to hand over a transceiver and a transmitter. But I don't have anything like that! It's obvious that I don't. But they insisted. They're mad!"

The three of them were in torment. It was agonizing watching Nainai as she struggled to move the bricks without being allowed to help her.

Nainai again urged them to go home.

But they refused. If they stayed, at least they could talk to her!

At one point, when Nainai was carrying ten bricks onto the gangplank of a wooden boat, she almost slipped and fell in the river. Without a moment's thought, the three of them rushed over to steady her. They could feel her legs trembling as she walked along the narrow, wobbling board. But when Nainai turned around, after putting the ten bricks down on the boat, there was a smile on her face.

That was the Nainai they knew. That was Océane.

When they were saying goodbye, Nainai said to Mama, "Take Ah Mei back with you."

Ah Mei heard her. "No! Nainai, I want to stay in Shanghai. I want to stay with you." She didn't want to go to Yibin.

Nainai was still smiling, but there were tears glinting in her eyes.

The sun finally disappeared behind the tall buildings on

the west bank of the Huangpu. In the distance, the last gold and red rays of the evening sun streaked the night sky.

The adults were not allowed to cross the river and see Nainai again. They were warned that if they did not comply, Nainai's punishment would be doubled. However, the people at the brick field were not concerned about Ah Mei turning up. And when she appeared, timid and shy, and smiled widely at them, it even seemed that they liked her.

Ah Mei learned how to take the ferry across the river by herself. The first couple of times she went to see Nainai she was too scared to go alone, and Mama or Xiaogu went with her as far as the brick field. But the third time, she let them see her onto the ferry, then asked them to go back. "I can do it now!" she said. When she reached the other side of the river, she climbed ashore, walked through the fields and villages, over one bridge then another, straight to her destination, the enormous brick field. As soon as she saw the smoke from the brick kilns rising in the distance, her heart filled with excitement: "I'll see Nainai very soon!" When she saw the columns of smoke rising higher and higher until they formed clouds, her heart raced and she quickened her step.

Ah Mei had brought some overalls for Nainai. Dabo had bought them from a woman who worked at a textile mill. Nainai asked Ah Mei to keep a lookout while she nipped behind a wall of bricks and changed.

"Beautiful!" cried Ah Mei, when Nainai appeared in the overalls.

Nainai twirled around. "Really?"

Ah Mei nodded. "Océane, you look beautiful whatever you wear."

Ah Mei had also brought five pairs of gloves for Nainai. Xiaogu had bought them in a shop. They were white.

"What was she thinking? I'm moving bricks! These gloves will be dirty in no time."

"Xiaogu says you look good in white gloves, and when they're dirty and torn, you can throw them away, and she'll buy you some more."

Xiaogu had also told Ah Mei, "When she puts on the overalls and the white gloves, you might see a different nainai, but she'll be as wonderful as the nainai who wears a qipao." When Xiaogu talked with Ah Mei about Nainai, she'd said, not without envy, "Your nainai has a natural beauty!" Ah Mei wasn't exactly sure what that meant, but thought she sort of understood.

When no one was looking, Ah Mei took two salted ducks' eggs out of her school bag. "Mrs Hu asked me to give these to you. She said this batch is ready to eat now, the yolks are nice and rich." Nainai took the eggs, held them under her nose and sniffed, then looked around to check no one was watching and hid them in the grass.

Every time Ah Mei went to see Nainai, she took best wishes from her cousins, and the whole family. Ah Lang sent Nainai a handkerchief with little blue flowers on it. "It doesn't seem the kind of gift a boy would send," said Nainai. It broke her heart to think of Ah Lang. "You must go and see him as often as you can," she told Ah Mei. "I know," said

Ah Mei. Nainai pictured the whole family, dozens of them, standing in front of her. And as she did so, her mood lifted, and she felt grateful beyond compare. These people, related by blood or marriage, were her children and grandchildren, and no one could take that away from her. She felt honoured and blessed to have them.

"Aina, you must go and see Yeye," said Nainai.

"I've been," said Ah Mei. "But he doesn't want me to visit. He said the pig farm stank, and he wanted me to stay away. He said that if I was going to see you, then I had to change my clothes." She looked Nainai in the eye. "Yeye said you'd be able to smell pig muck on my clothes. He said your nose…"

"He said *what*?"

"He said, 'Your nainai has the nose of a dog!'"

"Du Meixi!" Nainai grit her teeth indignantly, but there was clearly a smile in her eyes.

Ah Mei was like a puppy, happily trotting along in front or behind. It was a shame that she couldn't help Nainai move the bricks. As soon as she touched a brick, the supervisor standing on the high wall would shout out, "What are you doing, little girl?" Nainai would respond immediately. "Put it down!" And Ah Mei would have no choice but to do as she was told.

"Talk to me instead," said Nainai. "That will be just as good."

With Ah Mei to keep her company, moving bricks was not the ordeal Nainai had imagined. Her face might be covered in sweat, but she looked relaxed, not worn out or exhausted.

They talked about this and that, and of course, Nainai would always mention Yeye. Every now and then she'd remember things from the past. She repeated these stories again and again. Ah Mei wanted to tell her, "Océane, I've heard that story fifteen times already," but she just smiled and pretended she was hearing it for the first time, listening attentively. And when Nainai stopped in the middle of a story and said, "I'm sure I've told you this one," Ah Mei would reply, "I haven't heard it before."

Sometimes, Ah Mei would wander off, and follow a weasel. There were weasels and rabbits in the grass and among the piles of broken bricks around the field. For a moment, Ah Mei would forget about Nainai, but Nainai never let her out of her sight.

Ah Mei could make Nainai believe that this heavy, mechanical, dull moving of bricks was not wearing her down physically and mentally. These people wanted to break Nainai with hard labour, so that she would give in, tell them where the transceiver and transmitter were, and confess to being a spy.

But a different scenario was playing out – one in which an adult worked and a child played. And although this was a common enough scene, onlookers still found it fascinating.

Nainai was always saying, "Aina, you should go to school. Don't come and see me all the time."

Ah Mei told Nainai that there were basically no lessons in school any more. Some teachers were busy shouting, "Down with…!" everywhere they could, and others had already been brought down.

"It's better not going to school," said Ah Mei. "It's much better not going to school!"

"Once upon a time there was a girl called Aina, and once she started talking nonsense, she kept on talking nonsense!" said Nainai.

"A lot of my classmates don't go to school any more," said Ah Mei.

Bewildered, Nainai shook her head, let out a sigh and carried the ten bricks in her arms to the riverside.

Ah Mei followed her. Whatever it was that Ah Mei was thinking about, she was in a very good mood, and she began to sing.

That afternoon, it started to rain. The rain fell harder and harder.

Nainai told Ah Mei to run into a disused kiln to keep dry while she carried on moving bricks. She had no choice but to keep working in the rain, because her quota had been increased by five hundred bricks, and she had to fulfil her quota.

Ah Mei didn't do as Nainai said. She stayed outside.

"Go and shelter from the rain, Aina."

Ah Mei shook her head. She looked up at the sky, and saw the dense mass of raindrops coming towards her. They splashed on her face, and a few caught in her throat and made her cough.

"Quick, run to the kiln over there," said Nainai.

"No!" replied Ah Mei, walking towards Nainai. She kept her eyes on the ground. When she saw a piece of broken brick in Nainai's way, she picked it up and threw it into the distance. When the ground was slippery, she picked grass from near by and spread it over the mud.

Seeing Ah Mei's little figure darting about in the rain, Nainai felt a gentle warmth course through her body. The wet bricks were heavier, but Nainai gritted her teeth and carried on. As long as Ah Mei was there, Nainai could keep going. No matter how hard it got, she would carry on.

This girl gave her a very special kind of strength.

Ah Mei looked back through the rain at Nainai. Then, seeing she was too far ahead, she took a few steps back, singing aloud.

Nainai had never walked on such a muddy path before. She moved cautiously, one careful step at a time, keeping steady and calm.

The rain kept falling. Both sides of the Huangpu were shrouded in smoke – a river-smoke.

All of a sudden, Nainai slipped. The bricks went flying.

Ah Mei ran as fast as she could, and pulled Nainai to her feet. Nainai had hurt her arm, and it was bleeding badly. The pouring rain washed the dark red blood from the wound, and a pale red watery liquid ran over the mud.

"STOP WORKING…!" boomed a voice in the distance.

"They're telling you to stop," said Ah Mei.

Nainai shook her head. "No, I'm going to stay in the rain, and let the rainwater wash me. I'm so dirty, so dirty I can't bear it…"

Ah Mei helped Nainai pick up the bricks she had dropped. She passed seven to Nainai, and carried the other three herself.

No one tried to stop her.

Ah Mei helped Nainai to move another load of bricks. Again, no one tried to stop her.

Sometimes they walked in single file, sometimes side by side. The early autumn rain was fresh, if a little cold. Nainai felt so much cleaner, and as a result, so much happier. She started singing aloud in French.

Ah Mei didn't understand Nainai's French songs, but she liked to hear them, especially in the autumn rain.

"What are you singing?" Ah Mei asked Nainai.

"It's a folk song from Provence," said Nainai. "It's about the rain falling in the lavender fields. It says the lavender fields are purple as far as the eye can see. When the rain falls, the lavender releases its beautiful perfume, which fills the air across the land."

Nainai said that when she sang this song, she felt so much cleaner, and didn't stink any more. She said the first thing she'd do when she went home would be to ask Mrs Hu to fill a hot bath for her, and she'd soak in it for three days and three nights.

With Ah Mei's help, Nainai soon finished moving her quota of bricks.

The rain was still falling. Nainai lifted her face to the sky to catch the pure rainwater, and instinctively used her hands to wash her arms and face. Then she pulled Ah Mei to her, and, with her rough hands, washed Ah Mei's face too. When she finally felt clean again, she took Ah Mei inside the low building that was the workers' accommodation.

As if by magic, the rain stopped.

It was getting late, but the sky was clearing.

When Ah Mei left Nainai, she was wearing the overalls that Dabo had bought for Nainai. They had been washed the day before, and were clean and soft. They were too big, but she wore them anyway. She carried a string bag, stuffed with her dirty clothes. She walked through the villages and fields and took the ferry across the river, with everyone staring at her, looking her up and down.

Swinging the bulging bag, Ah Mei happily made her way home.

CHAPTER 16

Perfume

When Nainai finally came home, there was no sense of closure. The group that had initially detained her, then sent her to do hard labour on the other side of the Huangpu, had disappeared, never to be seen again.

"It's outrageous!" said Yeye resentfully, on Nainai's first day back home. He had returned before her.

Apart from grumbling about not being able to wash properly across the Huangpu, Nainai would simply smile gently whenever the ordeal was mentioned. She didn't utter another word of complaint. It was as though the impetuousness and boorishness of those young people was forgivable, and the inhuman hard labour was not a big deal.

She did not spend her first three days and nights at home soaking in the bath, as she had told Ah Mei she would. But she did spend a long time washing, and then sprayed herself with three times as much perfume as usual.

It was only as she poured a drop of perfume onto her

finger and dabbed it behind Ah Mei's ear that she realized she had finished her last bottle of perfume.

Nainai looked at the empty bottle, and showed Yeye the empty palms of her hands.

Yeye understood, and immediately went to telephone Xiaogu. "Your mother's out of perfume – do you have any at your house?"

"I've got almost half a bottle, but it's a very small one. And she only wears that particular brand. She might not like the one I use."

"Could you let her have it anyway?"

"Yes, I'll keep it for her," said Xiaogu.

"She can't live without perfume!"

"I know," said Xiaogu.

From that day on, Yeye's priority was to find perfume for Nainai. But where would he be able to buy a bottle given the current situation in Shanghai?

Mrs Hu picked some jasmine flowers, and steeped them in fresh water. The little flowers looked lovely floating about in the water as though they had lives of their own. The following day when Mrs Hu held the water in front of her nose, it smelled faintly of jasmine.

"Madam, try this," she said to Nainai.

After that, Nainai washed her face in this scented water every morning. She dipped her fingers in it and flicked it on her clothes.

"I feel as though there's a strange smell around me all the time," Nainai told Yeye. She looked at him. "Surely you must have noticed … an unpleasant odour?"

"Not at all!" said Yeye.

"When you're young, it doesn't matter if you wear perfume or not, because when you're young, you smell nice. But –" Nainai unclasped her hands, letting Yeye see their wrinkly backs – "I'm old now! And old people smell."

"In that case, I'd better use perfume too," said Yeye.

"You don't smell," said Nainai. She leaned towards him and sniffed. "Honestly, you don't."

"Neither do you."

"But I do. I know I do."

Ah Mei just happened to be walking past.

Nainai called her over. "Tell me, do I smell?"

Ah Mei sniffed Nainai, like a cat, from head to toe, from left to right. Then she said, "You smell lovely."

Nainai pushed her away gently. "You little fibber!" Then she looked round at Yeye. "And you're a *big* fibber! Cheats, the pair of you."

That evening, when Ah Mei had finished playing the piano, she asked Nainai, "Are all French people so keen on cleanliness?"

"No, no," Nainai told Ah Mei. "In the past, French people were really quite filthy. There was human waste all over the streets of Paris – the stench was unbearable, utterly revolting. Can you believe that people who lived on the first floor would open their windows and empty their chamber pots onto the street? In those days, French people washed only once every few days, and they smelled terrible. That's why perfume was invented, to cover the terrible smell."

"That's disgusting!" said Ah Mei.

"Of course, that was in the past. But it's not because I'm French that I like to keep clean. Your yeye keeps clean too, you know! That's what drew me to him in the first place. A man who looks after himself is very attractive. When you grow up, you must fall in love with a man who looks after himself."

"I don't want to fall in love!" said Ah Mei shyly.

"Let's wait and see," said Nainai. "You might change your mind."

They went back to talking about perfume.

Ah Mei realized just how important perfume was to her grandmother.

There was a shop on Huaihai Road that sold perfume, many different brands of perfume, including the one Nainai liked. However, this shop was only open to foreigners and only accepted foreign currency.

Yeye began to find any excuse to walk past the entrance to this shop. Foreigners went in and out, and as the men and women walked past, their perfumes would waft through the air. Yeye could identify most of the brands. For the past few days he had thought of nothing else. How wonderful it would be if he could get a bottle of perfume for Nainai! He had even been dreaming about it. One time, he had dreamed about the entire manufacturing process behind a single bottle. His sole reason for being part of the process, from start to finish, had been to get a bottle for Nainai. But in the end he wasn't able to fulfil his wish, and he'd woken up disappointed. He had resolved then and there that, whatever it took, he would get a bottle of perfume for Nainai!

One day, Yeye managed to slip inside the shop with a large group of foreigners.

He found the perfume counter, and immediately spotted the brand that Nainai liked.

The salesperson came up to him. "Would you like to buy some perfume, sir?"

Yeye shook his head and moved away.

The salesperson watched him suspiciously.

Acting as though nothing had happened, Yeye went from counter to counter, pretending to be looking at different products, although the only thing he was thinking about was perfume. He wanted to go back to the perfume counter, but in the end he didn't, and walked out of the shop instead. Once outside on the main street, he berated himself. *Are you really such an idiot! You haven't a penny in foreign currency, and yet you go looking around that store. Ridiculous! The good news is, they have the perfume. The bad news is, you can't buy it! You old fool.*

He started to laugh out loud.

Passers-by turned their heads to stare at him: the old man must have gone mad!

Yeye laughed and laughed, but his heart was swelling with sadness. He wanted desperately to cry. *All this over a bottle of perfume?* he chided himself. *How ridiculous!* He gave a single sigh, then walked down the main road as if there was nothing wrong. But as he walked, he was thinking of Nainai – his other half, his Océane. He started to feel unsettled again, all knotted inside. *She has given me so many children and raised a big family for me. She has given me the best years of her life with no complaints or regrets. What have I given her? And now, I can't even buy her a bottle of perfume!* Yeye felt so ashamed.

Without thinking, he walked to Nanjing Road, the most prosperous street in Shanghai.

The wind blew off the river onto the Bund, and then down the length of Nanjing Road, messing up people's hair, and whipping their clothes.

For some reason, walking this way, battling against the wind, made Yeye feel better inside, and helped to firm his resolve: *I must get a bottle of perfume for Océane, no matter what.*

Perfume was her life-force.

All of a sudden, he thought he caught a whiff of perfume.

He sniffed the air. He followed the scent through the crowds, and spotted a Western woman hurrying towards the Bund. Instinctively, he hurried after her, after the scent. It wasn't Nainai's favourite, but it was one she liked.

Yeye followed the woman down Nanjing Road. The crowd seemed to fall away, disappearing into shops, and thinning as they neared the Bund.

Yeye guessed she was young. This brand of perfume suited women of her age. He had recognized it immediately; Nainai had worn it when he first met her.

The woman realized she was being followed, and glanced back in alarm. She was relieved to see a tall, elegant figure, who wasn't at all intimidating. She even smiled.

Yeye smiled back, apologetically. *I was following your perfume, that's all.*

The woman walked on.

Yeye smiled again, and stopped where he was. The scent of perfume became fainter and fainter.

It was dusk by the time Yeye started for home.

Trams rumbled past, and from far away, perhaps the horizon, came the blasts of ships' whistles.

An idea was forming in Yeye's mind. He was so excited about it that when he got home, Mrs Hu took one look at him and asked, "Did you find a pot of gold when you were out today, Sir?"

Nainai looked at him, wondering what could have happened.

Yeye smiled, took off his jacket, handed it to Mrs Hu and went straight to Ah Mei's room. "Ah Mei!" he called.

"Yeye!" said Ah Mei, rushing to the door. She was also surprised by the look on his face.

"Inside! Inside!" Yeye waved his hands.

He gave her a gentle shove to hurry her up, and closed the door behind them.

She looked at him, her eyes blinking fast.

Yeye sat down on a chair, and stood her in front of him. "Ah Mei, there's something important I need to talk to you about, something I need your help with."

Nainai and Mrs Hu looked at each other, then at the closed bedroom door, and wondered what on earth was going on.

Yeye was in Ah Mei's bedroom for a full hour.

That evening, while they were eating, Ah Mei and Yeye kept making eye contact. From the way they squished their eyebrows and rolled their eyes, it seemed that they were still making plans, or had made plans, and were caught up in the excitement of it all.

The next day, after breakfast, Yeye said he was going out for a walk with Ah Mei, and off they went, hand in hand.

They had a mission to complete: to get Nainai a bottle of perfume.

Yeye had included Ah Mei in the plan because while he'd been hanging around Nanjing Road and the Bund the day before, he had noticed the patrols. These teams wore red armbands, looked holier than thou, and walked around in silence, on the alert, their eyes swivelling this way and that, scanning the place and the people, ready to leap into action when the moment called. Yeye needed Ah Mei because he planned to hang around on Nanjing Road and the Bund, waiting for an opportunity to approach foreigners – female foreigners, in particular.

They were the only way he would be able to get some perfume.

By taking Ah Mei along, the two of them would look natural, inconspicuous – a grandfather and granddaughter out for a stroll were unlikely to attract attention and arouse suspicion. The previous day Yeye and Ah Mei had gone over all the things that could possibly go wrong.

Yeye had told her exactly what to do if they were to find themselves in any of those scenarios.

"Don't be afraid. Keep calm and use your brain," Yeye repeated several times.

"I get it, I get it," Ah Mei answered him again and again.

"Good," said Yeye. "It's important."

Every so often Yeye would slip his hand into his trouser pocket. There was a piece of jade in there that he loved, that he kept in his pocket and took out from time to time, that he would hold in his hand or play with. The jade had a soft warmth to it – he couldn't say whether it was a natural attribute or the result of being taken out and handled so frequently – and it was developing a rich depth as well. He had decided to exchange this piece of jade for a bottle of perfume.

Ah Mei knew when Yeye's hand disappeared into his pocket that he was holding that piece of jade.

They walked down Nanjing Road towards the Bund, looking out for foreigners who might help them realize their plan.

By five o'clock they had had no luck despite having been there since the morning. What with the language barrier, and the patrol teams that kept walking past, they hadn't been able to find someone to help them. And now that the sun was sinking lower and lower, they were preparing to go home empty-handed.

Yeye looked at Ah Mei. She was tired.

"Ah Mei, can you hold out a while longer? I mean, if, on our way home, the right person just happened to walk past?"

"Yes, I can, Yeye!" said Ah Mei. She put her hands on her hips and straightened her back. Her muscles had been getting stiff, but now she felt a new rush of energy. She jumped up and down.

They gazed at the big clock on the Customs House, then at

the river. They walked up the Bund and back down again. If anyone had been watching them, they would probably have thought they were lost, this old man and his granddaughter.

All of a sudden, Ah Mei tugged at Yeye's jacket, and pointed.

A blonde middle-aged woman, with a bag over her shoulder, was crossing the road, heading for the river.

Ah Mei was so nervous her hand started shaking. Yeye gripped it tightly, and they stood there watching the woman.

She walked over to the river, gazed across over the water for a while, then turned and, leaning back against the railing, looked up at the architecture on the Bund.

Yeye checked all around for patrol teams and scanning eyes, then led Ah Mei by the hand, as though they were simply out for a stroll, and headed towards the woman.

The woman heard footsteps and looked round. When she saw Ah Mei, she raised her hand and waved.

Yeye told Ah Mei to use the English she had just learned, and say hello to the foreign woman.

The woman took a moment or two to respond, before greeting Yeye and Ah Mei in rather stiff English.

When she spoke, Yeye almost slapped his hand on the railing in excitement: she spoke with a heavy French accent, a Parisian accent. Yeye recognized it immediately. His French came flooding back, and although it was by no means perfect, it was good enough to manage a conversation.

When Yeye greeted the woman in French, she gasped in surprise.

Yeye used the simplest language, and in a very short

time had given her a string of information: his wife Océane was French and from Marseilles; they had lived in Lyons for fourteen years; in late autumn 1939 they and their four children had left Lyons and come back to Shanghai.

With this string of information, and Ah Mei smiling at her throughout, the Frenchwoman and Yeye very quickly established a bond.

When Yeye had finished speaking, he glanced all around.

The Frenchwoman could see that he was on the alert. She seemed to be aware of the situation in China, of what was happening in Shanghai, and subconsciously glanced around too.

Then she and Yeye smiled in recognition.

Yeye took the piece of jade out of his pocket.

"I would like to use this piece of jade to buy a bottle of perfume for my wife," he said, earnestly. He gave her the name of the perfume, and immediately added, "And if not this brand, then another brand will do."

The Frenchwoman said, "It's a pity I didn't bring any perfume with me today. I have some, but only half a bottle, and it's at my hotel."

Yeye slumped in disappointment.

Ah Mei kept her eyes on the Frenchwoman, pleading with her silently.

The woman was moved by Ah Mei's eyes, and said to Yeye, "Tomorrow, tomorrow morning at ten, here, I can bring a bottle of perfume for your wife. All right?"

"OK, OK," Yeye answered quickly. He tried to give her the piece of jade.

She pushed it away.

"I heard it's from the Warring States period," said Yeye. He explained in simple French that the Warring States period was a very long time ago.

The woman pushed the jade away more firmly.

But Yeye was determined to give it to her.

While all this was going on, Ah Mei kept her eyes on the street. It was what Yeye had repeated so many times: when he talked to a foreigner, she was to keep a lookout, and to tell him the moment she saw a patrol. Yeye said that now he was old, his sight wasn't so good, whereas Ah Mei was still a child, and had sharp eyes.

To convince Yeye that she would do her absolute best to get a bottle of perfume for his Océane, the Frenchwoman agreed to take the jade for the time being.

Having confirmed once more the time they would meet the next day, Yeye grabbed Ah Mei's hand and quickly left the Bund. On the way home, he was as happy as a little child. He sang as he walked, quietly when there were people around, and loudly when there weren't:

> Sing a song of sixpence,
> A pocket full of rye.
> Four and twenty blackbirds
> Baked in a pie!
> When the pie was opened,
> The birds began to sing
> Now wasn't that a dainty dish
> To set before the king!

Ah Mei couldn't make out the words properly, and asked Yeye, "Is it a French song?"

"It's an English one," he replied. "When your baba and the others were little, your nainai used to sing these odd little nursery rhymes to them."

Yeye sang odd little nursery rhymes all the way home.

The next morning, Yeye and Ah Mei were on the Bund at eight o'clock.

They didn't go straight to the agreed meeting point, but watched for a while from the entrance to Nanjing Road, then walked north towards Waibaidu Bridge. Then they wandered around, a short distance from the meeting place.

Every now and then they would look up at the hands on the Customs House clock, and glance at the entrance to Nanjing Road, where the Frenchwoman had appeared the day before.

In the distance, from the roof of a tall building, a loudspeaker was broadcasting songs with an unmistakable rhythm and a forceful tone. From time to time, trucks full of people wearing red armbands went past. The trucks were fitted with loudspeakers too.

There seemed to be loudspeakers everywhere.

Yeye was anxious. He kept seeing patrols. They didn't march briskly, but walked slowly, as though examining everyone. Yeye felt that if they spotted someone suspicious, they'd question them immediately, or arrest them on the spot.

It seemed that the patrols had been ordered to stay in

groups of six or seven people, and that each had their own patch.

Yeye kept glancing at the clock. So did Ah Mei. She wished the hands would move a little faster, so they could collect the perfume from the Frenchwoman as soon as possible. Yeye wished the hands would move a little slower: he hoped the woman would not arrive until the patrols had moved on.

At 9.45 a.m. the Frenchwoman appeared at the entrance to Nanjing Road.

She glanced over at the river, crossed the road and headed towards the meeting point. But just before she got there, she changed her mind, and, acting as though she was out for a stroll, began to walk by the railings, slowly heading north. She seemed to have sensed something was not right.

Ah Mei wanted to run over to the Frenchwoman, but Yeye gripped her hand tightly. Then he led her to the side of a kiosk.

"Do you really want to get a bottle of perfume for Nainai?" he asked.

"Yes!" said Ah Mei.

"Then you must do as I say."

Ah Mei nodded.

"You must wait here, and not move away. You must watch me, quietly. Over there – can you see? – there's a dustbin. When I've got the perfume, I'll crouch down next to it to tie my shoelaces. Then, I'll head south, towards the wharves at Shiliupu. I don't know how long it will take me to get back to you. If I'm not back after two hours, you must go home by yourself, in case I've had to find another route home. Remember, ten minutes after I've moved away from the bin, you're to walk towards it, as though you're playing some kind of game. Go straight to the bin—"

"Yeye, I know what you're going say!" Ah Mei said excitedly.

"What?"

"The perfume will be in the bin!"

Yeye nodded. "Then you're to go back to the kiosk and wait for me there." He watched as a smile brightened Ah Mei's face.

"We'll be just like the underground workers in the movies?"

Grief swept over Yeye's face. He gave a long sigh.

The clock seemed to *cur–lick* loudly as the hands reached ten o'clock.

Ah Mei felt an invisible hand clenching around her heart. She glanced at the clock. "Yeye, it's ten o'clock."

"I know." He looked at the meeting point. The French-woman was walking towards it.

The loudspeakers were broadcasting.

A patrol was heading northwards, stopping occasionally to scan all around.

The Frenchwoman reached the meeting place. She stared across the river for a few minutes, then slowly turned around. A little anxious that Yeye and Ah Mei hadn't appeared, she turned back towards the river again.

Yeye waited until the patrol team had gone past, then impressed upon Ah Mei once more: "Don't be scared. Keep calm, and use your brain." He started to walk towards the Frenchwoman. The Customs House clock said twenty past ten. By now there were many sightseers on the Bund. Yeye felt a pang of regret: he shouldn't have arranged to meet here. He should have picked a more secluded place. His choice of location was a mistake. But it was too late now, he had to hold his nerve amid the staring eyes of the crowd, and head over to the Frenchwoman.

If he left it any longer, she would assume something had happened, and walk away.

When Yeye had nearly reached the Frenchwoman, he greeted her quietly.

In an instant, she had turned around and opened her bag, then, checking that the coast was clear, she took out a paper bag containing a bottle of perfume and handed it to Yeye. "Your wife is very lucky, she can have a bottle of her favourite perfume. The friend who came to China with me just happened to have one."

Yeye quickly took the perfume, and put it in his jacket pocket.

"My very best wishes to your Océane! But I'm sorry, I can't keep this piece of jade." And without letting him answer, she pressed the jade into his hand. "You are a remarkable husband." Then, with a puzzled look, she asked, "Where's your adorable granddaughter?"

Yeye didn't answer.

The Frenchwoman smiled. "Goodbye! My best wishes to the girl." Then she turned around and headed back towards the entrance to Nanjing Road.

"Thank you so much!" whispered Yeye, although he knew she could no longer hear him.

Yeye waited until the Frenchwoman had crossed the road and disappeared into the crowd, then he set about following the agreed plan of action, which was to head for the dustbin. He had no idea what eyes might be watching him from the crowd – these days there could be any number of informants in the area. He had to lose that bottle of perfume as fast as he could. He glanced over his shoulder, and immediately started to worry. There was a middle-aged man watching him from a distance. When their eyes met, the man quickly looked elsewhere.

Damn! Yeye said to himself. He looked up at the Customs House clock, took a deep breath, turned around and began to walk towards the dustbin. Just before he got there, his shoelace appeared to come undone. When he reached the bin, he crouched down and took his time tying the laces that didn't need any attention in the first place, then stood up, staying as close to the bin as he could. His loose jacket had long, wide sleeves, and when he put his hand in his pocket and pulled out the perfume, it was so subtle you could have been standing near by and still not have noticed. Nor would you have noticed him discreetly passing the bottle, still in its paper bag, through the slot in the side of the bin. He had even managed to slip the piece of jade into the paper bag too. Having completed the task, he adopted a leisurely manner, and walked off towards Shiliupu.

Ah Mei, peering round the corner of the kiosk, had not taken her eyes off Yeye. Her heart was pounding.

Yeye walked fifty or sixty metres, then snatched a look back. He saw those eyes again.

And again those eyes looked away.

Yeye felt anxious, but more than that he felt blessed. Thank goodness he had managed to put the perfume in the bin. His worry now was whether Ah Mei would be able to retrieve it.

He hoped it would be straightforward, and that nothing unexpected would happen.

He moved further and further away, and soon disappeared in the crowd.

Ah Mei kept her eye on the clock. Time seemed to pass incredibly slowly, one long second at a time. She wanted to go straight over to the bin, but Yeye had told her to wait ten minutes before fetching the perfume, and she had promised to do as he said.

With two minutes to go, Ah Mei glanced at the dustbin. An old rubbish-collector with a sack on his back was walking towards it. Now she couldn't follow Yeye's instructions any longer. She ran towards the bin, and once she'd overtaken the old man, slowed down, pretending she had come to the Bund to enjoy herself.

About thirty metres from the dustbin, Ah Mei looked up. The old man wasn't hurrying towards the bin at all – he was picking up things people had dropped, things that he could sell. *Don't be afraid. Keep calm, and use your brain...* She repeated Yeye's words over and over, and as though enjoying her walk, moved closer and closer to the bin.

It was half past ten.

Ah Mei arrived at the bin. She checked all around her, and when she was sure there were no eyes watching, put her hand through the slot in the side, all the time looking the other way. She felt around and found the paper bag. She knew in an instant that it was the bag Yeye had left for her, and she knew what was inside it – the perfume!

Nainai's perfume.

Very quickly, Ah Mei took the paper bag out of the bin and put it in the school bag on her back.

No one had noticed, except for the old refuse-collector. "Hey, what're you doing?" he called out.

Ah Mei stepped back in surprise.

"That's my bin! Go find your rubbish somewhere else!"

Afraid that he might come after her, Ah Mei ran off. She realized immediately that she was heading in the wrong direction – it was the same way Yeye had gone. She was supposed to go the other way, back to the kiosk, to wait for him there. Holding her school bag in one hand, she looped round, running towards the road, then back to the kiosk. When she looked round, she saw the old man rummaging through the bin.

She started to laugh.

All she had to do now was to wait for Yeye. Reaching into her school bag, it suddenly occurred to her to check inside the paper bag. What if it wasn't a bottle of perfume? She tensed at the thought. What if the perfume was still in the bin and the old man had found it? What would they do then? She had to check! She put her hand into her school bag and felt around. She found the paper bag, opened it and slipped her hand inside. There was a slim, rectangular cardboard box, and there was something else, too. Was it Yeye's jade? Yeye had let her touch it once, and this thing in the paper bag felt the same. But she wasn't interested in the jade; she wanted to know what was inside the box – whether it was a bottle of perfume … or not. Then a smile crept over her face, and her heart fluttered – she had caught a whiff of the perfume. And she recognized the scent. It was the very same scent that followed Nainai wherever she went.

Océane! Yeye and I have got you some perfume! The one you wanted!

Ah Mei could have wept.

She pulled out the other object. It was Yeye's jade! The Frenchwoman hadn't taken it after all.

Ah Mei could feel a card inside the paper bag too. She took it out. It was folded, like the Christmas cards Nainai kept in the little leather suitcase. She opened it, and saw two lines of fresh handwriting, which she recognized as being French, though she couldn't read them.

Later, Nainai would tell her what it said: *For Océane, the epitome of elegance (as your husband described you) – from your French compatriot.*

Ah Mei put everything back in the paper bag, fastened her school bag, and waited patiently for Yeye.

She didn't know that Yeye was in trouble. He was being questioned by a patrol team.

Standing behind Yeye was the man who had been watching him. He had followed Yeye. He had seen a patrol approaching, run over to them and reported Yeye. "That old man, can you see him?" he'd said, pointing to Yeye. "Just now, over there, he was exchanging something with a foreign woman. He was acting suspiciously from start to finish. You should stop him and question _him_. There's definitely something going on there!" When the patrol team had looked dubious, he'd slapped his hand on his chest: "There was an exchange. I saw it with my own eyes, clear as day."

The patrol team had put their heads together, discussed what to do, then walked at speed towards Yeye.

When Yeye looked round, and saw them and the middle-aged man, he knew immediately what was happening. He didn't panic, just carried on walking, keeping an eye on the Customs House clock. If he could keep moving, playing for time, Ah Mei would be able to collect the perfume and get back to the kiosk safely.

"Halt!" the team leader shouted at Yeye.

Yeye carried on walking.

They rushed up in front of Yeye. "Halt!"

Yeye pointed his finger at his chest. "Are you talking to me?"

"Yes, you!"

The middle-aged man came over and pointed at Yeye: "That's him! The shifty-looking old guy. You can see it in his eyes: he's a cunning thief, a sneaky rat."

But that was not how the patrol team saw Yeye. They saw an old man who had a certain air about him, a man who must have been quite handsome in his day. They waved their hands impatiently at the middle-aged man as if to say, _You can go now._

But the middle-aged man didn't want to go. "Why should I leave? It was me who spotted him, who kept my eye on him!"

Then the questioning started.

"Did you make contact with a foreign woman just now?"

"What do you mean 'make contact'?" Yeye said. "It was a chance meeting, nothing more."

"You were talking for some time. Can you speak a foreign language?"

"No." Yeye didn't want them to know he could speak French.

"They were talking to each other!" the middle-aged man said. "Quite easily, from the look of things."

"Actually, we each spoke in our own language, and neither of us understood what the other was saying," Yeye said.

"That woman gave you something. Right?"

Yeye shook his head. "No. Why would she give me something?"

"You low-life!" The middle-aged man was still standing behind Yeye. "I saw it with my own eyes. I'm not blind, you know!"

Yeye laughed. "I don't know whether you're blind or not. But I did not receive anything from her."

"Then you gave her something?"

"No," Yeye replied. "What would I give her? I don't even know her!"

One of the patrol members turned to stare at the middle-aged man.

The man recalled the scene: "I didn't see him handing something to her. But she did give something to him – there's no doubt whatsoever about that. Heaven strike me with five thunderbolts if I tell even half a lie."

"Are you going to hand it over voluntarily? Or are we going to have to search you? Perhaps it was an exchange of information? Or perhaps she gave you something very important, something you can use: a part for a transmitter, for example?"

Yeye laughed out loud.

He was still laughing when a fist landed in his face. It belonged to one of the patrol team, a big, strong man, who looked like a dockworker.

Yeye's tall body lurched backwards, and almost keeled over.

Blood trickled from the corner of Yeye's nose. Once he had recovered his balance, he jabbed his hand towards the man. "You're not even human!"

Then, raising his hands ready to fight, he advanced on the man who had hit him. In an instant, the group lunged forward, and after a bout of kicking and punching, Yeye was pinned to the ground. The patrol searched him from head to toe, but found nothing. Then they turned again to stare at the middle-aged man who had been kicking Yeye with them.

The man kept blinking. "No, no, no... Let me me think, let me think... What actually happened just then? I definitely saw that foreign devil give something to him, so it must be somewhere. Have you done a thorough search?"

"Yes! Didn't you see us turning his pockets inside out?"

Suddenly the man's eyes lit up. "You're in luck today, beause you've met an old fox! Come with me, come on!

I remember, yes, I remember now. He might have noticed me watching him, because he crouched down beside a dustbin and tied his shoelaces. It must have been an act! He must have thrown whatever that woman gave him in the bin. I was standing to the right of him, and couldn't see the other side of the bin. Quick! Don't let the refuse-collector get it first!"

The man was almost leaping up and down with excitement.

The patrol team believed him, and pushed Yeye brusquely towards the dustbin.

"That's the one," said the man, pointing to a bin not far from where they were gathered.

Ah Mei watched the entire scene from the kiosk.

Yeye was dragging his feet. He was worried that for some reason or other Ah Mei might have been delayed, and might not have been able to retrieve the perfume, or that something had gone wrong. What if a beggar had managed to get to the dustbin before Ah Mei, and had walked off with the paper bag? Yeye could think of so many "what ifs". His biggest worry of all was that Ah Mei, having collected the perfume, might suddenly come running towards him.

When Ah Mei saw a bunch of barbarians marching Yeye towards the dustbin, that was exactly what she wanted to do. But she remembered what Yeye had said. *Unless you see me coming towards you, do not, under any circumstances, come out; and if, after two hours, I haven't come back, you're to go straight home by yourself.*

Yeye had repeated this many times.

The patrol team pushed and shoved Yeye towards the bin.

People were milling around, watching, and asking, "What's happening? What's going on?"

The middle-aged man had become separated from the patrol team. He was pointing excitedly at the tall figure that was Yeye. "They've captured a secret agent, and I was the one who found him. Just now, right here, he made contact with a foreign woman, and may have been given an assignment…" He spoke animatedly, his imagination firing his excitement.

The news spread quickly – a secret agent had been captured! An old secret agent! Among the crowd, excitement was mounting.

"If you have hidden something in this dustbin, confess now, and it will be considered a voluntary handover. But if we have to look ourselves, and we find something, can you imagine the consequences?"

Yeye suddenly shouted loudly, "I DID NOT HIDE ANYTHING IN THE BIN!" His voice was ear-deafeningly loud. Loud enough for Ah Mei to hear. He knew that if she heard, she wouldn't move from the kiosk. She was too smart to do something stupid like that.

The strong man who had punched Yeye kicked over the dustbin.

"Start looking, old man!"

"I did not hide anything in the bin!" Yeye shouted again.

They insisted that Yeye rummage through the rotting pile of rubbish, and find the so-called "information" or "component" or whatever it was, but Yeye refused point blank. They were infuriated that their words had no effect whatsoever. How dare this old man humiliate them in front of all these people! The strong man charged at Yeye and landed another punch, this time on his chest. Then the entire team went for Yeye, knocking him to the ground, then dragging him to the bin and forcing him to rummage through it and produce the evidence they wanted.

Yeye was battered and bruised. He resisted the urge to fight back. Then, just as the patrol team thought he was yielding, he pulled himself up till he towered like a pylon. The seaman's spirit surged through his ageing body – he had battled wind and waves in his time. He gripped his shirt with both hands and ripped it open with a terrific noise, revealing his broad chest, as though the oppression, frustration, adversity and humiliation that had been building up inside for centuries, nay millennia, was suddenly exploding. Then, waving his fists in the air and roaring, he charged at the patrol. He might be an old man, but his first punch threw one man to the ground, and his second floored another.

The entire patrol froze.

"Now the special agent's started fighting!" shouted the middle-aged man. He rushed towards the bin, leaned over, and without worrying about getting dirty, plunged his hands into the rubbish, searching for whatever it was he had seen earlier. "This old man's going to fight to the bitter end – no coffin, no tears!" He was convinced that whatever the foreign woman had handed over was in that pile of rubbish. He had to find it; he wanted that old man to hang his head.

Yeye was knocked to the ground again.

Ah Mei could see and hear the merciless attack on Yeye,

but there was nothing she could do. She tugged at her hair and choked back sobs, and struggled to keep a hold on herself.

A mournful ship's whistle blasted in the distance.

As the middle-aged man swept aside the last handful of rubbish, he began to feel confused. "It doesn't make sense, all that effort, and there's nothing but a pile of rubbish," he muttered to himself. He brought his hands together, brushed off the dirt, then wiped them on the back of his trousers. "I saw it with my own eyes. With my own eyes!" he said, backing away.

A member of the patrol marched up to him. "Did you or did you not see an exchange between this old man and a foreign woman?"

"I'd sooner be run over by a car than lie to you about what I saw!" said the man nervously, clearly hoping to beat a retreat.

The patrol let go of Yeye, and made for the middle-aged man instead.

"I saw it, I definitely saw it, in broad daylight. I'm not lying!" He continued to back away, then turned and started to run.

Soon after that, the crowd dispersed.

A few people who had been part of the crowd came over and helped Yeye to his feet.

"Go home now."

"Do you have far to go? Can we see you home?"

"It's not far," said Yeye. "I can make it home by myself. Thank you. Thank you." He clasped his hands together in front of his chest, and made a deep bow.

He staggered to the railing and leaned against it. He'd wait a while, check there was no danger, then go back to Ah Mei. He was so worried about her. He desperately wanted to walk over and give her a hug, but it was safer to stay here a little longer. He wished he hadn't had to involve her in this terrifying incident. She was only a child. He suddenly felt overwhelmed with guilt.

He looked up at the Customs House clock. It was already twelve.

He had left Ah Mei on her own for almost two hours. He had put her in danger by asking her to collect the bottle of perfume from the dustbin. What an ordeal it must have been for her.

He kept his eyes on the clock, and held out. The longer he could wait, the safer it would be.

As the two-hour time limit approached, Yeye started to walk towards the kiosk. He knew she would be there waiting for him.

No one paid him any attention as he approached the kiosk.

When he was just a few metres from the kiosk, Ah Mei couldn't hold back any longer. She ran like the wind, and threw her arms around him: "Yeye, Yeye!"

On the way home, Yeye replayed in his mind the scene in which he had raised his fists and knocked those men to the ground, and it gave him a good deal of pleasure. "I feel like singing," he said to Ah Mei.

"You mean those funny little songs?"

"Don't you like them?"

"Yes. Go on, Yeye, sing."

They walked hand in hand, the perfume safely in Ah Mei's school bag on her back, her little hand in Yeye's big, cool one. She walked slightly ahead of him, as though she was leading him home.

"Ah Mei, when we get home, if Nainai asks where all my cuts and bruises have come from, I'm going to say that I tripped and fell over, and you must say the same, all right?"

Ah Mei nodded.

When they were almost home, Ah Mei let go of Yeye's hand. She couldn't wait to get inside. She ran a few steps, then stopped, suddenly thinking of him limping along.

"Go on," said Yeye, waving her away. "I'm fine."

Can you really manage by yourself? Ah Mei asked with her eyes.

Yeye waved her away again. "I'm fine. I'll catch you up." He shook his head and smiled.

In the blink of an eye, Ah Mei was inside the house.

She stood in front of Nainai and held up a bottle of golden perfume. Nainai seemed to go into a trance – she must be dreaming, she thought. It just didn't seem real.

But it *was* real. Ah Mei was holding a bottle of perfume – and it was exactly the brand she loved!

Nainai had run out a while back, and as a result her nose for perfume was extremely sensitive. She could pick up the scent even though the bottle was sealed.

Ah Mei stood there, grinning and holding up the perfume.

Nainai reached out to take it, but Ah Mei dodged to the side.

"Give it to me! Give it to me!" said Nainai, like a child.

Ah Mei dodged again, this time holding it up high.

Nainai chased her round and round the room, following the perfume like a torch in the dark.

"Don't be silly," chided Mrs Hu. "Hurry up and give it to Nainai!"

Nainai lunged forward, and caught Ah Mei at last. "Give it to me!"

Ah Mei chuckled as she handed her the perfume.

Nainai held the bottle up to the light. The midday sun was pouring through the window. The colour of the perfume, and the light bouncing off the angles of the bottle, was enchanting.

Nainai closed her eyes, and pressed the bottle of perfume to her chest. She held it there for a long time.

"Where did you get it?" It seemed she still couldn't believe it was real.

"It's a secret!" Ah Mei said. "We can't tell you."

"Where's Yeye?" Nainai asked.

"I'm here!" Yeye had reached the bottom of the stairs. He didn't go straight upstairs, however, because he didn't want Nainai to see him limping.

"Why don't you come up?" asked Nainai.

"I need to rest a moment. Have you seen the perfume?"

Nainai held it up.

"I've brought your life back," said Yeye.

Nainai twirled around.

"You look younger than Ah Mei!" said Yeye.

Without letting go of the perfume, Nainai took Ah Mei's hand, and they did a little dance together, grandmother and granddaughter wiggling and waving.

Yeye laughed.

"Why don't you come upstairs?" said Nainai again, letting go of Ah Mei's hand, and looking dubiously at Yeye.

Yeye had cleaned himself up on the way home, washing his face and hands at a public water-tap, but Nainai could see his injuries. "What happened?" She rushed downstairs, then helped Yeye climb the stairs, one step at a time, each one an effort.

"What really happened?" demanded Nainai, when they had made it up the stairs.

"I tripped and fell. It's nothing," said Yeye.

Nainai asked Mrs Hu to bring a bowl of salt water so she could tend to the cuts all over his body, and helped him to a chair. Then she turned to Ah Mei. "Tell me, where did all these wounds come from?"

"Yeye t-t-tripped … a-a-and fell," Ah Mei stuttered.

Nainai looked into Ah Mei's eyes. "You're not telling me the truth, are you?"

Nainai's piercing gaze was too much for Ah Mei. She burst into tears.

Nainai hugged her.

Through her tears and sobs, stammering and stuttering, Ah Mei told Nainai everything.

"Little traitor," muttered Yeye.

With a clean towel dipped in salt water, Nainai cleaned

Yeye's wounds. "So you think I can't live without perfume?"

Yeye winced. "You can, but life's not the same without it."

Tears burst from Nainai's eyes. They landed on Yeye's wounds, making them sting even more.

"Your tears are worse than the salt water! Are you trying to pickle me?" said Yeye, pulling a face, an exaggerated grimace.

Nainai shook her head vigorously, and, like rain shaking from a tree branch, tears showered onto Yeye's skin.

"Ow! Ouch! Ow! Ouch!" squealed Yeye.

"It's medicinal," said Nainai, through her tears.

CHAPTER 17

One Gone

The educated youth were leaving the cities; the relocation programme had started. Universities had stopped taking students, and secondary school pupils were being sent to the mountains, grasslands, deserts and remote rural villages to do hard physical labour. Except for children without siblings, all students aged eighteen or under had to go.

Thousands and thousands of families across China were packing their children's bags.

As an only child, Ah Lang could stay in Shanghai. But Ah Lang wanted to go. His father asked all the relatives to come and help persuade him to stay, but each time, Ah Lang repeated the same four words: "I want to go!" Yeye and Nainai went to plead with him too, but again, he gave the same determined answer.

Ah Mei went to see him. She didn't try to persuade him to stay, just sat by his side, keeping him company. They were like brother and sister.

Ah Lang hadn't left the house for a long time, but now he

wanted to go out. "Let's go for a walk."

Ah Mei nodded.

Ah Lang found it difficult to get used to the outside world. He stood for a while with his hand on his forehead, shielding his eyes, struggling to open them in the sunlight. When his eyes had adjusted, he started to walk. The streets were crowded, and Ah Lang seemed to have forgotten how to move aside and let people pass – people bumped into him, or he bumped into them. "Can't you look where you're going?" a few people said crossly. But that just made it worse. Ah Mei took his hand, and led him through the crowd. It wasn't long before they were moving in time with each other, weaving through the crowd like fish swimming through water.

They walked aimlessly along main roads and side streets. Shanghai is like a grid with streets running north-south and east-west, and it seemed that Ah Lang wanted to walk the length and breadth of the city. He'd speed up. He'd slow down. Sometimes, he'd see a wutong tree and stop to look at it for ages, until Ah Mei tugged at his shirt, and then he'd start walking again. At other times, he'd fly ahead, until he heard Ah Mei calling from behind, "Ah Lang, wait for me!"

Eventually they found themselves outside Ah Lang's school.

It was Sunday, and the school gates were closed. They would probably have been closed even if it wasn't a Sunday – they had been closed for weeks. There were no teachers, and no students.

Ah Mei pushed at the gate. Unexpectedly, it opened.

There was no one in the office.

"Do you want to go in and have a look around?" asked Ah Mei.

Ah Lang shook his head. "I can see from here."

He looked at the school from that single spot, tilting his head to see it from different angles.

He was wearing his mask.

Ah Mei followed his gaze, and when he stared at something, she stared too, following his line of vision to a corner of the teaching block, a flowerbed between two buildings, the flagpole. Ah Mei had often gone to the school with Ah Lang, and was familiar with it. He told her that many years ago it had been a mission school, run by an English man called John.

The last thing they looked at was a stained-glass window.

It had been smashed.

Ah Lang stared at the window for a long time.

As they walked away, Ah Lang kept looking back at his school.

Eventually, it disappeared from view.

Ah Mei said, "I saw your classmate Shu Xiu walking down the street last week."

Ah Lang's eyes lit up.

"She was wearing army clothes; she looked great."

Shu Xiu's father's in the army, Ah Lang wanted to tell her. But he didn't. He just listened.

"Will she be leaving Shanghai too?"

She's an only child, so she can stay in Shanghai, Ah Lang

wanted to tell Ah Mei. But he didn't. *It's possible that I may never ever see her again,* he thought, and he couldn't help looking back. But by then there were too many buildings between him and the school.

For a long time, he could see nothing before him but Shu Xiu.

Ah Mei took his hand, as though leading a blind person. "Ah Lang, I'm tired," she said.

But Ah Lang was still lost in his thoughts about Shu Xiu.

Standing on tiptoes, Ah Mei waved her hand in front of his eyes. "What are you thinking about?"

"I'm not telling you," said Ah Lang.

"I know what you're thinking about."

"And what would that be?"

"I'm not telling you."

"Where are we now?" asked Ah Lang.

"Sichuan Middle Road." Ah Mei pointed to the street sign.

"Then let's head north, to Suzhou Creek, and walk along the creek to the Huangpu."

"I'm getting tired, Ah Lang."

"It's not much further. When we get to the river, we'll sit down and rest. I want to take a good look at the Huangpu." For some reason, the last few words caught in his throat.

Suzhou Creek flowed on and on, as it always did.

They walked along the creek, talking as they went. They stopped now and then to lean against the railings and rest. At one point, Ah Lang turned his head to look at Ah Mei, just as she turned her head to look at him.

"You're beautiful, Ah Mei," he said.

"So are you, Ah Lang."

He gazed at the murky water, without saying anything.

"We both look like Nainai," said Ah Mei.

"She's beautiful too," said Ah Lang.

"That's why you're beautiful."

Ah Lang shook his head.

"You are so handsome, Ah Lang!" said Ah Mei.

He laughed. Ah Mei couldn't see his face, but she could hear the bitterness.

They walked on towards the Huangpu.

It was high tide. In the distance waves rose like brown horses galloping towards the shore.

Like brother and sister, they leaned against the railings, watching the river roll on and on.

There were a few seagulls in the sky. As they rose in the air, gusts of wind blew them off balance, sending them high and low, left and right.

"Do you have to go?" asked Ah Mei.

Ah Lang was staring at the vast river. There were tears streaming down his face, soaking his mask. When he heard Ah Mei's question, he began to sob.

Ah Mei didn't know what to do. "Ah Lang! Ah Lang!" she said, gently touching his arm.

Without taking his eyes off the river – he could see nothing else – Ah Lang suddenly unhooked the mask from his left ear, stretched his arms wide and, baring his face for the first time in weeks, shouted at the never-ending river, "I ... WANT ... TO ... GO...!"

He put his hands back on the railing, put his face in his hands, and didn't make another sound.

Ah Mei stood there, watching the seagulls.

Ah Lang slumped against the railings as though he had just crossed a desert and was too exhausted to do anything but sleep. His face mask flapped in the wind. Ah Mei worried that it might blow off into the river.

The Customs House clock struck six, the sonorous chimes lingering in the air.

Ah Lang raised his head, and fastened his mask. He turned around, leaned back, looked up at the tall buildings on the Bund and waved to them. Then he took Ah Mei's hand.

"It's time to go home," he said.

The image of Ah Lang waving stayed with Ah Mei all the way home.

Ah Lang could have joined his classmates who were going as a group to the Great Northern Wilderness in Heilongjiang. He could have gone to a well-populated area, to the villages in Jiangsu and Zhejiang. Instead, he chose to go to a small mountain village on the borders of Yunnan and Guizhou. The village was deep in the mountains, more or less cut off from the rest of the world, not so much a village, but a few dozen households scattered up and down the mountain. It was an ethnic minority area, where people didn't tend the land, but raised sheep, cattle and horses.

From Shanghai, it would take about two weeks to get there.

Everyone in the family urged him to give up on that place, and go to the Great Northern Wilderness with his classmates, or to Mrs Song's village. She had already cleared a room ready for him. But no one could make him change his mind. His mother, Nainai and Xiaogu were in tears, but there was nothing they could do.

"It's his choice," said Yeye.

Yeye told Nainai not to cry, but he was in tears himself.

Ah Mei was the only person who didn't cry, because Ah Lang had warned her, "If you cry, I won't love you any more."

During his last days in Shanghai, Ah Mei stayed at his house, and followed him everywhere, like a tail.

The whole family went to the railway station to see Ah Lang off.

The loudspeakers were broadcasting heartwarming songs – the kind that make you feel happy to be alive in this wonderful beautiful world.

The train sitting on the tracks was a long one. You couldn't see where it started or finished, and there were too many carriages to count. They were full of boys and girls all roughly the same age as Ah Lang. Youthful faces filled the open windows. There were faces streaming with tears. There were beaming faces with eyes glistening with excitement. There were bewildered faces with eyes staring blankly.

The station was crowded. All along the platform, as far as the horizon, people were crying. There were lengthy exchanges of instructions and promises.

Dabo and the others helped Ah Lang put his luggage in

the carriage, then they all went back to the platform. Ah Lang was still wearing his mask.

He was about to leave Shanghai, to leave his family and all his relatives. He would have a two-week journey to the mountain village. No one knew if he would ever come back.

The family stood together, the women at the front, the men behind. The men didn't cry – some looked away, smoking; others looked at Ah Lang, smiling. The women's faces glistened with tears.

Fifteen minutes before the train was due to leave, the adults suggested that Ah Lang make a move.

"You should get on now."

As he boarded the train, their hands reached out to touch him – to brush his hand, to tap his shoulder, to pat him on the back.

"Write to us!"

"Come home for New Year!"

"Wrap up warm!"

"Don't worry about us here!"

For a few moments, Ah Lang disappeared. Then he squeezed his way back out of the carriage, and ran towards Nainai, spreading his arms open wide.

Nainai opened her arms too.

He hugged her tight. He wrapped his arms around her neck, put his head on her shoulder and cried, just like when he was little.

Nainai patted him lovingly on the back. Her heart was breaking.

Ah Mei tugged at his shirt, as if to say, *Don't cry, please*

283

don't cry, though there were tears rolling down her nose onto her feet, and onto the platform.

"I'm sorry, Nainai."

Nainai held him tighter. "No, I'm sorry, Ah Lang. It's Océane who's sorry…"

Ah Lang shook his head vigorously. "I love you, Nainai. I love you, Océane!"

The loudspeaker told the passengers to board the train.

Ah Lang pulled away from Nainai, and leaned towards Ah Mei. "Aina! I know your other name, Aina!" He reached out his hand and gently wiped her tear-soaked face. "I'll write to you," he said, looking at Ah Mei as he stepped back towards the carriage door. And before turning to board the train, he played the piano in the air.

Ah Mei waved, and nodded.

The train started to move.

Ah Lang poked his head out of the window. All of a sudden he pulled off the mask and threw it into the air. It caught in the air current from the train, flashing and swirling and soaring like a white bird spreading its wings in flight.

CHAPTER 18

Another Gone

Exactly one month later, the family received notification that, on account of her registration documents having been sent to Yibin, Ah Mei could no longer remain in Shanghai as a student.

It was non-negotiable.

It was almost September, and the start of the new school year. Nainai telephoned Baba and Mama in Yibin, and told them the situation. Mama could hear over the phone that Nainai was upset, and tried to comfort her. "She'll miss you, but she can come and visit. And you'll miss her, but you and Yeye can come and visit us here. We all knew that Ah Mei would have to leave Shanghai sooner or later."

Two days later, Mama telephoned Nainai to say they had found a place for Ah Mei in a good school, in a beautiful setting, where you could see the Yangtze River from the window.

Yeye and Nainai knew that they couldn't keep Ah Mei in Shanghai. They wanted to make the rest of her time there as enjoyable as possible. This meant Ah Mei could eat her favourite food every day, including two French-style lunches, which, despite being extremely simple, she adored.

"Mind you don't eat the plate!" said Mrs Hu, who was standing near by.

By scrimping a little here and there, Nainai managed to put together enough money to buy Ah Mei some new clothes, and some material for Mrs Hu to make into a padded jacket and padded trousers for her to wear in the winter. Socks, shoes, gloves, stationery – all the things she needed, Nainai bought new.

"She's not going away for ever, you know," said Yeye.

"I know," said Nainai, but in her mind, Ah Mei was going far, far away. She didn't know when Ah Mei would be able to come back, and she wouldn't really be coming back, what with Shanghai no longer being her home. Her home was in Sichuan now, in Yibin.

In the short time they had before Ah Mei left Shanghai, Nainai wanted to indulge her granddaughter and shower her with love.

Ah Mei lapped it all up, and was even a bit babyish with Nainai at times.

On her last two days in Shanghai, each branch of the family prepared a special meal for Ah Mei. The first meal was at Dabo's. Ah Mei was in good spirits, and ate happily.

Yeye kept shaking his head. "I don't understand what all this fuss is about. You're only going to Yibin! It's not as though you can't come back whenever you want. There's a boat, and a train…"

"I'd like to invite Ah Mei to a restaurant," said Xiaogu, when it was her turn. "But I'm only taking one person." She smiled at Yeye and Nainai.

"It would be too much effort for me," said Nainai.

"I wouldn't go, even if you invited me," said Yeye.

Xiaogu chose the best restaurant. It was on Huaihai Road, and was still serving Western food, which Xiaogu knew that Ah Mei loved. When the family could afford it, Nainai used to make Western food at home, and would take Ah Mei to eat at the Red House and other famous restaurants in Shanghai. Ah Mei loved to eat with a knife and fork, and to hear the clink of the metal, and she loved how Nainai tucked a white napkin into her collar before she started to eat. These little rituals made a mealtime a special occasion.

At the restaurant, Xiaogu ordered a steak with all the trimmings for Ah Mei. She knew it was her favourite.

Ah Mei ate and ate. Xiaogu just watched, her eyes welling with tears. Eventually, the tears brimmed over and rolled down her face. She tried to wipe them away with her napkin, but they kept coming.

Ah Mei looked up at her aunt. "Why are you crying?"

"I don't know," said Xiaogu.

"This is delicious!" Ah Mei said bravely.

"I know this is all an act," said Xiaogu, pressing her finger gently on Ah Mei's forehead.

Ah Mei lowered her head, and very soon, there were tears falling onto her plate.

Xiaogu wiped them away with the napkin. "Do you know how awful it is, watching someone enjoy their food like that?

It's enough to make you cry!" She laughed through her tears. "Come on, let's eat together, and make it a real pleasure."

The people at the next table were looking at them.

"We're being watched!" Xiaogu whispered.

They two of them laughed and cried and ate.

Nainai emptied the little leather suitcase. She called Ah Mei to her room and held it out to her with both hands. "Aina, this is for you."

Ah Mei immediately hid her hands behind her back.

Nainai was insistent.

Ah Mei took a step backwards.

"I know you love this suitcase. I was going to…" Nainai paused, and smiled. "I wanted to give it to you when you got married. But I have other things to give you when you get married. I want you to have the suitcase now."

"You should keep it, Océane," said Ah Mei.

"No. I want to give you a present. Tomorrow you'll be leaving Shanghai, and me."

"But you've already given me clothes, socks, shoes … so many things," said Ah Mei.

Nainai smiled. "Those aren't presents. Take it. Take everything out of your little canvas case and put it all in this one. Give your canvas one to me – we can swap! That way, when I miss you, I can look at your little canvas case. And when you miss me, you can look at the little leather suitcase." Nainai stepped forward, and held the suitcase out to Ah Mei.

This time, Ah Mei didn't refuse. She held her arms out and took the little suitcase.

"Go on, go and pack," said Nainai.

Ah Mei went back to her room. She put the little leather suitcase down on her bed and opened it. She put the little canvas bag next to it, and moved one thing at a time into the leather suitcase.

Every single thing had been given to her by Nainai. Everything but her annual school reports, her awards, certificates and prizes, which had nothing to do with Nainai – except that they had everything to do with Nainai, because without Nainai her grades wouldn't have been so high, and she wouldn't have won so many prizes.

There was the little box containing the sweet-wrapper dolls with their tiny waists and long skirts. They were so bright and colourful, exaggerated but life-like.

Nainai had made them especially for her.

There had been a time when Ah Mei walked about with her head down, always looking out for pretty sweet wrappers on the ground. She used to pick them up and take them home, where Nainai's clever hands would turn them into lovely sweet-wrapper dolls. They stood in a line on the little table where Ah Mei did her homework, and on the windowsill in her bedroom. These tiny people had been part of her childhood. When she was bored, she would imagine conversations with them, and sing and dance with them. She put a few of them on the piano – when she was playing by herself, she felt they were listening. When the other children started to distance themselves from her, the little sweet-wrapper people were her friends. They hadn't abandoned her; they had kept her company from one lonely day to the next. There had been times when she'd woken from a nightmare, sat bolt upright and turned on the light – and one by one, they'd come alive, so vividly. She'd moved them around, talked to them and played with them until she felt sleepy again.

She had put them in a cardboard box the day before. She wanted to take all of her sweet-wrapper friends with her. Each one had a beautiful name – a name Ah Mei had chosen specially for her.

And there were thirteen brightly coloured stockings, all different sizes.

Nainai had placed a stocking by her pillow every Christmas Eve. She had knitted them herself with thick wool and put a small gift inside: some nougat, some prune drops, a pretty handkerchief or a brand-new pencil case. And every year, without fail, there had been a Christmas card, handmade by Nainai, with a personal message inside. For decades at the Blue House, they had celebrated both Chinese and Western festivals, at least to some degree. Each festival had a different atmosphere, and the children who had grown up in the Blue House loved them all. When Ah Mei was one, Nainai had placed a very small stocking by her tiny pillow. Mama had kept it for her. When she was three, she had started to keep them herself. She counted them now: thirteen, one for every year of her life.

Ah Mei continued taking one thing at a time out of the canvas case.

She came across a little green steamboat. It had been a present from Yeye.

The two of them had been obsessed with it. When she was about five or six, Yeye had come home one evening and called out, "Ah Mei! Where are you?" and she had leaped up and run to him.

"Let's go!" With a cardboard box tucked under one arm, Yeye had led Ah Mei to the tiny pond in the garden.

"I've bought you something," said Yeye. He opened the box, and lifted something out.

"A boat!" said Ah Mei.

"A steamboat," said Yeye. Then suddenly remembering, he turned around and shouted, "Mrs Hu, could you bring some paraffin?" Mrs Hu brought a can of paraffin. Yeye glanced at Ah Mei. "Don't worry, we'll have it in the water in no time." He poured just enough paraffin into the boat, and lit it. The propeller at the back started to whirr, and the boat came to life. Yeye put it gently in the water. It whistled, and started moving, leaving a fine trail in the water behind it. Ah Mei clapped her hands in excitement and jumped up and down by the side of the pond.

She watched the little steamboat move across the water, then ran over to the opposite side of the pond, and lay down on her front, reaching for the boat. "Turn it around!" Yeye called to her. Ah Mei did as he said, and the boat moved back across the pond to Yeye. Every so often it would whistle, a strong, vigorous sound.

"We can keep the paraffin can by the pond," said Yeye.

After that, the two of them would come to the pond whenever they could and watch the steamboat moving about on the water.

Once Ah Mei had stopped jumping up and down, and flailing her arms and legs about, she spent most of the time lying on her front by the pond, quietly watching the steamboat, imagining herself on board, travelling to places far, far away.

Yeye would sit on the grass, looking lost in thought too.

Nainai soon realized that the steamboat was as much Yeye's gift to himself as it was to Ah Mei.

Sometimes she would join them by the pond. "Are you going as far as Marseilles?"

Yeye would nod. "I can just about see the shoreline. That's Marseilles."

When Nainai wasn't around, Yeye would regale Ah Mei with his memories of the past: waves glistening like jewels, shoals of fish, the sky full of seagulls, the ports, an island in the ocean, a ship in the distance ... but he didn't elaborate on his former life of freedom.

Ah Mei knew she would never forget watching this little steamboat moving about on the pond.

Of course, Yeye was too embarrassed to play with the boat by himself, and when the last drop of paraffin was spent, he wiped it clean with a dry cloth, and handed it to Ah Mei. "It's a present from me to you – look after it."

The little steamboat had been lying in Ah Mei's canvas suitcase for eight years.

As Ah Mei gazed at the steamboat, and pictured the two of them watching it by the pond, she remembered Yeye's expression. He must have been thinking of the boundless sea. She smiled, then felt sad. Yeye was getting old, he was ageing faster than Nainai. An image of her tottering Yeye swayed before her eyes.

All of Ah Mei's most treasured possessions were now packed in the little leather suitcase.

Before, it had been filled with Nainai's memories of home. Now, it was filled with Ah Mei's memories of Shanghai, of Yeye and Nainai. So many memories.

Ah Mei's departure was the following evening.

Ah Lang had left Shanghai by train. Ah Mei was to leave Shanghai by steamer.

She was making the journey to Yibin alone. For one thing, they couldn't afford another ticket. Secondly, she was at middle school, and old enough to travel on her own. Thirdly, the boat followed the river upstream, so there was no danger of her getting lost on the way. Also, one of the sailors was Yeye's friend's son, and Yeye had asked him to look out for her. Baba and Mama couldn't come all the way to Shanghai to fetch her. Mama said that neither she nor Baba could take time off work, but they would meet her off the boat at Chongqing, and take the next steamer with her to Yibin.

Ah Mei's journey would take eighteen days.

There was endless fussing: *Remember to do this … you mustn't do that…*

Ah Mei nodded obediently.

When they went aboard, Yeye's friend's son came over. He picked up Ah Mei's luggage and stowed it in the cabin. Then he turned to Yeye. "Don't worry, Uncle, I'll be here the whole way."

There was an iron guardrail around the deck. Ah Mei stood by the guardrail with the little suitcase, waving at Yeye, Nainai and everyone else in the family. She didn't cry, but kept a big smile on her face the whole time.

Those on the quay were doing their best to contain the pain in their hearts, to contain the tears that were ready to burst out at any moment.

The ship's whistle blew, on and on, as though it might continue all century, an angry roar and a helpless lament combined. Then the gangplank was removed, and, very slowly, the boat started to pull away. Finally, with its bow facing east and its stern facing the Bund, the ship began to move.

The family stood on the Bund, like a forest of trees. They watched the boat moving away, gradually blurring into the distance, until eventually it disappeared.

Ah Mei stood by the guardrail. No matter how much Yeye's friend's son tried to persuade her, she would not go to her cabin.

She watched as Nainai and the others shrank to tiny black dots. After some time, the towering buildings on the Bund blurred and finally faded from sight.

Ah Mei's wrist ached from carrying the little leather suitcase by her side, so she switched to holding it in front of her with both hands. As dusk fell, and darkness spread, with only the sound of water, and nothing to see but the twinkling lights on the river, Ah Mei stood there, trying as hard as she could to see Shanghai.

CHAPTER 19

The Robbery

Ah Mei did not adjust well, and within a short time had become so thin and weak that it took all her strength just to keep going to school. Fortunately, Nainai was not there to see this, as it would have upset her very much. Ah Mei was physically in Yibin, but her heart was in Shanghai – day and night, she thought about Yeye and Nainai, all her relatives, and her teachers and classmates in Shanghai … and as she grew thinner and weaker, she grew more and more emotional, often bursting into tears for no apparent reason.

Weeks passed, and she was still finding it difficult to adapt to Yibin. She was used to the bustle of Shanghai and the peace of the Blue House. She missed the air in Shanghai. She missed everything from there. Here, the sun shone so brightly that it hurt her eyes – it scared her. It burned so fiercely that she felt sure it would burn itself out of the sky, whereas in Shanghai the sun was soft and gentle – it rose and fell beautifully, and never hurt the eyes. There was a particular kind of tree in Yibin that was planted in rows that were frighteningly tall. When Ah Mei walked beneath these trees, she would start to panic, and run like a scared rabbit. She missed the trundling rumbling of the trams, and the sound of the Customs House clock – she had heard the clock several times in her dreams, and it had sounded so real. She missed the air in Shanghai, that subtle sweetness. The air in Yibin seemed to be full of chilli, and made her want to cough all the time. The smell of Sichuan pepper wafted through the streets and alleys, and she found it overwhelming. But what she missed most of all was the soft, friendly sound of Shanghainese. People here spoke so loudly, and so emphatically, that it sounded like they were constantly arguing.

Not a day went by without Ah Mei feeling anxious and lost.

"Yibin is your home now," said Mama. "You have to get used to the way of life here. When you've settled in, you'll find it's actually a very beautiful little town."

True as that might be, Ah Mei found it hard to get used to Yibin. Thirteen years in Shanghai had bound the city to her heart: the Bund, Nanjing Road, Huaihai Road, Suzhou Creek, all the Western-style buildings with their gardens, the Western restaurants, the patisseries, the theatres, cinemas, trams, neon lights, the gramophone music from people's windows… At thirteen, she was already attuned to the rhythm of Shanghai. She loved that special rhythm, and had been shaped by it. You could tell at a glance that she was a girl from Shanghai.

Ah Mei was surprised to find that the dreams she had here

were different from her dreams in Shanghai. In Shanghai she had dreamed of the moon, butterflies, bees, winding alleys, pigeons, long dresses and silk scarves. But in her dreams now there was always the huge sun, a black cat, lots of chilli flakes, and baskets. Big baskets on people's backs; baskets of ducks with their legs tied together... There had been a few times when, before going to sleep, she'd said to herself, *Let's go back to Shanghai*. But those dreams were as rare as swallows in winter.

Memories tugged at her heartstrings.

"I miss Yeye and Nainai," she told Mama.

"I know," said Mama.

"I miss Xiaogu."

"I know."

"I miss Dabo and Erbo..."

"I know, I know," said Mama.

"And Mrs Hu."

"I know you do." Mama hugged Ah Mei, "I miss them too. I've been here a long time and I still miss them. Sometimes I miss them so much I can't sleep. But I tell myself, *You mustn't miss them like this, or you'll never be able to get on with things, and you have to be able to get on with things!* It's not as though you'll never see them again – you will. Try not to miss them so much, Ah Mei. Your baba and me, we're here for you, we're a family!"

Ah Mei nodded, but she could feel tears swirling in her eyes.

Sometimes, she would tell herself, *I mustn't think about them, I must think about my Ah Lang!*

She opened the little leather suitcase, and took out the letter from Ah Lang. Her cousin had kept his word – he had written to her, and in his letter he'd said he would write to her more often in future. He hadn't written to Yeye and Nainai, or even his parents, but at the end of his letter to Ah Mei, he had asked her to let them know how he was.

It had taken about a month for the letter to arrive by post. Ah Mei had received it just as she was preparing to leave Shanghai.

In the letter, Ah Lang sounded happy. He wrote that the scenery there was enchanting: clouds curled through the mountains, mist hung in the hills. He said the people there were wonderful, so honest, so generous and kind. He said he'd seen a leopard, and that it was beautiful. It had seen him and been scared, but instead of running off, it had wandered slowly beside a stream, looking back at him after every few steps. And there were so many kinds of birds! There was one that hid among the leaves, and sang beautifully. He had never imagined that a bird could sing so sweetly.

Ah Mei had shown Ah Lang's letter to Nainai.

"I don't know if he's telling the truth," Nainai had sighed.

But Ah Mei was convinced that everything Ah Lang had said was true. She always knew whether or not he was telling the truth. If Ah Mei believed that everything he wrote was true, Nainai said she would believe it too. Nainai took the letter, and read it again. She had lost weight at Ah Lang's departure, and now that Ah Mei was about to leave, she looked thinner than ever. She read the letter again, and this time there was joy in her eyes.

Before leaving Shanghai, Ah Mei had written back to Ah Lang, and given him her new address. She hoped to hear from him again soon.

Gradually Ah Mei found a solution to her sadness. She would separate her thoughts. She would think about Yeye and Nainai and the others in Shanghai. Then, the next time she felt sad, she would think about Ah Lang. It was less upsetting this way.

Ah Mei wanted to be happy in Yibin.

From now on, although she missed them, she would send them her best wishes every day, from her heart.

The situation in Shanghai was growing increasingly serious.

There was shouting every day. "DOWN WITH…! DOWN WITH…!" You heard it everywhere: in the streets, in the alleys, in school playgrounds, in churches, in factories, in meeting rooms… And as the shouts went up, so did a forest of fists, as though in formation, trying to punch holes in the Shanghai sky.

People were rushing around like an angry rash – not thinking, just rushing. They were not eating or drinking or sleeping – they were living on their nerves. They split into groups, they brandished their fists, punching the air, excitement erupting into violence. Fists also punched forward, into the enemy's face, smashing their glasses, even breaking their nose. Those on the receiving end retaliated in rage.

The whole of Shanghai seemed to be fighting. People began using sticks instead of fists, then super-strength slingshots, using scraps of iron as shot, firing from windows in one building to the windows opposite. Iron whizzed through the air, setting everyone on edge.

Then word went around that people had guns.

One day, a truck stopped near the Blue House. An army of dozens leaped down, and stormed into the house, shouting slogans.

It was a different group from the last one. Yeye and Nainai did not recognize a single face. Still shouting, they charged through the rooms and up the stairs.

Yeye put his arms out to protect Nainai, but half a dozen of them surged forwards, and without any explanation pushed him to the side, and marched him down the stairs and into the garden.

The group split into two, and started their interrogation. It was similar to the last time.

Upstairs, they questioned Nainai.

"Where have you hidden the transceiver and the transmitter?"

Nainai answered coldly. "The house has already been searched. They searched everywhere, even under the floorboards, but found no trace of a transceiver or a transmitter."

"That's because they were useless! We won't leave empty-handed."

"In that case, please, be my guest," said Nainai.

"Your Chinese is very good."

"I am a Chinese citizen," replied Nainai.

The interrogator slammed his hand down on the table. "NO! You are an international spy! We have all the evidence we need."

Nainai did not make eye contact. "If that's the case, then arrest me."

"Search the house!" ordered the interrogator, with a wave of his hand.

"You'd be better off razing the house to the ground," said Nainai.

"What makes you think we won't?"

"Go on. You'll stop at nothing," said Nainai.

Mrs Hu was standing beside Nainai. She gave her a quiet nudge.

A middle-aged man, his face tanned, his clothes immaculate, was standing silently to one side. There was a strange look in his eyes, and he was staring intently at Nainai's necklace with the dragonfly eyes. It was Yeye's birthday, and Nainai had dressed up specially, and was wearing the necklace that Yeye had given her all those years ago. The gang had stormed upstairs so suddenly that she hadn't remembered to take it off. And by the time the thought occurred to her, they were already standing in front of her. So she kept it on. She wanted to face them like this, dressed up in her best clothes.

The middle-aged man kept shifting position, but continued to gaze at the dragonfly eyes.

The gang rummaged through chests and turned cupboards inside out.

"Stop! There's nothing in there!" Mrs Hu shouted.

But they paid no attention.

"Let them do what they want," Nainai said to Mrs Hu. She was more concerned about Yeye. Where was he?

Yeye's interrogation was different from the previous time. His interrogators had encircled him, and were demanding he tell them how he had exploited workers in the past.

"Back then," said Yeye, "if you worked at my company, you could provide for a big family. I'm sorry, I don't know the meaning of the word 'exploit'."

"So you were actively exploiting people?"

"That's not what I said," said Yeye.

"How could you have such a large silk company, on an international scale, *without* exploiting people? You had enormous mills, employing upwards of eight hundred people in each!"

"I gave everything to the state. I didn't keep so much as a silk scarf," said Yeye, as though it was a badge of honour.

Apart from revealing their ignorance, this so-called interrogation yielded nothing. The interrogators were not happy at all.

The apricot tree that Yeye had planted for Nainai was covered in lush green leaves, the result of Yeye's tender care and attention. All year round, he tended this tree: loosening the soil, spreading manure, watering it, pruning it and killing insects. At the first sign of winter, Yeye worried it might freeze to death, and always wrapped a thick grass rope around the trunk, to give it a padded jacket.

Yeye cherished this tree.

He loved nothing better than to see Nainai sitting under the branches reading the newspaper, or checking manuscripts, or knitting sweaters for the family. It was the loveliest sight in the world.

At such moments, Yeye felt, Nainai's face wore the same expression it had in Marseilles.

And at such moments, Yeye, who had always felt guilty for inflicting so much on Nainai, would feel more at ease.

At the first sight of spring, the apricot tree had burst into life. Its tender leaves had begun to unfurl before the weather turned warm, covering the branches like a flock of birds arriving home from afar, and clamouring for space. When the breeze blew, the leaves rustled, as though sharing their experiences of winter. Then, almost overnight, the tips of the branches had filled with white blossom, and for a few days in a row, Nainai had either gazed at the blossom or sat beneath the tree, bathed in its perfume, her eyes closed. Yeye had somehow managed to get a small bag of coffee beans, which she ground carefully, and, using the metal coffee pot from France, she would make two small cups of coffee. As the aroma of coffee wafted through the house, Yeye would move a small table and two chairs under the apricot tree.

As they sat under the apricot tree, sipping strong coffee, and talking about before, about the past, about Marseilles, which was the other side of the horizon and which they would probably never see again, the tension and sadness on Nainai's face would dissolve, replaced by feelings of happiness, of being blessed and of hope for a wonderful future ahead.

But the group who stormed people's homes in broad daylight did not understand any of this. When their interrogation of Yeye achieved nothing, they found their attention drawn to the apricots on the tree. They were like emeralds half-hidden among the leaves, a subtle red colour peeping through, each fruit gleaming as though it had been polished. The group had already smelled the sweet fragrance in the air – perhaps that was why they had marched Yeye into the garden – but in their efforts to appear serious, they had exercised self-control, pretending not to be interested in the tree full of fruit, and resisting the temptation to go and take a look.

Yeye had seen the delight on their faces, however. He had seen their eyes light up, their mouths gape in surprise. Not just one or two, but every single one of them. They had been surprised to find an apricot tree like this in the city, in Shanghai!

The interrogators dropped their serious approach, and took their eyes off Yeye. At first, they simply gazed appreciatively at the apricot tree. Then they started to pick the apricots. They each tried a fruit, rubbing them on their shirts, holding them up to their mouths and taking a bite. "Delicious!" they declared, picking a second one, then another, and another...

Yeye let them pick as many as they wanted. After all, the apricots were for eating.

Soon, all the apricots within arm's reach had been picked. Some had been eaten, but many had been stuffed into pockets. Perhaps the group had come prepared, because their clothes had plenty of pockets, of all different sizes. There were still many pockets to fill, so they went up to the tree trunk, stood around it, and shook it with all their might, hoping to shake down the apricots that were out of reach.

At this point, Yeye put out his hand to stop them. "Don't do that!"

He feared their collective force would loosen the soil around the tree's roots and cause the tree to fall. He couldn't bear to see it swaying so violently.

They didn't listen – they just wanted to shake the tree so the apricots would come showering down.

The apricots fell on their heads, and covered the ground.

Some of the men continued to shake the tree. Others picked the fruit off the ground, and stuffed their pockets eagerly, with an element of competition. Those shaking the tree didn't have to compete: looking up, they saw plenty more fruit. They could afford to let the others take what they wanted; they would fill their own pockets later.

Yeye was furious. He charged at them, forcibly pushing them away from the trunk. Then he stood in front of the tree with his legs and arms stretched wide, and glared at them.

The young people were affronted. How dare this man, this capitalist who was nearly in his coffin, push them away and stop them picking a few of his apricots!

A pale-faced one with glasses, who looked like a poet, pointed at Yeye's nose. "Move aside!" he ordered.

Yeye stiffened his arms.

The Poet spoke in a slow and measured way: "You cruelly, inhumanely exploited us poor people in the past, and now you begrudge us a few of your apricots! You are as scheming as ever! This land does not belong to you and your family. The apricots that grow on this land do not belong to you and your family either."

"I planted this tree with my own hands, and this land does belong to me and my family," said Yeye.

The Poet started to laugh. "To you and your family? How come our families don't have a big piece of land like this!" He turned to face the group. "Hey, do any of your families have a big piece of land like this?"

They all shook their heads.

"Did you see that? Not one of us! So what gives you the right?"

"Go and ask the government!" said Yeye.

"The government belongs to the people! And we are the people! When the people say you no longer merit such a large piece of land, then it's no longer yours. We'll start right now. I declare this apricot tree to be public property!" The Poet pointed at each of the tree-shakers. "What are you waiting for?" Then he turned around, and pointed at Yeye again, still looking at his accomplices. "Take him away! He has the nerve to resist, so there's no need to treat him with respect."

They crowded around Yeye. Grabbing, twisting, pushing, gripping, and shoving, they dragged him to one side and pinned him to the ground, face down, his mouth in the mud, his arms behind his back. He looked like a big bird that had been caught.

"Thieves! You're a band of thieves!" yelled Yeye, but with his mouth pressed in the mud, the words sounded like stones rolling round and round in his throat.

There was another bout of vigorous tree-shaking, and another shower of apricots, but after that, the downfall dwindled. Eventually, no matter how hard the group shook the tree, not a single apricot fell. But when they looked up, they could still see fruit on the higher branches.

By this time, the beautiful apricot tree had been ravaged beyond recognition.

Before Yeye's eyes, the tree that just a short while ago had been joyously bursting with life, had started to droop.

He stopped trying to fight, and just lay on the ground, overwhelmed with despair for the world as he knew it, for the uncharted future ahead.

Then the youths who were pinning him down suddenly let go. They walked back to the tree, perhaps wanting to stuff their pockets with more fruit, perhaps thinking the old man had given up the fight.

Yeye sat up slowly.

He could see the Poet looking up at the top of the tree, wanting to pick all the apricots. He watched him spit in the palms of his hands and mutter, "I won't leave a single one," as he started to climb.

Yeye managed to get to his feet, but he swayed unsteadily.

When the Poet reached the top of the tree, he stood with both feet on a branch, wrapped one arm round the tree trunk and tried to pick the apricots at the top. He couldn't quite reach them, so he pulled as hard as he could on the branch above. With a crack, the branch snapped. As the Poet fell, he grabbed the branch he'd been standing on. It tore from the tree trunk, stripping the bark from the trunk, almost down to the roots.

For Yeye, it was like watching an arm or a wing break, or seeing a sail-mast come tumbling down.

The Poet rolled about on the ground, groaning.

By now, Yeye was standing beneath the apricot tree. The Poet staggered to his feet, and as he did so, Yeye raised his old seaman's fist and punched him right in the face.

The Poet fell to the ground.

Everyone was stunned.

The Poet felt across the ground for his glasses. His hands were still shaking when he put them on. The left lens was shattered, as though a bomb had hit it. The Poet didn't go for Yeye immediately. He pulled the branch clean from the tree, then, taking his time, he stripped away all the shoots and leaves, so that very soon he had a stick in his hands. He wanted revenge. He ran his hand up and down the wood, and said, to no one in particular, "I'm going to use this stick to teach the world a lesson: the Chinese people stood up twenty years ago!"

Gripping the stick, he paced slowly towards Yeye. He paused in front of him, then all of a sudden he drew the stick through the air with both hands and whacked it against Yeye's legs. It happened so fast. Yeye screamed. The pain was excruciating.

When Nainai heard him, she dropped everything, charged downstairs and ran straight to her husband's side.

The Poet's hands were hurting too, and wouldn't stop shaking.

No one stood in Nainai's way.

When she was within touching distance, Yeye reached out with his hand, but then fell.

Nainai dropped to her knees and saw that his trousers were soaked with blood.

"They're … a bunch of thugs!" she said.

The youths suddenly decided it was time to go. They left Yeye and Nainai where they were and headed for the gate. One of them looked over his shoulder on his way out. "We'll be back!"

Mrs Hu had run into the garden with Nainai, and when she saw the blood oozing from Yeye's leg, she hurried back inside to fetch a cloth to use as a bandage.

As Nainai got up to take the cloth from Mrs Hu, the man who'd been staring at her earlier came running out of the house with five or six others behind him, gasping and panting. They stopped in front of Nainai.

"Haven't you done enough?" Nainai asked angrily.

The middle-aged man made no eye contact, just looked at the dragonfly eyes on Nainai's chest. "Times have changed! And you're still wearing those old things!" he said, snatching at the dragonfly eyes with such force that the necklace broke, and the other beads scattered. The youths immediately bent over and tried to grab a few.

Nainai froze momentarily, then shouted, "GIVE THEM BACK!"

But they turned and ran out of the gate.

Nainai went after them, but another group rushed up and blocked her way. As they were blocking her, they were edging towards the truck on the street outside the house. When the engine started, they leaped on board, and the truck drove away.

Nainai shook her fists as the truck sped off. "Thugs!"

Mrs Hu hurried over to Nainai, took her arm and together they walked back to Yeye.

"That was robbery!" said Nainai, dragging her heavy feet.

"Do you want to report it?" asked Mrs Hu.

Nainai shook her head. "Who would we report it to? Who would pay any attention to us?"

"Madam, I don't understand this world any more, I don't understand…" Tears were welling in Mrs Hu's eyes.

Dabo and Erbo took Yeye to hospital. Two thousand kilometres away, a young girl walked to the riverbank, and placed a paper boat on the gently flowing water of the Yangtze River.

The boat was a letter.

Dear Yeye and Nainai,

It's me, Ah Mei. How are you both?

Are the apricots on the tree ripe yet? I used to love standing under the tree at this time of year, looking up at all the fruit. I could stand there for ever. Nainai loved it too, even more than I did. I know why Nainai loves that tree so much – because there was an apricot tree in her back garden at home in Marseilles.

Don't worry about me. I'm gradually starting to like it here. The Yangtze is clear, and green, almost blue. And there are fish, all kinds of fish, including some enormous ones, and there are always fishing boats out on the river, and lots of people standing, watching, on the riverbank. I've made some new friends – let me count, ten new friends. There's a girl called Xiu Xiu who's very pretty and has big twinkly eyes, and she often comes to my place to play, or I go to hers. Her nainai is an amazing cook, and I love eating at their house. I eat so much that Mama says

I'm a greedy puss, always eating! She says I've put on weight.

I've already talked to Baba and Mama, and as soon as the summer holidays start, I'll take the boat to Shanghai to see you and the whole family. Oh, and I've had a letter from Ah Lang since I've been here. He says he's a shepherd in the mountains, looking after 120 sheep, and that he's very happy there, very, very happy. You don't have to worry about him any more.

Baba's fine, and Mama's fine.

Please say hello to Mrs Hu. The clothes I'm wearing today are the ones Mrs Hu made for me. Xiu Xiu says they're lovely and she'd like to wear them too.

There are apricots for sale everywhere here, but they don't taste as good as the apricots from our tree. I would love, love, love to eat those apricots.

I hope you are keeping well and healthy.

I hope you are having a nice, peaceful time.

Your granddaughter, Ah Mei

CHAPTER 20

The Search

The hospital confirmed that Yeye had a comminuted fracture – his left leg was shattered. He needed a plaster cast, and would have to stay in hospital for ten days.

"Don't tell them in Yibin, especially not Ah Mei. She'd be beside herself if she knew!" said Nainai.

So no one mentioned Yeye's broken leg to the family in Yibin.

Ten days later, Yeye was discharged from hospital. It would be a long time before the plaster cast could be removed, and even longer before his leg had fully healed. Now he was home, he could concentrate on his recovery. The family breathed a sigh of relief. But there was something Nainai needed to do urgently, and that was to locate the dragonfly eyes and get them back, no matter how much it might cost. She had not stopped thinking about them as she'd gone to and from the hospital every day.

Where were the dragonfly eyes?

Yeye and Nainai tried to think who the gang members

might be. Could they be anyone they knew? They weren't from their neighbourhood, or they would have recognized some of them. Were they from the publishing house Nainai had worked for? That didn't seem to be the case. She had worked with the publishing house for many years, and was always coming and going; if this big group had been from there, surely she would have seen a familiar face among them. Were they from Yeye's company? Yeye tried to think, but that didn't seem likely either. He couldn't be sure, though, because the group were almost all young people, too young to have worked for the company before he handed it to the state. It was such a large company, and he had long been on the periphery, so it stood to reason that he wouldn't recognize them. But it was a middle-aged man who had snatched the dragonfly eyes, and in theory, if he had worked for Yeye's company, then he would have seen him before.

There wasn't a single lead to go on.

The whole family threw itself into the task. Days passed, and still there was nothing.

"Forget it," said Yeye, who had his foot up, resting on a chair.

But Nainai refused to let it go. She was determined to get the beads back. It wasn't because of their monetary value – she had no idea how much they were worth – but because of their extraordinary significance. They were part of the necklace that Yeye had given her to wear at their wedding, and they had been his father's most treasured possession. She would never forget how he had looked at them as he was dying, and how he had held them in his trembling hands.

He had invested so much emotion in them, and so much hope for the future.

Nainai was determined to get them back, no matter what.

One day, Mrs Hu came back from the market with a piece of news. The group that had raided the Blue House that day were indeed from the company that Yeye had handed over to the state.

Mrs Hu had been asking around in the market when she went shopping. You could get all kinds of news and information there. She had learned that the man who snatched the dragonfly eyes was the son of a man called Zhu Sancheng.

"Zhu Sancheng?" said Yeye. "I know him! He was an employee at my company, a very good man. What's his son's name?"

"They weren't too clear about that," said Mrs Hu.

"I reckon that when Zhu Sancheng retired, his son took his place," said Yeye. He paused for a moment to think. "We may be able to find this man. Zhu Sancheng was always interested in antiques, and perhaps some of it's rubbed off on his son."

Yeye had someone take a letter to a man who had worked at the company in the past, and with whom he was still in touch, asking him to come to the house. When he arrived, Yeye explained the situation.

"Yes, Zhu Sancheng's son did take over from him at work many years ago," the man told Yeye.

"I wonder if it would be possible to find Zhu Sancheng, and ask him to have a word with his son about returning our dragonfly eyes."

The man shook his head. "Zhu Sancheng died the year before last." He paused for a moment. "However, I could find out his son's name and address, and you could ask him directly. Back then, you treated his father well. He should remember that."

Yeye nodded. "Could you try?"

It took only two days for the man to learn that Zhu Sancheng's son was called Zhu Daxiong and that he lived on Changning Road. He was even able to get the exact address.

The first person to pay Zhu Daxiong a visit was Dabo. But Zhu Daxiong denied it outright. "When am I supposed to have snatched these dragonfly eyes? And what *are* dragonfly eyes in the first place? I've never heard of them before. What would I do with that kind of thing?"

"If you valued our fathers' friendship, you'd give them back to us," said Dabo.

Zhu Daxiong was outraged. "How can you say that? What kind of friendship could our fathers have had? Your father was a capitalist; my father was just a worker – he was exploited!" It was very clear from the tone of his voice and his body language that he wanted Dabo to go.

Dabo had no choice but to leave Zhu Daxiong's house.

Then Dagu and Xiaogu went to see Zhu Daxiong. He let them in, then left them on their own while he went to talk to one of his friends. There was a table with some paintings on it, and the two of them were talking business. "Look after them, these are good paintings!" said the friend. "I daren't think how much these paintings will be worth when the

situation changes, but it will be a phenomenal amount."
When his friend had finally gone, Zhu Daxiong poured two
cups of hot water, gave them to Dagu and Xiaogu, and asked
the two women the purpose of their visit. This time he didn't
deny it. He admitted that he had taken the dragonfly eyes
that day, then added, "As soon as we were out of the gate,
I threw them away. What would I want with two lumps of
glass? I took them simply to show your old lady that it's
not appropriate to wear things like that these days, that it
will cause trouble." Then, without any sense of shame, he
said, "I was doing you all a favour." When they asked where
he'd thrown them, he said, "I threw them in the long grass
at the corner of your wall." Dagu and Xiaogu didn't know
what to say: they knew he was lying. When they got home,
they called Nainai and Mrs Hu to join them, and made a
thorough search of everywhere that had any grass. But no
dragonfly eyes came to light.

"In other words, he looked you square in the eye and lied
through his teeth!" Yeye was furious. "Zhu Daxiong's father
had a lifelong interest in antiques, and his son would have
seen and heard all kinds of things as he was growing up. He
would have recognized those dragonfly eyes when he saw
them. He says he threw them away? Who does he think he's
kidding! He just doesn't want to give them back! That man
is nothing like his father!"

Next, Erbo and Sanbo paid a visit to Changning Road.
They took two cartons of cigarettes, three bottles of alcohol
and a whole stack of nice words. Zhu Daxiong accepted all
of it, but didn't change his tune. "If only I'd known those two

lumps of glass were something special, I would never have thrown them in the grass. What an idiot, what a stupid idiot I've been."

There was nothing Erbo or Sanbo could do. When they left, Sanbo walked down the road, the anger rising inside him. He wanted to go straight back to Zhu Daxiong's place and beat him up, but Erbo wouldn't let him. "If you do that, he's bound to return to the house with his friends and take revenge on Yeye and Nainai. They can't go through that again."

The two of them restrained themselves and swallowed their pride.

Nainai could not stop thinking about the beads. She was always touching her neck, or glancing down. She had been wearing the dragonfly eyes for years, and had come to take them for granted; they were a part of her. Now, her neck and chest felt bare without them. She was bereft, as though she had lost part of her life – the warmest and most beautiful part. The necklace was gone, leaving an empty space that could never be filled.

The beads were such a part of her that one morning Nainai got up early and automatically looked for the necklace. She searched all over the house, until Mrs Hu reminded her that she'd been robbed, at which point Nainai sat down on a chair, somewhat taken aback, and laughed at herself. "Oh dear, my memory is playing tricks on me!" Then, shaking her head, she said, "I'm not going to think about it any more."

"Don't worry," said Yeye, "we'll get them back. I'm going to tell Zhu Daxiong that his father and I used to drink together. I'm going to tell him that when their home caught fire, I gave his father fifty silver dollars." He looked down at his leg. "When I can walk, I'll go and see him myself, and ask for them back. No, I won't ask for them, I'll demand them!" said Yeye, banging his stick on the floor.

Then, using the stick, he hobbled over to Nainai, and put his hand on her shoulder. "I'll bring them back to you."

It never occurred to anyone in the family that Yeye might not be able to keep his promise to Nainai.

With only ten days left before the summer holidays, Ah Mei was beginning to get excited. But she was anxious as well as excited, and her anxiety was growing by the day, as though something urgent was calling her to Shanghai. Baba and Mama didn't know what to do. They tried to reassure her: "The holidays will be here soon. Be patient, just a few more days and the holidays will start and you can go back to Shanghai to see Yeye and Nainai." Mama drew Ah Mei in front of her, then turned her around, and, using both hands, gently massaged Ah Mei's shoulders.

It hurt a little, but it felt good, too. Gradually, she began to relax.

"What are you so worried about?" Mama asked as she worked her fingers over Ah Mei's shoulders. "You can spend the entire summer holiday at Yeye and Nainai's. This evening, I'll help you start packing."

"I've already packed," said Ah Mei.

Mama's fingers suddenly dug into Ah Mei's shoulders, which made Ah Mei flinch.

"You'll be sprouting wings next," said Mama, "and flying straight back to Shanghai."

That was exactly what Ah Mei longed for! At night she dreamed about flying through the air. During the day, she tried to imagine what it would feel like to fly. She wanted to soar high in the sky, to fly fast and with ease. She imagined looking down on the Yangtze as it wound its way through the land, which was how she remembered it from the boat. She would follow the Yangtze, so as not to get lost, and when she'd flown to the end of the river she'd be in Shanghai. She imagined what it would look like from the air, and how lonely she would be, making this journey by herself. But the birds would keep her company: big birds and little birds. She would fly all the way to the Blue House and land in the apricot tree. She'd call out "Nainai, I'm back!" and Nainai would run outside, wondering where she could be, checking everywhere. And Ah Mei would leap out of the tree and surprise her.

Ah Mei loved losing herself in the world of make-believe. Time was passing, and Ah Mei was growing up by the day, but instead of leaving that world behind, she was going deeper and deeper into it.

Ah Mei's anxiety grew. She felt the tension rising inside her, as though something terrible had happened in Shanghai. She kept asking Baba and Mama to buy her boat ticket as soon as possible.

One morning, Baba went out very early to go and buy Ah Mei's ticket. It was midday by the time he got home.

Ah Mei could see from his face that something was wrong.

319

She looked him straight in the eye.

"They told me the tickets would be available three days in advance. But then they changed it to four days in advance, and by the time I arrived there were none left."

Ah Mei burst into tears, then roared at Baba and Mama. She picked up her pillow and hurled it onto the floor.

"I told you to get the tickets! I told you!" Ah Mei stamped her foot in frustration.

"Baba went out first thing this morning to buy your ticket!" said Mama. "They'd told him that tickets would be available three days in advance. He couldn't have known they'd start selling them a day earlier. You're at middle school now, Ah Mei, you're not a little girl any more. You need to be reasonable."

"I won't be reasonable. I won't!" she screamed, then stormed out.

"You don't think anything could have happened in Shanghai, do you?" Baba asked Mama.

Mama looked at Baba, puzzled.

"I mean, Ah Mei's quite … special." Baba was trying to find the right word.

Mama knew exactly what he meant. She thought there was something intuitive about Ah Mei too. And there was something else niggling her. "Shanghai is so far away," she sighed.

Ah Mei walked all the way to the quay.

She arrived just as a boat was pulling away. The whistle blew and then blew again. Slowly, the boat moved to the middle of the river, and joined the Yangtze as it flowed downstream. There were a lot of people standing on the deck, waving to friends and family on the riverbank as they set off on their long journey.

The water flowed endlessly, carrying them east.

Ah Mei sat on the quay, watching the boat gradually fade and disappear in the distance.

She looked at the river again, then, remembering that she should be going to school, stood up and started to head back. But after a few steps she stopped, turned around, and walked towards the waiting room. She knew that was where the ticket office was.

There was a long queue of people at the counter, all wanting to buy tickets.

However, they were all buying tickets for the day after Ah Mei's original departure date – four days away. Tickets for any earlier were all sold out, as the sign at the window very clearly said.

Four days! Ah Mei couldn't wait four days. That was too long!

Ah Mei felt her hair would turn white if she had to wait four whole days.

Then she noticed a man pacing up and down by the counter, asking the same question over and over: "Anyone returning tickets? For today, tomorrow, the day after?"

Not a single person responded.

Ah Mei watched the man, with growing impatience, as though she had come looking for a returned ticket too.

He was persistent and unrelenting.

After a while, Ah Mei began to feel his approach was pointless.

She was just thinking that nothing would come of it, when an old man walked in and asked, "Does anyone want a ticket for the day after tomorrow?"

Both Ah Mei and the man rushed over to him.

In her hurry, Ah Mei caught her leg on the bench and fell. As she lay on the ground, she reached her hand towards the old man, and said, "I want it, sir!"

The old man kindly hurried towards Ah Mei, helped her up and then said to the man who'd been asking for a ticket, "The girl was first."

The old man opened his hand, and revealed the ticket.

Ah Mei reached for it immediately, then stopped with her hand in mid-air, slowly pulled it back, and hung her head. "I didn't bring any money with me," she said.

The old man sighed, and shook his head.

"I can go home and get some!" said Ah Mei.

The old man asked where she lived. "That's quite a distance. I'm sorry, young lady. I need the money now. I was going to take a trip, do some business out of town, but my little granddaughter's suddenly fallen ill. She's in hospital and we're trying to save her life."

Ah Mei didn't say another word. She just nodded, turned around and ran home.

When she saw Baba, she said, "Ba, if you give me the money for the ticket, I can wait for a returned one."

"It's not easy," said Baba. "I waited a whole morning for nothing."

"I can still try," said Ah Mei.

Baba and Mama had to go to work. They didn't have time to go and wait for a returned ticket. Baba considered Ah Mei's suggestion. Then he took out the money for Ah Mei's ticket, counted it in front of her, put it in a little cloth purse and handed it over. "All right, try it and see. Who knows, perhaps you might be lucky. Look after that money! If you lose it, you won't be able to go back to Shanghai."

Mama helped Ah Mei tuck the cloth purse into her inside pocket, and told her, "Don't let anyone see it, especially at the quay – there are lots of pickpockets there."

Ah Mei nodded, turned around and went back to the quay.

She stayed there until the last person had gone, and the ticket counter had closed, but there were no more returns that day.

The next morning Ah Mei got up early to go to the quay again. "I'll go," said Baba. "I'll buy you the earliest ticket I can get. It'll be a few days later than we planned, but the summer holidays are long. Otherwise, we might not be able to get a ticket for next week either."

But Ah Mei insisted. "I'm sure I'll be able to get a returned ticket."

She tucked the little cloth purse into her inside pocket again, and went back to the quay.

By the late afternoon, however, Ah Mei had lost hope, and was walking slowly towards the ticket counter to buy the earliest available ticket, when a young woman ran into the waiting room. "Does anyone want a ticket for tomorrow?" she asked.

"I do!" said Ah Mei, rushing over to the woman, her legs trembling.

And so, Ah Mei ended up with a ticket to travel a day earlier than originally planned. She and Mama went to the school together, and made up an excuse for why she had to miss the end of term.

Baba and Mama told the family which day Ah Mei would arrive in Shanghai.

As soon as Yeye got up that morning, he made some fresh coffee for Nainai. A few days earlier, Xiaogu had asked an old school friend to help find some coffee, and had somehow managed to buy about a kilo of coffee beans. This meant Nainai could have coffee for a while yet. Yeye was walking again, although not very steadily, and as he tottered towards Nainai, the coffee kept spilling over the top of the cup and into the saucer. He tried his best to keep his balance, but the coffee kept sloshing over. It wasn't just because of his leg, but also his hands. Recently, Yeye's hands had become very shaky, and he couldn't control the tremors.

When Nainai looked up and saw Yeye coming towards her with the coffee, she hurried over, and took the cup from him. "I've told you to stop bringing me coffee, but you won't listen."

Yeye was upset. "I used to be able to bring you a cup full to the brim, and breeze over to you without spilling a drop. I'm getting so old, Océane."

Nainai put the coffee down, and quickly helped Yeye onto a chair. "You're not old! How can you say that? I had coffee yesterday, didn't I? And now, here you are, making me another one! Take it slowly – when this coffee is finished, who knows when we'll be able to get any more. Those coffee beans are more precious than gold."

"Today is a special day. You must have a cup of coffee, because in a few hours, your darling granddaughter will arrive, and I want you to have the happiest day." There was colour in Yeye's cheeks; he looked happy and healthy. The plaster cast had been removed two days earlier, and, looking at his leg, you would never know it had been in plaster.

Yeye took Nainai her coffee at eight o'clock. At ten o'clock, as Mrs Hu was about to head down to the kitchen, she heard a series of bumps and thumps. She rushed onto the landing and saw Yeye lying at the bottom of the stairs. His stick had slipped from his hand and was lying across the steps.

"Madam!" she cried out in shock.

Nainai hurried out of Ah Mei's room. Mrs Hu had cleaned it, and Nainai was just checking it was ready for Ah Mei. When Nainai heard Mrs Hu, she rushed straight out.

By then, Mrs Hu was running downstairs, gasping and panting.

When Nainai saw what had happened, her legs turned to jelly, and she almost dropped to her knees. Clutching the banister with one hand and reaching out to Yeye with the other, she made her way awkwardly towards her husband. "Meixi! Meixi...!"

Yeye lay there without moving, as though fast asleep.

"Meixi! Meixi!"

"Sir! Sir!"

Nainai and Mrs Hu called his name over and over, but Yeye did not open his eyes again.

As soon as Ah Mei woke up that morning, she left her cabin, and, pressing her hands on the guardrail, gazed out in front of her. The early morning mist over the river had yet to lift, and although she thought she could see the riverbank, it was a little too dark for her to be sure. Sometimes she thought she could see it, sometimes she couldn't. When she spotted a crew member she asked, "How soon can we get to Shanghai?"

"Is there an emergency, Miss?" he asked.

Ah Mei shook her head.

The crew member smiled. "Be patient. We'll be there today."

"They said we'd arrive at around nine o'clock in the morning."

"Unfortunately, the wind's been against us the whole way, and that slows the boat down. I'm afraid we won't be there by nine." He tried to reassure Ah Mei. "Enjoy the scenery. It won't be long now, and then you'll see the shore, and Shanghai, clear as can be."

Ah Mei leaned on the railing, picturing Yeye and Nainai, imagining how they'd react when they saw her. And all her uncles and aunts and cousins … the whole family. She pictured every single one of them. And Mrs Hu. *I wonder what Mrs Hu will look like? And whether she'll have cooked something nice for me?*

Gradually the mist lifted. In the east, a huge sun was rising from the vast surface of the water. She knew the sun is largest when it first appears, and gradually becomes smaller as it rises. But this sun was enormous! She had never seen it so large. By the time it had formed a semi-circle on the horizon, there was a path of light hanging beneath it, the slats on the water a metre or two wide. As the sun rose, it drew the path with it. Ah Mei watched the slat nearest the horizon rise slowly, and saw the wobble as it was finally pulled from the water. She could imagine, at every upward beat of the sun, a shower of water droplets pitter-pattering down.

By this time, many passengers had emerged from their cabins to see the sunrise.

Just as the crew member had said, the land eventually came into sight, and, as the sun rose higher, the view became clearer. Soon, they could see buildings and trees, little forests by the river, villages along the banks – a warm world, bathed in sunlight.

It was three o'clock in the afternoon when the tall buildings on the Bund came into view. Shanghai! She could see Shanghai! Ah Mei had been standing on the deck since early morning.

For hours, every time a crew member walked past her, they had said the same thing: "It's windy out here, Miss. You should go back inside."

And Ah Mei had said, "I'll go in soon," though she had no intention of doing so. She couldn't wait to see Shanghai.

Who will come to meet me? Ah Mei wondered.

Yeye would come. Nainai would wait for her at home, but Yeye would definitely come to the quay.

Xiaogu would come too. And probably her cousins, if they weren't at work. It was only natural that she should think about Ah Lang, too. If he were in Shanghai he would definitely have come to meet her off the boat. He would probably have told the others, "None of you need to be there. I'll go by myself to meet Ah Mei." But he wasn't there, he was thousands of mountains and rivers away.

In the little leather suitcase, as well as the presents for Yeye and Nainai and the rest of the family, there were six letters from Ah Lang. Since she'd been in Yibin, Ah Mei had received six whole letters from him! She wanted to let Yeye and Nainai read them. Perhaps they would be the best presents she could give them. She had tried a few times to decide whether she should let them read the letters themselves, or whether she should read the letters to them. Better to read them aloud, she thought, because every one of Ah Lang's letters was so beautifully written. She would often read them aloud to herself. Once, late at night, she had been reading one of his letters aloud to herself when Mama had pushed open the door and come in. "What are you reading?" she'd asked. "It's so beautiful!" Ah Mei told her it was a letter from Ah Lang. Mama took the letter and read it, then she pulled Ah Mei towards her and the two of them read it again together.

Ah Mei could see the Customs House clock. She could even see the hands on the clock.

The Huangpu was a light brown colour, and the closer they came to the Bund, the browner the river became. It was easy to see why it was called the Huangpu; *huang* means yellow or light brown, and *pu* means the mouth of a river.

Finally, the long journey reached its end.

The ship's whistle blasted, and the boat slowly pulled up at the quay. At either end of the boat was a crew member standing by, with a coil of mooring rope in his hands, ready to cast it towards the shore at the right moment.

There were people on the quayside ready to catch the ropes, and two iron bollards, glistening in the sunlight.

People shouted and waved as they spotted their friends and family. Sometimes it was the people on board who cried out first, sometimes it was the people on the quay.

Ah Mei soon spotted Xiaogu, then one after another, her relatives appeared before her eyes.

Ah Mei called out to them in a loud voice.

As soon as Ah Mei was off the boat, one of them took the little leather suitcase, another took her other luggage, and there was kissing and hugging, as though, right there, on the quay, they were giving her all the love they hadn't been able to show her for such a long time.

Ah Mei's happiness was boundless.

But she couldn't see Yeye. At first, she thought he might be standing at the back, hidden in the crowd. So she stood on tiptoe, searching for him. Her aunts saw what she was doing, but didn't comment.

Gradually, the crowd thinned, but there was still no sign of her grandfather.

"What about Yeye?" Ah Mei asked.

No one said anything.

"What about Yeye?" she asked again.

"Yeye's waiting for you at home," said Xiaogu, looking

away as she spoke, not wanting Ah Mei to see her eyes – she couldn't hold the tears back any longer, and she quickly wiped them away. "Ah Mei, let's go home," she said.

Everyone said the same thing: "Let's go home."

All the way home, they carefully avoided mentioning Yeye. There was a tacit agreement, they would wait until Ah Mei was home before telling her that her grandfather had died.

As soon as she saw the Blue House, Ah Mei forgot everything else and ran towards it. Her voice flew inside before she reached the door: "Yeye! Nainai!"

Nainai was standing by the door, waiting for her.

"Nainai!" Ah Mei cried, throwing herself into her grandmother's arms.

The relatives who had met her off the boat came inside. The relatives who were upstairs by Yeye's side came down. When they saw Ah Mei and Nainai, their hearts ached. Tears streamed down the aunts' faces.

Nainai lowered her head, and gently kissed Ah Mei.

Ah Mei rose up on tiptoe and kissed Nainai back.

After a long hug, Ah Mei asked, "What about Yeye?" She called up the stairs: "Yeye, I'm back!"

No one said anything. Dagu and Xiaogu began to cry. They came over to Ah Mei and stroked her arm.

Ah Mei looked at each of her aunts in turn, and then back at Nainai. "What about Yeye? Where is he?" She ran upstairs.

They all followed.

"Yeye! Yeye!" Ah Mei called his name as she ran into her grandparents' bedroom.

There was a pure white sheet on the bed. Yeye was lying on it, pencil-straight. He was wearing the blue serge trousers he had worn on the ship in winter, and the matching blue serge overcoat with the buttons made of brass. On his feet were a pair of old, but well-polished boots, the ones he had worn on deck as a seaman.

Lying there, Yeye looked so serene.

"Yeye…" Speaking in a very quiet voice, and taking very slow steps, Ah Mei inched towards him, as though scared she might startle him in his sleep. "Yeye, it's me, Ah Mei. I'm back…" And then, she stood by Yeye's side, no longer trying to greet him, and looked at him in silence. There was no more calling out his name now. At first she was too stunned to cry, but very soon, tears gushed from her eyes.

Xiaogu came over, and, placing her hands on Ah Mei's shoulders, said to her father: "Ba, Ah Mei is here. She's come back. Ah Mei, perhaps you knew that Yeye was going to leave us? Maybe you sensed something, a thousand *li* away, and hurried here as fast as you could to say goodbye…"

Ah Mei bit her lip hard. Tears rolled down to the corners of her mouth, and slipped between her lips. She tried to choke them back, but this made her cough. Her face, ashen a few moments before, turned bright red, as though she was about to be sick. Dagu rushed over, and urged her to move back.

Ah Mei cried for the rest of the day. She kept repeating the same words: "They said we would reach Shanghai at nine o'clock this morning…"

At the end of the evening, Nainai said to them all: "Let

me spend some time alone with him. Go home now, and get some sleep."

They did as Nainai asked.

Ah Mei stayed where she was.

"Ah Mei, you should go to bed too," said Nainai. "Mrs Hu has made your room ready for you."

But Ah Mei wouldn't go.

"Go on, Ah Mei. I'd like to spend some time alone with your yeye."

Ah Mei left the room.

Nainai sat on the chair beside the bed, and looked at Yeye. There were no more tears, just an endless stream of words: "You went without saying goodbye, and left me behind. Well, maybe that's not such a bad thing. But the children and I, we'll miss you, because you were a good father, a good baba, a good man, a good husband! You go on ahead, I'll catch you up soon. I won't stay here much longer. Wait for me over there… Ah Mei is back, and it's such a shame you couldn't have waited a few more hours to see her. She's taller, and has grown up a lot. Her baba and mama won't be able to get back in time to see you. They'd need a couple of weeks to get here by boat. And Ah Lang's not here either. It's not that he doesn't want to see you, it's just that he's so far away. That place is so remote they don't even get telegrams. And even if we sent him a telegram, what could he do? But you don't need to worry about him. I've read the letters he wrote to Ah Mei. There were six of them, all very long. Reading between the lines, I can tell that he's happy there, very happy. You mustn't worry about him, he's a grown man now! But you left too soon… You said you were going to get the dragonfly eyes back for me! All your life, you've been a man of your word. You said you'd love me your entire life, and you have. But you broke your promise this time. I'm still waiting for the dragonfly eyes! Thank you for making and bringing me coffee all my life. Thank you for planting the apricot tree for me…"

Ah Mei couldn't sleep. She couldn't stop thinking about Yeye. She walked across the landing to Yeye and Nainai's bedroom. She didn't go in, but sat on the floor by the door.

Nainai heard a sound outside the room. She knew it was Ah Mei. She opened the door, reached out to her granddaughter, pulled her up and led her into the bedroom.

"You can come and help me keep Yeye company."

Ah Mei pulled up a chair, and sat down next to Nainai.

"Are you scared?" Nainai asked.

Ah Mei shook her head.

Outside in the street, all was quiet, save for the occasional sound of a car driving past.

"Let's wash Yeye's face and hands again," said Nainai.

Ah Mei went with Nainai to fetch a fresh bowl of water.

Nainai put a clean white towel into the new water, then wrung it out, and started to wash Yeye. As she did so, she said, "Actually, he doesn't need a wash. Your yeye's a very clean man. I've never in my life met another man as clean as him. Shanghai men have a thing about being clean, and your grandfather was the cleanest." Nainai gently wiped his face and hands. "Look, can you see how clean the water is?"

When she had finished, Nainai sat down again, putting

her arm around Ah Mei's shoulders, drawing her close. "Back then, when we met in the café, he used to wear this uniform. He just needs the cap now, that's all." Nainai looked at Yeye's head of white hair.

Nainai told Ah Mei the same stories as always. But when she came to the question of who was waiting for whom outside the café, she stopped. Ah Mei smiled, and looked quizzically at Nainai.

Nainai shook her head. "I won't ever be able to correct him again."

It was getting late. Now and then they heard the distant blast of a whistle on the river, a note of sympathy on a night when the world seemed so sad and forlorn.

When they stopped talking, they just leaned against each other, quietly looking at Yeye.

Ah Mei fell asleep in Nainai's arms, and soon after that Nainai fell asleep too.

Waigong, Ah Mei's other grandfather, came from Hangzhou for Yeye's funeral. Afterwards, he asked Ah Mei to take him to a public telephone so he could call her parents in Yibin, and reassure them. When Mama sobbed down the phone, he said, "Don't cry. Crying isn't going to help, is it? Crying isn't going to bring him back. He's gone now. We have to think about the living instead." He was referring to Nainai. Then he asked, "Did you know about this business with the dragonfly eyes?"

"I've only just heard," said Mama.

"We need to hurry up and get them back. If we can get

them back, it'll help her keep going."

"The whole family has been trying to think of a way."

"I have an idea," said Waigong.

"What can you do?"

"Leave it to me," said Waigong. "Don't worry about things here. We can manage." When he finished speaking, he hung up.

Then he made another phone call, this time to Hangzhou, and asked for six of his paintings to be sent to him straight away. Six of his best ones.

On the way back to the Blue House, Waigong told Ah Mei, "Now that your yeye's gone, it's even more important that we get the dragonfly eyes back. Do you know what kind of man your yeye was?"

Ah Mei shook her head.

"Think of your yeye as a kite-flyer. And your nainai as a beautiful kite. And the necklace as the kite-string. When the string breaks, the kite will fall, down into the dust. Do you understand what I'm saying, Ah Mei?"

"Yes, I understand."

Ah Mei wanted to ask Waigong to save Nainai, but she didn't, because she could already see the determination in his straight back, his strong stride and the expression on his face.

As soon as the paintings arrived from Hangzhou, Waigong and Ah Mei set off for Changning Road, taking the address that Dabo had given him. Waigong didn't want anyone else to go with him, just Ah Mei. "I can't believe that a black heart won't melt on seeing Ah Mei and her eyes!"

They reached Zhu Daxiong's house.

Waigong was carrying a cardboard box containing his paintings. He introduced himself.

Zhu Daxiong was surprised. "An artist?"

"No, just a painter."

Zhu Daxiong quickly pulled up a chair and invited Waigong to sit down.

"To cut a long story short," said Waigong, sitting on the chair, "I would like to exchange one of my paintings for the two dragonfly eyes." He opened the box. "Or two paintings, if you wish."

Zhu Daxiong's eyes lit up. But, after a moment, he said, "The truth is, I really did throw those two lumps of glass in the grass."

Waigong laughed. "I've heard about your father's lifelong interest in antiques; that he was a connoisseur. I can't believe that you didn't know what those lumps of glass were."

Zhu Daxiong rubbed his hands together nervously.

Waigong went a step further. "Here in Shanghai, there are probably only a handful of people who know what dragonfly eyes are. Fewer than have heard of me and my work, wouldn't you say?"

Zhu Daxiong examined the six paintings carefully, then asked rather uneasily, "May I have three paintings?"

"Yes, you may."

"Wait here," said Zhu Daxiong, then he went up to the attic.

Waigong sat calmly on the chair.

Ah Mei did not take her eyes off the staircase.

It was quite a long time before Zhu Daxiong came back downstairs, but his hands were empty. He walked towards Waigong, rubbing his hands together again. "I'm afraid I've changed my mind... It's true that there are only a few people in Shanghai who know the value of dragonfly eyes, but so what? I know their real value." Zhu Daxiong's eyes were on the paintings in the box. He put on a somewhat apologetic expression, and looked at the six paintings again, one by one, as though he had forgotten the deal he had just made with Waigong. "Every single painting is excellent. I like them all."

Waigong stood up. He gently put the lid back on the box. "Ah Mei, please lift this box with both hands, and place it in the hands of the uncle in front of you."

Ah Mei didn't move.

"Didn't you hear what I said?" Waigong asked.

Ah Mei walked over, lifted the box with both hands and took it to Zhu Daxiong. She stood in front of him, looking at him with big, bright, tear-swollen eyes.

With those eyes watching his every move, Zhu Daxiong gave a long sigh, took a few steps back, turned around and went back upstairs to the attic. It was not long before he came down again, holding a beautiful wooden box in his hand.

Ah Mei's gaze followed the little box the entire time. Meanwhile, Waigong was looking down at his shoes. The leather was so old and scuffed that there was no shine at all. He didn't look up until Zhu Daxiong opened the little wooden box, and said, "Please, take a look." He saw the dragonfly eyes in the box, carefully held in place on a cushion of white silk. He nodded at Zhu Daxiong.

Ah Mei's eyes glistened as brightly as the dragonfly eyes.

Zhu Daxiong said, "You can keep the box. It's made of the best red sandalwood. It's quite old." He closed the lid, and handed the box to Waigong.

Waigong took the box, examined it carefully, and ran his hands over it a few times. "Indeed!" he said, as he opened the box, and took out the two dragonfly eyes, checking each one in turn. They were flawless. He took out a clean handkerchief from his breast pocket, wrapped them up carefully, and put them in his inside pocket. Then he placed the box on the table, and slid it carefully towards Zhu Daxiong. "When you took them, they were not in this box." Waigong held his hand out to Ah Mei. "We can go home now," he said.

They walked home, arm in arm, Ah Mei's right arm squeezing Waigong's left arm as tightly as she could, all the way to the Blue House.

CHAPTER 21

The Reedlands

Mrs Hu had kept in touch with Mrs Song after she left the Blue House. They had become such good friends during the years they worked together that they were like sisters, and their relationship remained strong after Mrs Song went back to the countryside.

Mrs Song felt a similar attachment to the Blue House. Although she was no longer an employee there, she still cared about the family, and the family had not forgotten about her, either. At New Year, Mrs Song always found someone to take some specialities from her region to the Blue House, perhaps some local fish or game, and in the autumn when the rice was harvested, the first bag of new rice always went to the Blue House. And the family supported Mrs Song's family, in so far as they were able, and so the relationship was never broken.

Mrs Hu was expecting a telephone call from Mrs Song. They had arranged that she would phone when she visited her son in the county town at the end of the month. Eventually Mrs Song's call came through.

"Would you be able to have Madam to stay for a while?" Mrs Hu asked Mrs Song. She explained how Shanghai was getting more and more chaotic, and that the situation was looking more and more dangerous. For the last few days, she'd been worried that a gang might charge into the house at any point and seize Nainai. She'd been waking up in a cold sweat from nightmares about Nainai being taken captive. She told Mrs Song that when she'd gone out two days earlier, she'd seen an older woman standing in the back of a lorry, her head half-shaved, being paraded around the streets. From the comments she'd heard, it seemed the woman was a university professor. She said that if Nainai were to be taken captive by those out-of-control hooligans with their poisoned minds, and have her head shaved "yin-yang" style, it would be the death of her.

"If only we could remove her from this awful city, and keep her out of the limelight for a while. This madness can't last for ever, and when the situation calms down, we can bring her back. She's just lost her husband, and is very low. If she could stay with you for a few days, it would take her mind off things."

"Yes, yes, of course she can. Let her come to the countryside for a while, out of harm's way, where she can relax. I miss her so much," came Mrs Song's voice on the other end of the line.

"Ah Mei is in Shanghai. No doubt she'll want to go too," added Mrs Hu.

"They can come together. I really miss that little girl," said Mrs Song.

"She's growing up, you know. You won't recognize her when you see her," said Mrs Hu.

As they were discussing when to fetch Nainai, Mrs Song said, "As it happens, one of my cousins will be setting off tomorrow to take a boatload of water chestnuts to a food-purchasing station. I can give him the address and ask him, when the boat is empty, to quickly go and collect Madam and Ah Mei."

"Let's do that," said Mrs Hu.

"That's settled then. And when they're here, you can stop worrying," said Mrs Song.

Mrs Hu told Dabo and the others about her plan. They were all in support. They had been worrying day and night about the current situation. Nainai did not object, but said she would consider it, and by the evening she had begun to pack – for herself and Ah Mei.

Three days later, a wooden boat from the wetlands of northern Jiangsu stopped in Suzhou Creek. It was not a large boat, nor a small boat, and the water chestnuts had already been offloaded.

"I'll go and get them. You watch the boat," Mrs Song's cousin told his son, who'd come with him to drive the boat.

At three o'clock that afternoon, with Nainai and Ah Mei on board, the boat set off on its journey to the wetlands of Subei.

Three days later at around three or four o'clock in the afternoon, the boat reached the never-ending marshes and turned into the waterways that meandered through the reedlands. The reeds grew tall and lush, a deep dark green as far as the eye could see. There were broad expanses of water, and narrow ones too. With the broad ones, the reeds in the distance formed a swathe of black-green, where the reeds themselves were no longer visible. In the narrower places, they could hear the swish of the reeds rustling and jostling, until the wind calmed, and the reeds stood still, like a tall green wall. Now and then, they would spot a water bird about to land, or take flight, or dive underwater as the boat approached.

Nainai seemed happier already.

Ah Mei's cares and worries vanished as soon as they entered this world. She looked at the sky, at the water, at the reeds, at the birds taking off and landing, her eyes constantly drawn to aspects of the natural world she had never encountered before.

At dusk they reached Mrs Song's hometown.

As the sun moved to the west, the sky filled with the black silhouettes of birds flying home.

The evening scent of the wetlands was intense. The reeds, lotus leaves, water chestnuts, waterplants and sweetflag, and the rice and other plants, emitted their own fragrances, which merged together in the moist air. Ah Mei's nose was on the alert, greedily taking them all in.

The air was clean and fresh; pure and unadulterated.

Mrs Song had been waiting for them since noon. Every so often she had gone to the water's edge to look out towards the river, and now that she could finally see the boat, she raised her hands and waved to Nainai and Ah Mei.

Nainai and Ah Mei saw a figure waving in the distance.

They knew immediately that it was Mrs Song, and waved back. As the figure of Mrs Song gradually came into focus, a smile spread over Nainai's face, like ripples spreading across the water.

People gathered at the water's edge.

When the boat was twenty metres from the bank, the air filled with the popping and snapping of firecrackers. The *pi-li-pa-la* went on for a long time, and when Nainai and Ah Mei looked at the bank again, the group were surrounded by smoke.

Mrs Song had arranged it especially, to give them a grand welcome, and to scare away bad luck – there had been so much of that in Nainai's family recently.

The boat stopped at a small island, which was home to just four or five families, and surrounded on all sides by reeds.

In this little world of its own, it was not long before Nainai's heart found peace, and the sadness vanished from Ah Mei's eyes.

Just after nightfall, in the vastness of this tranquility, the tension began to ease in Nainai's body and mind. She took Mrs Song's hand and started to cry.

Nainai and Ah Mei were not ready to turn in for the night. They never went to bed so early in the city. Besides, night-time in the countryside was too enchanting.

There was a full moon. They had never seen such a pure moon in such a pure sky. They gazed up at the night for the longest time, long after their necks had grown stiff. There were no clouds in the sky, except for a few drifting past the moon.

The sky was so clear, and reached so high and so far that the world seemed to have grown.

When the wind blew, the reeds rushed forward, a dark tide of green waves. At their feet, the water rushed too, a white tide of glistening crystals. In the distance there were boats moving on the water, their lamps twinkling in the dark, flickering as they passed behind the reeds. For the people driving these boats through the night, crooning their weary songs, it must have seemed a lonely world. There were noises, too. Deep in the reeds, there was a noisy flapping of wings as a bird took to the sky. It seemed to have been startled, perhaps by a rabbit or fox. Its eyes unused to the dark, it flew awkwardly for a short distance, then came down to land again.

Ah Mei and Nainai sat on little stools very close to the water's edge, and watched it flow in front of them, its gurgling as clear as could be. A wooden boat moored to an old willow tree bobbed to and fro.

Mrs Song chivvied them a few times. "You must be tired after your journey, and it's getting late, why don't you go to bed?"

And each time, Nainai would say, "I want to sit here a little longer."

Nainai had never seen such an enchanting sky in her life. Or perhaps she had, but at the time had not been in the calm state of mind she was now, and it had not left a deep impression on her. In recent times, in recent years, her mind had become as bleak as a wilderness, and as tangled as the undergrowth. To see a sky like this now made such a strong and vivid impression.

The moonlight, like water, washed over all those dark memories in Nainai's mind.

She was so grateful to Mrs Song for giving her this world. That evening she felt like a boat, buffeted by the wind and the waves, that has finally come to shore. Although it was only a temporary arrangement, and Nainai was exhausted in mind and spirit, her heart was filled with gratitude.

There were fireflies everywhere. Yellow fireflies with a subtle blueness, sparkling like tiny diamonds in the air.

The night sky here was truly dream-like.

Ah Mei had forgotten her sadness and sorrow. She sat beside her grandmother, listening to Nainai and Mrs Song talking. Then she got up and tried to catch the fireflies.

The moon started moving to the west. Nainai and Ah Mei finally went to bed.

Although they were in a house on the riverbank, they felt as though they were on a boat, on an immense sea, where the wind and the waves were still and calm.

Moonlight shone through the lattice window onto Ah Mei's face. Nainai could see her granddaughter was still awake. She looked so young, but had known such sadness.

"Night-night, Aina," she said.

"Night-night, Océane," said Ah Mei.

In no time at all, they were fast asleep.

The next day, when the sun was already high in the sky, and the birds had already flown off to look for food, Ah Mei and Nainai were still fast asleep.

*   *   *

Mrs Song had four sons and a daughter. Her youngest son had moved away to the town. Her other three sons and her daughter still lived near by, and had families of their own. So although there were five families on the island, they were in fact all Mrs Song's family. Her sons had houses on the little island, and were living their own lives. Her daughter had married a local man, and they had a house on the island too. Mrs Song had told her children countless times, "You may have your own houses and your own lives now, but don't forget the gentleman and the lady in Shanghai." She had been a servant at the Blue House for so many years, and her pay from Yeye and Nainai had always been the highest among her peers. On top of the monthly pay, Yeye and Nainai had always supported her family through difficult times. The scenery here was beautiful, but you can't eat beauty. The moon was stunning, but the moon can't satisfy hunger. Although there were reeds everywhere, reeds are not crops. You can build houses of reeds, and put them on the fire to cook rice, but you cannot eat them. There were fish, shrimp and wild ducks, but you can't live on these things alone, all year round. And they had to have clothes and send the children to school, and to see the doctor when they were ill. Everyone here was poor. Of all the families in this backwater, Mrs Song's family had the best life. Those years when Mrs Song was working as a servant, there was always money arriving from Shanghai. It meant that her sons and daughter did not go cold or hungry, that they grew up healthy and strong. Her youngest son had not only been to school, he'd passed his exams and gone to teaching college, and after graduation he had been assigned a job in the town. Mrs Song had used her savings to build each of them a house, so that they could hold their heads high and marry well. They had never been to Shanghai, let alone the Blue House, but they held them in the highest esteem. And the gentleman and the lady were often in their thoughts.

Now the lady and her granddaughter had come to stay, they would look after them as warmly as they could. They would do everything possible to give them a happy time here.

Red water chestnut, water caltrop, lotus root, shrimps as translucent as jade, and all kinds of fish, wild duck, pheasant, ducks' eggs and pheasants' eggs ... they wanted their guests to try all the foods of the wetlands. After a few days, Nainai's pale face was noticeably different, and Ah Mei, who had arrived looking gaunt, slowly began to put on weight.

Mrs Song had grandsons and granddaughters, and they all called Nainai "Nainai", and Ah Mei their sister. The older ones called her Meimei (little sister), and the younger ones called her Jiejie (big sister). There were dozens of family members on this island, and every day seemed like a festival, full of joy.

"After all that family has done for us, heaven's finally giving us a chance to repay their kindness," Mrs Song said to her husband.

Nainai was content, and she smiled. Ah Mei was happy as can be, and it showed. She smiled from morning till night, as though she'd been reunited with the smile she'd been robbed of these past few years. She played all day with Mrs Song's grandchildren, going out on the boat to catch fish, to collect water chestnuts, to weave through to the densest part of the reeds to look for wild ducks' eggs. With fish leaping about in the net, Ah Mei would lean over the side of the boat, and search among the water chestnut leaves floating on the surface. A red water chestnut might appear before her eyes, or a nest of wild ducks' eggs … and each of these vivid discoveries would make Ah Mei cry out in delight. With one excitement after another, Ah Mei's face, rosily nourished with fish and shrimp, became even rosier.

They were staying in village houses with mud walls and thatched roofs, bamboo fences and wooden gates, but in Nainai and Ah Mei's eyes, this was heaven.

After two weeks, Ah Mei was going barefoot, rolling up her trousers and sleeves, and fishing and shrimping with Mrs Song's grandchildren, drenched in water and spattered with mud.

Three weeks flashed past.

One day, Mrs Song's third son took Nainai, Ah Mei and some of his children out on the boat to see the gorgeous lotus flowers that had just opened in a stretch of water deep in the reeds. They had only been gone a short while when Mrs Song's cousin, the one who had brought Nainai and Ah Mei from Shanghai, arrived on the island. He looked flustered. As soon as he saw Mrs Song, he pulled her to one side.

"Where's the old lady and the child?" he asked.

Mrs Song said, "My son's taken them to see the lotus flowers."

Her cousin gave a sigh of relief. "There are some people

from Shanghai looking for them."

"*What?*" Mrs Song was alarmed.

"There are some people from Shanghai looking for them! They're talking to the village committee and the cadres, saying the old lady fled here, and they want to seize her, take her back and parade her through the streets for all to see."

Mrs Song was panic-stricken. She didn't know what to do.

"They're bound to come here. Best to hide the old lady and the child."

"Hide them where?"

Her cousin said, "The reed marshes here are so big, you could hide seven or eight people, not just one or two. I'll go and find them, and tell them to stay where they are and enjoy the lotus flowers. We just have to get through today. If the party from Shanghai can't find her, they'll have to go back."

"We'll see if any of them dares come ashore!" said Mrs Song.

Her cousin drove off on his boat.

Mrs Song quickly gathered her husband, her sons and their wives, her daughter and her husband and the older grandchildren, and told them that some people from Shanghai had come to seize the old lady, and that they might cross the river at any moment. As soon as her family heard this, without waiting for Mrs Song to go into detail, they disappeared off, returning shortly, not with their usual wooden yokes but armed with shovels and fishing spears.

"Let's see if they dare touch anyone!"

"If they get out of that boat, they won't be going back to Shanghai!"

"They won't be seizing anyone from this island!"

Mrs Song's husband was holding a scythe. The long blade atop the long handle glinted in the sunlight.

An hour and a half later, a large boat crossed the water to the island. The head of the village was standing at the front of the boat, and behind him were seven or eight people from Shanghai, all of whom looked very young.

"They really are coming!" Mrs Song's husband went first. The children and grandchildren each picked up a tool, and followed him to the riverbank.

"Do you see that?" said the village head. "Everyone in that family is a brute. Don't think that they're holding those tools just to scare you. They'll use them. But it's up to you. If you've made up your minds, and you're not scared, go ashore."

The people from Shanghai hesitated. They didn't want to turn back, but they weren't sure how to proceed.

The village head continued, "I suggest that I go ashore first to mediate, and ask them to hand the two of them over. That way, you can avoid being attacked, and we can prevent a bloodbath. This family – well, they're not easy to deal with."

"All right," said the people from Shanghai.

When the village head was ashore, he turned and waved to the villagers driving the boat, suggesting they should move it away from the shore. Then he turned back and roared at Mrs Song's family on the bank: "Is this how you greet people? By picking a fight?" He glowered at Mrs Song's husband and her sons and grandsons. "Step back, all of you!"

They all took a few steps back.

Then the village head moved forward, and quietly asked Mrs Song, "The old lady and the young girl, are they safely hidden?"

"Yes," said Mrs Song.

"I've seen the girl but not the old lady, and the moment I saw her, I knew that her nainai must be a good person," said the village head. "If we were to let them take a good person captive, we villagers would never be able to look anyone in the eye again. They're talking about arresting them – but that's the public security bureau's job! What right do they have to arrest people? These people from Shanghai are so demanding."

After this conversation, the village head turned back. His expression suggested that the situation was hopeless and he was not happy. He walked briskly towards the river, beckoning for the boat to come closer, climbed aboard, and as though expecting yokes and shovels to be hurled at him at any moment, quickly slammed his foot against the bank and pushed the boat out onto the water. Then, as if brushing his hands clean, he said, "There's no talking with them! If I'd stayed much longer, things would have got nasty. Have you seen the old man's scythe – that blade on the long handle? It's for cutting reeds ... like this!" And he mimed the action, making a big circle so the people from Shanghai could picture the slashed reeds falling to the ground. "That family's wild, you can't reason with them." He looked at the visitors. "I think you'd better forget it. The old lady can't hide out here for ever."

"Then let's see how long she lasts here. We'll show her who rules the world now!" said one of the group. "We'll head back to Shanghai, but, who knows, we might be back in a few days, and then it won't be just a few of us, it'll be a whole company. A whole regiment!"

"How soon will that be?" asked the village head.

"We have a lot of things to do in Shanghai," they replied, avoiding the question.

"Have something to eat before you leave," said the village head. "There's a special kind of fish that you can only find here, nowhere else in the world. You can't eat it in Shanghai."

"No, no, we need to head back," said the group.

"As you wish," smiled the village head. "Maybe next time."

From that day on, Mrs Song's family was on the alert. They took it in turns to keep watch, twenty-four hours a day, to keep an eye out for any suspicious activity. They got hold of a bronze drum, so that as soon as they spotted the people from Shanghai, they could beat it, and everyone could hurry back from wherever they were working. In the evening, as soon as it got dark, the family hung a paraffin lamp from a tree on the riverbank so they could see any boats approaching. Not far from the lamp, in an open shelter, a pair of eyes watched the river. And the family did all of this without letting Nainai and Ah Mei sense there was any danger. They took it in turns, and whoever was on duty would pretend to tidy the yard and stack firewood, or sit in the shelter pretending to doze, and yawn when they saw Nainai and Ah Mei.

"Let them stay as long as they can," Mrs Song told her

family. "You can see it's good for them."

One day, Ah Mei asked Mrs Song, "Why do you keep a paraffin lamp lit all night?"

"There are so many insects at night," said Mrs Song. "When the lamp is lit, the bugs fly over there." She didn't tell her the real reason.

Time passed quickly. Soon, Nainai and Ah Mei had been there a month and a half, and the tree with the paraffin lamp had become like a lighthouse.

It was a world of cockerels crowing and birds singing, of rivers gurgling, of live shrimp and fresh fish, of water chestnut and lotus root. The scent of fresh reeds filled the air, as though it was steeped in green. Mrs Song's family treated Nainai and Ah Mei as family, and did everything they could to look after them and make them feel at home. Nainai and Ah Mei were able to forget their sorrow and grief for a while. Nainai put on a little weight. And after six weeks, you would think Ah Mei was a village girl, if it wasn't for the fact that beneath her rosy cheeks, her skin was pale.

"No matter how poisonous this big sun, it's not going to tan that young girl!" Mrs Song sighed with feeling.

But Nainai and Ah Mei could not stay there for ever, and just as Nainai was thinking about returning, there was a telephone call from Shanghai. Mrs Song went to the village committee office to take the call. It was Mrs Hu. "Madam and Ah Mei can return. A lot of the gang that beat up our master have been arrested, and the gang leader has been scared off. He's gone now."

Mrs Song's husband and their third son took Nainai and

Ah Mei back to Shanghai.

The day they left, there wasn't a dry eye on the bank or the boat. Mrs Song's entire family came to see them off, walking along the bank as far as the bend in the river, after which thick reeds blocked the view, and even then, the family carried on waving. For Mrs Song, the boat soon went out of focus, as she saw only a blur of green through her tears.

CHAPTER 22

The Silk Scarf

After three days in Shanghai, Ah Mei headed back to Yibin to start the new school year.

When Ah Mei was safely on her way, Mrs Hu told Nainai what had happened that summer.

Two days after Nainai had left Shanghai, the same gang had come to raid the Blue House a second time, shouting that they were going to drag Nainai out and parade her through the streets. They said that she had refused to hand over the spy equipment, that they could not let her get away with it so easily and that she needed to be taught a lesson. When they realized she wasn't there, they turned on Mrs Hu. Mrs Hu told them she didn't know where Nainai had gone, and that she had herself been looking all over for her. Of course, the gang didn't believe her, and wanted to force Nainai's whereabouts out of the old housekeeper. They wagged their fingers at her. "If you don't tell us where she's gone, we'll tie you up and parade you in the streets!"

"Wait! Stay right where you are!" said Mrs Hu. She turned around, went into the kitchen, grabbed a cleaver and then returned, brandishing the knife. "I've spent a lifetime working here, being completely exploited by that family! After all that, do you think I'll let myself be bullied by you? I'd rather die!" They raised their hands in the air, took a few urgent steps backwards, then turned and fled. Afterwards, although Mrs Hu didn't know this, they made enquiries and somehow learned that many years previously there'd been another servant at the Blue House called Mrs Song, and that although she'd long since left, the family was still in contact with her. Nainai had probably gone to stay with her, they concluded. They asked everywhere for Mrs Song's address and eventually found it.

Ten days before Nainai and Ah Mei's return, Dabo had come to the Blue House and told Mrs Hu the news: the gang had been arrested, and the leader had been scared into hiding. Exactly who had arrested them, Dabo couldn't say for sure, but the news was true, and the gang had been split up. Nainai and Ah Mei could return to Shanghai!

It was only when they were back home that Nainai learned of the group from Shanghai who had come looking for her while she and Ah Mei were staying with Mrs Song. She thought about the paraffin lamp that shone all night, and about the shelter, where there was always someone watching the river, and her heart swelled with gratitude for Mrs Song's family. How could she hate the world when there were such good people in it?

But ever since her return, Nainai's mood had been low.

Still grieving for Yeye, she had to face the departure of Xiaogu and Ah Mei on the same day.

Those three days that Ah Mei had been in Shanghai she had spent mostly with her aunt, because Xiaogu – who had worried Nainai by being single all these years – was about to leave Shanghai to get married. Five years earlier she had met a cellist from Hong Kong at a concert. After the orchestra had finished its performances in Shanghai, Xiaogu and the cellist had seen each other briefly a couple of times, and he had filled a space in her heart, like a cloud that refuses to move. She didn't say a word about him to the family, but kept him secret, a secret that made her face blush and her heart flutter. They stayed in touch by letter, their correspondence infrequent but unbroken. While Nainai was away from Shanghai, the cellist had called Xiaogu, a call that had lasted three hours and had infuriated everyone else wanting to use the phone. In fact, Xiaogu had merely listened as the cellist stuttered and stammered, and incoherently poured his heart out to her. Xiaogu was silent throughout, her hand trembling as it gripped the phone. He invited her to join him in Hong Kong: now, the sooner the better. And with tears in her eyes, and two sighs of joy, she accepted.

She didn't ask anyone in the family for their opinions, she just went ahead and made arrangements. She'd assumed the process would be as hard as climbing to heaven, and never expected it would be so easy!

When Nainai returned to Shanghai, it was almost a fait accompli.

Nainai wept, partly because marriage meant letting her daughter go, and partly because this daughter would be going so far away. The thought of not knowing when she might see Xiaogu again filled her heart with sorrow.

Those last few days, Ah Mei did not stray from her aunt's side. When they weren't out and about, she would quietly gaze at Xiaogu's face.

"What are you looking at!" Xiaogu pretended to tweak Ah Mei's nose.

Ah Mei shrugged her shoulders, and smiled. "You look different."

"Nonsense! What makes you say that?"

Ah Mei couldn't put her finger on it, but whatever it was, she preferred her aunt's face this way. If Xiaogu's old face had reminded her of the moonlight in autumn, her new face was like the sunlight in spring.

Before each going their separate ways, Ah Mei and her aunt spent their last evening together, neither of them talking. That night they shared a bed, and Ah Mei snuggled up as close as she could to her aunt. She could hear Xiaogu breathing, her particular way of breathing that Ah Mei had loved since she was little. Ah Mei listened to her soft, warm breath carefully, as though after that night, she might never hear it again.

Ah Mei left Shanghai in the morning. Xiaogu left in the afternoon.

After their departure, Nainai felt the Blue House was empty, utterly empty.

* * *

Autumn arrived, planting its cool, dark feet all day and all night. The wutong trees started to drop their leaves, and flocks of geese appeared in the Shanghai sky on their way south.

Since returning from Mrs Song's, Nainai's life had been quiet.

The news she received from different sources led her to believe that this chaotic world was already heading towards its end. No one knew what would happen next. It was like being in a nightmare, that moment of absolute terror, that moment when you are falling into the abyss, and all of a sudden you wake up.

Nainai hadn't been to church for decades. She'd almost forgotten they still existed. But, one morning as she was walking past a church, she stopped, and stood for a long time. She looked up at the steeple, and said a silent prayer in her heart. She prayed for her children and grandchildren, for Yeye, for Mrs Hu, for Mrs Song and her family, and for the whole world.

She stood there for an hour. She spent the next hour walking home.

Her feet were barely through the door when she was seized and taken away. There was no explanation. They didn't say who they were, and Nainai didn't ask. Because even if she knew, what good would it do?

They took her to some kind of warehouse. But unlike the last two gangs, they didn't interrogate her.

A few hours later, they pushed an elderly man into the room.

"Mr Jin!" Nainai knew immediately what was going to happen next.

Mr Jin was Yeye's barber, and he had been coming to the house for years.

"Madam," he said quietly, then lowered his head. He couldn't bear to look up.

Nainai tried to see what was outside the door, but the view was blocked by the gang's bodies. She was their prey, surrounded, trapped in a tiny space with no way to escape. She didn't try to break through. Instead, her entire body started to shake, until eventually she could hold out no more, and sat down on a chair in the middle of the room.

The ringleader rolled up his jacket sleeves, revealing an immaculate white shirt. He had a neat parting, not a hair out of place. His hair looked oiled: it was black as could be, sleek and shiny. He said to the barber, "Tomorrow she'll be paraded around the streets!"

Mr Jin stood there, numbly.

"Leave one side on, shave the other side off, half and half. Make sure you do a good job!" said the man with the parting.

Mr Jin didn't move.

"I heard you used to go to the house to cut their hair." The man with the parting rubbed the sole of his shoe on the concrete floor.

Mr Jin shivered, and opened the bag that was tucked under his arm. Inside was a set of clippers.

Immediately, two strong young men stood behind Nainai, making it clear that they would hold her down if she struggled. The barber took out a white cloth and shook it. Freshly laundered, it was pristine, and the neatly pressed folds left a pattern of perfect squares.

Nainai remained sitting on the chair, and put up no resistance at all. She knew very well that to resist would only lead to more humiliation. She lowered her head, and before the clippers even came out, ice-cold tears had already started to fall.

Mr Jin carefully placed the cloth over her shoulders. It began to blur in front of him.

Nainai could feel his hands shaking.

Mr Jin picked up the clippers, but his hands were trembling even more. He turned around and asked the man with the parting, "Would it be all right to have a cigarette?"

"Yes," replied the man.

Shaking, Mr Jin took a cigarette from his pocket. He fumbled with the matches, and had to strike three before one lit. Then he took his time, as though he wanted that cigarette to last for ever.

Some of the gang seemed impatient – coughing, or tapping their feet on the ground.

Nainai sat there, not moving, like a stone.

"Get on with it!" The man with the parting pointed angrily at the old man. "Or would you rather we gave you one of those haircuts? But, you know, we're not skilled like you are…"

Mr Jin's clippers trembled in the air above Nainai's head.

Then a racket erupted outside, and the man with the parting rushed out.

Everyone else left too, except for a young woman of seventeen or eighteen, who wore a lilac chiffon scarf around her neck. She had flinched and turned aside when Mr Jin had raised his clippers, and she was still shaking.

Still trembling, Mr Jin stood beside Nainai, his hands by his sides. Whatever had happened, the gang didn't return.

It was almost evening when a bent old man came in and spoke quietly to Nainai.

"They were going to parade you around the streets, but the two sides started fighting. I hear the hospital's full of people who've been beaten up. Go home, no one's going to parade you now. Go on, go home! What they've done here is sinful, and there'll be retribution. Go on, go home." Then he turned around and left.

Mr Jin lowered his head, and removed the white cloth from Nainai's shoulders. "You should go, Madam. Leave Shanghai if you can. These animals aren't going to leave you alone."

It was a long time before Nainai looked up. And when she raised her head, the young woman quickly looked away.

Mr Jin and Nainai walked out of the building. They had barely gone any distance when the young woman caught up with them, the lilac scarf floating behind her, only this time she was not wearing it around her neck, but holding it in her hands. She held it out to Nainai without a word, but Nainai could understand the message when she looked in the woman's eyes: *Don't let them see your hair.*

"Thank you," said Nainai, accepting the scarf.

The woman edged away from her, then finally turned and ran.

Nainai carefully tied the chiffon scarf around her head.

There was a chill in the autumn air, and there were many women wearing silk scarves tied around their heads or around their necks. Mr Jin walked Nainai home. On the way, he spotted a bin. He went over to it and threw away the barber's kit that had been with him all his life. "I won't be needing that again," he said, returning to Nainai's side.

A truck drove slowly down the street, its loudspeaker blaring. Nainai couldn't bring herself to look at the people being paraded in the back of the truck.

When Mr Jin said goodbye to Nainai, he repeated what he had said earlier: "Madam, they aren't going to leave you in peace."

Nainai got home before dark. Mrs Hu had been looking out for her by the door.

"Madam, where have you been?"

"I went for a walk," said Nainai. She grabbed hold of the banister and with some effort began to drag herself upstairs. Mrs Hu rushed to help her.

Nainai said she wanted to sleep, so Mrs Hu went to get the bed ready for her.

It was night-time before Nainai got up. She washed, put on clean clothes, then opened the canvas suitcase she had swapped with Ah Mei, and took out a dark blue silk scarf. Yeye had bought it for her in Paris all those years ago. She had seen it in a shop and fallen in love with it, and when Yeye had examined it, he had said it had been made by his silk company. "We make them in a range of colours, how many would you like?" he'd asked. "Just this one," she'd said. "I'd like you to buy it for me as a present." And Yeye had nodded, and bought it for her.

The blue silk scarf had gone from China to France, then from France to China, and all these years it had been lying quietly in Nainai's suitcase.

It was as blue as it had always been, the deep blue of the sea. As she shook it gently, Nainai could see the rolling waves.

Had it been waiting in her suitcase all those decades just for today? she wondered. As her tears fell, dark blue circles spread on the silk.

She folded the young woman's scarf neatly, and placed it in a drawer in the wardrobe. "Perhaps there'll be a chance to return it to her," she said to herself.

After her ordeal that afternoon, Nainai could not stop thinking about her hair. It may have lost most of its colour, but it was her hair, it was her life. Right now, she felt she had to protect it from the cold winter wind if she was to survive. She wore the blue headscarf at supper. When she noticed the children looking puzzled, she said, "I seem to have caught a chill, and feel I'm going down with a cold. And I have a slight headache. At my age, I need to be careful."

Nainai looked beautiful in the silk scarf and no one gave it a second thought.

It was after supper that Nainai discovered the piano room was empty.

Mrs Hu told her what had happened. "Yesterday, dozens of people came, determined to take the piano away. They said it might be part of your spy equipment. I tried to argue with them, to fight them off, but it was useless."

Mrs Hu didn't tell Nainai that when they had tried to take the piano out of the house, she had lain down in their way. They'd punched her and kicked her, then picked her up and thrown her onto the grass.

They were from the same gang that had seized Nainai. As soon as one group had taken her away, another had charged into the house just as Mrs Hu was on her way home from the market.

"They rampaged through the house, and made such a mess you couldn't see the floor." Mrs Hu showed Nainai the metal coffee pot she had brought with her from France. "They trod on it."

Nainai looked at the squashed coffee pot and sighed.

For the next seven days, Nainai wore her headscarf all the time. She went out early in the morning and did not return until late. She searched the whole of Shanghai, but found no trace of the piano.

Then, one day, she didn't go out. She called for Mrs Hu: "It's Ah Mei's birthday on the eighteenth of October. I haven't been to see the three of them in Yibin yet. I'm going to take the boat tomorrow, which should get me there in time for her birthday. I'll stay a few days. You haven't been home to see your family all year. When I've gone, lock the house and go and spend some time with them."

"I'll start packing for you," said Mrs Hu.

Nainai pointed to a suitcase. "There's no need, I've already packed."

Mrs Hu was about to turn around and set about tidying the house when Nainai called her back. "Mrs Hu, won't you sit down for a while? You've always been so busy, rushing around. Let's sit and chat."

Nainai and Mrs Hu talked for a long, long time, like sisters.

Nainai wouldn't let Dabo and the others put a call through to Yibin, or send a telegram, to tell them she was on her way. "I want it to be a surprise for Ah Mei," said Nainai. She knew exactly what she wanted to do, and didn't want to put her children to any trouble.

Nainai arrived in the evening on 17 October, struggling with her suitcase. Baba and Mama were still at work, and Ah Mei had been by herself since she came home from school. Ah Mei couldn't believe her eyes when she saw Nainai at the door. For a moment, she thought she was dreaming. She looked at her grandmother in a daze, speechless.

"Aina!" Nainai called her name.

Ah Mei's mouth fell open. Her eyes couldn't stop blinking.

"Aina, it's Océane! I've come to see you!"

"Océane!" Ah Mei finally cried out, hugging Nainai. "Océane! Océane!" she said over and over again.

When Ah Mei went to meet her parents from work, she told them Nainai had come. They didn't believe her at first. It couldn't be true! But Ah Mei was so excited they had no choice but to believe it. They hurried home, Ah Mei leading the way.

When they saw Nainai, a myriad of emotions surged through their hearts, and tears burst from their eyes. Thinking of Yeye, and how they hadn't been able to get to Shanghai to see him one last time, Mama was overwhelmed. She grabbed Nainai's hands and shook them uncontrollably. Eventually, remembering that Nainai had made a long journey and must be exhausted, Baba pulled over a chair so she could sit down.

Nainai said she had come to celebrate Ah Mei's birthday.

She still hadn't taken off her headscarf. "I seem to have caught a chill, and feel I'm going down with a cold. I have a slight headache, and at my age, I need to be careful," she explained calmly.

"As if!" said Ah Mei. "Nainai's wearing it to look smart."

Nainai laughed. Mama agreed – the blue scarf suited Nainai's pale skin, and she did look smart. If Nainai wanted to keep it on, why shouldn't she? After a while, they thought nothing more about it.

The next day, Nainai arranged a birthday party for Ah Mei. That evening, they had cake, and candles, and sang Happy Birthday – thanks to Nainai it was a very special and happy scene in the little town of Yibin.

Ah Mei served the cake, and when she came to Nainai there were tears in her eyes. "Thank you, Nainai!" she said. Then, whispering in her grandmother's ear, "Thank you, Océane!"

Nainai's eyes glistened with tears. "Look at you, all grown up!"

Baba and Mama moved things around so that Nainai and

Ah Mei could share a room: one big bed and one little bed. Mama told Ah Mei not to chatter all night and keep Nainai awake, as she'd spent so long on the boat and was bound to be tired. But Nainai had so much to tell Ah Mei. She kept talking, and sighing, and telling Ah Mei what she must and mustn't do, and laughing over memories of the past.

Then, suddenly, she stopped. After a long pause, she said, "Aina, Océane's so sorry she wasn't able to keep the piano safe for you. She's so sorry…" They were the last words that were spoken that night.

Nainai promised Ah Mei she would stay for a few days. Before Ah Mei left for school, and Baba and Mama left for work, they gave her a house key. Mama had got up very early and already been to the market to buy food so that Nainai could make herself whatever she liked. She and Baba would come home early that evening, and they'd eat together as a family.

Nainai nodded in agreement.

But when they came home that evening, they found a letter from Nainai addressed to Baba and Mama. On top of the letter, holding it securely on the table, was a beautiful little cotton-covered box.

The letter read:

I'm leaving, and going back to Shanghai.
The day before yesterday, when I got off the boat,
I went straight to the ticket office and bought a ticket for
today. I didn't tell you because I knew you would have tried

368

to return the ticket, and have me stay for longer. But I have to go back. Before coming to Yibin, I heard that there are people in Shanghai who are starting to occupy houses. I can't help worrying while our house is empty, so I must return. Please forgive me for leaving without saying goodbye.

In the box are the two dragonfly eyes, my gift to Ah Mei. Please look after them for her, and keep them for her wedding. Find some pretty gemstones, and make her the most beautiful necklace in the world. A beautiful necklace for my beautiful Ah Mei!

Now that I have seen Ah Mei, and celebrated her birthday with her, I can go.

I love you.

Mama

Baba and Mama were surprised by Nainai's decision, but when they thought about it, it seemed plausible: the house was the only thing she had left. And it wasn't just a house, or a place to live, it had so many beautiful and happy memories, and so many sad and painful memories. It was where Nainai had brought up her children. She had dedicated her youth, her whole life, giving her heart, her hands and her head to the family property. All the other property the family had owned belonged to the state now, though its glorious history was in their hearts.

Nainai had found the most persuasive reason for her urgent return to Shanghai.

But after dinner, when they were reading through the letter again and chewing it over, they found lots of things that gave them cause to doubt and worry. Nainai seemed to be hiding something, and that something made their insides feel tight. And when they pondered over the dragonfly eyes that Nainai had left for Ah Mei, that feeling only tightened. Ah Mei was only fifteen; she would not be getting married for years.

That night, Baba and Mama barely slept.

Before dawn, they had come to a decision: whatever the situation, they had to go to Shanghai and they had to leave that day.

Baba left Mama to do the packing, and to go to the factory and to Ah Mei's school to ask for time off, while he went to the quayside. The boat would leave at ten. He would buy tickets if there were any, or wait for returns. And if there weren't any returns, he would talk to the captain, and see if he would let them on board first, and sort out the tickets later. They would find a way.

Baba told Mama that he would stay at the quayside and wait there for her and Ah Mei.

In the end, he got two returned tickets. They were still one short, but the captain said, "You're a family of three, and we can't leave one of you on the quayside, can we?"

It wasn't until they were on board that Baba and Mama realized they should have telephoned Shanghai first. They could have kicked themselves! They couldn't contact anyone now they were on the boat.

They regretted it all the way: why had it taken them so long to realize something was not right? If only they had seen it when they first read the letter, they could have phoned the family in Shanghai then, but they hadn't wanted to worry them. They'd been so stupid. What kind of brains did they have? Pigs' brains?

Ah Mei was too young to fully appreciate why Baba and Mama were so concerned. But seeing them weighed down with worry, she couldn't help feeling anxious for Nainai too, though she didn't know why. She couldn't explain it. Baba and Mama couldn't explain it either.

Baba and Mama's moods kept changing all the way to Shanghai. There were times when they felt they were worrying over nothing, and times when every detail gave cause for doubt. The more they rubbed away at it, the more they felt that Nainai's behaviour was abnormal.

Their mood affected Ah Mei, too. All she could do the whole journey was watch the expression on their faces. Baba and Mama were like a boat, and Ah Mei was sitting on the boat. When the boat lurched, she lurched too.

Eventually Baba and Mama realized this, and agreed privately that they would do their best to appear relaxed in front of Ah Mei. They hoped it would help them relax too.

"We might be overthinking it," Baba said to Mama.

"There might be no problem at all," said Mama.

And for a while, they were able to enjoy the scenery along the riverbanks.

Ah Mei was able to enjoy it too, as if the boat trip wasn't for Nainai's sake, but a holiday for the three of them. But Baba and Mama struggled to keep up their pretence, and suddenly the mood would become tense again, because they'd thought of some detail or remembered the wording of the letter. What did she mean: "I can go now"?

They spent almost two days pondering something else: why had Nainai worn a headscarf the entire time she was there? That blue silk scarf lodged in their minds, as though demanding their attention. And it was still on their minds as the boat lined up at Shiliupu Wharf in Shanghai.

For some reason, the little leather suitcase was also on Baba and Mama's minds. When they were packing Mama had insisted that Ah Mei not use the little leather suitcase, the reason being that it was on the heavy side, and didn't hold much. Ah Mei had originally done as Mama said, but just as they were about to leave, she had changed her mind, and become determined to take it, as though it were a matter of life or death. Mama was annoyed: "I have so much to carry, it'll be hard enough as it is. I was counting on your help, but if you take the little leather suitcase, you won't be any help." But it was no use: Ah Mei was adamant. Mama got cross, but Ah Mei, in tears, gripped the little leather suitcase with both hands and refused to let go.

On the boat, the next time Baba and Mama saw the little leather suitcase, they felt – although they had no grounds whatsoever for this feeling – that the little suitcase signified something. Mama felt it especially.

One afternoon, when the boat was going past Wuhan, someone suddenly shouted: "Man overboard! Man overboard!"

Then others joined in. "Man overboard! Man overboard!"

Ah Mei had been standing out on the deck. She saw someone bobbing up and down in the water. She was so shocked that she turned and ran back to the cabin, calling, "Ba! Ba!"

Baba and Mama were just coming outside. "What's wrong? What is it?" they asked.

Ah Mei pointed to the river: "There's a … man … in the r-r-river…"

Mama put her arms around Ah Mei, and patted her on the back. "Don't be scared. Don't worry."

Baba went out, but told Mama and Ah Mei to stay in the cabin.

The boat slowly came to a stop, but by then the man was far away. A little boat sped towards him, a rescue boat for saving lives on the river.

After a while, the passenger boat continued on its way.

The passengers were deeply affected by what they had seen, and didn't know if the man was alive or dead. The discussion went on for a long time.

Mama hadn't seen what happened, but she felt as if she had seen it, and it was vivid in her mind. She comforted Ah Mei, and then, when Ah Mei was able to be left quietly with the little leather suitcase, she went to join Baba. She met him on his way back to the cabin. She glanced back to check Ah Mei was out of hearing and said, haltingly, "Nainai … she … she wouldn't have … got off the boat … would she?"

Baba immediately put his finger on her lips. "Please, don't let your thoughts run away with you like this! In a few days, we'll be in Shanghai. She's bound to be safe and sound."

The night before they arrived in Shanghai, Ah Mei refused to sleep. She sat by the window, looking out through the oval porthole, silently watching the river under cover of night. The sky was clear, the wind was low. The full moon had followed the boat all the way – not trailing behind, but casting its light ahead of the boat, laying a path of broken silver across the water, leading the boat to the east.

When Ah Mei grew tired, she rested her elbows on the little leather suitcase beside her, and propped her chin on her hands, but her eyes were still looking out.

"Ah Mei, it's late, go to sleep," said Mama. She pulled Ah Mei towards her. "Why won't you go to sleep?" she asked.

"I miss Nainai," said Ah Mei, silently starting to weep.

Although Ah Mei didn't make a sound, Mama knew she was crying. "You'll be able to see her tomorrow."

"But I miss her," said Ah Mei.

Mama patted Ah Mei gently on the back, just as she had patted her to sleep when she was little.

Ah Mei finally fell asleep, but not for long, and Mama didn't sleep at all.

"Mama, I miss Nainai," said Ah Mei, the moment she work up.

They heard the whistle blowing – warning another ship that it was coming too close. The sound of the whistle over the autumn river was like the low *mou mou* of an old buffalo on a grey rainy day.

Mrs Hu did not return to Shanghai on the day Nainai suggested, but came back a week early.

Such a big house needed someone to look after it. What if a pipe had burst? What if children, throwing stones for fun, had broken a window and there happened to be a storm?

In the garden, the flowers needed watering, the apricot tree needed watering, the table and windowsills needed to be dusted…

She arrived at the Blue House around ten o'clock in the morning.

The house was quiet and still, but as soon as she had put the key in the door and opened it and both feet were over the threshold, she felt something was not right. Someone had been in the house, and they had been in not so long ago. She checked the time in her mind. Dagu was supposed to come to the house that afternoon. Before she and Nainai had left Shanghai, they had arranged that Dagu would call at the house once a week. But Dagu was only free to come on Wednesday afternoons, and today was Wednesday but it was only the morning.

So who had been in the house?

Mrs Hu still had the big sack of food that she'd brought with her from home on her back, and the loofah-sponge she'd brought for washing the pots and pans in her hand. She took them into the store room, wondering who it could be.

Half an hour later, she was standing at the door to Nainai's bedroom.

It was unlocked.

Mrs Hu hesitated, then gently pushed the door open. The light was dim and for a while she couldn't see clearly. She felt her way across the room and drew back the curtains. All at once, sunlight shone into the room, and the scene in front of Mrs Hu set her entire body shaking.

Nainai, wearing a brand-new qipao, a blue silk headscarf and spotlessly clean shoes and socks, was lying on her bed, still as could be.

This time, Mrs Hu was not shaking from terror.

The moment she saw Nainai, she knew.

"Madam…" Mrs Hu called out quietly.

Nainai looked as though she was sleeping.

Mrs Hu could sense Nainai's smile hanging from the corners of her mouth.

"I'm back, Madam…" Tears rolled down her face.

She placed her finger under Nainai's nose. There had been no breath for hours.

She looked down at Nainai, her employer, her sister.

She recognized the qipao as being one of the three that Mrs Song had made before leaving the Blue House, the one with the slightly thicker fabric, the one she had never worn, the one most appropriate for this season.

She didn't touch the silk scarf tied around Nainai's head. She knew why Nainai was wearing a headscarf. When her children and grandchildren came, she would tell each and every one of them, "Don't touch your mama's silk scarf." "Don't touch your nainai's silk scarf."

They mustn't touch it!

"There's a chill in the air," said Mrs Hu. She opened the wardrobe, took out a light silk bed cover, and gently placed it over Nainai.

As the cover came down, the scent of Nainai's perfume rose, wafting through the cool air. It was fainter than it had once been, but it still seeped into her lungs.

"I'll go and inform the children."

Mrs Hu walked towards the stairs, one slow step at a time.

At two o'clock, not long after the family in Shanghai had assembled, Ah Mei and her parents arrived at the Blue House.

Dagu went straight up to Ah Mei and gave her a hug.

Baba and Mama didn't ask; they could read what had happened from the solemn, sad faces.

Dagu took Ah Mei's hand, and led her slowly upstairs to Nainai's room.

Ah Mei looked at her grandmother. It was a long time before she started to cry, and then a stream of enormous tears rolled down the sides of her nose, and spattered on the floor.

Ah Mei's family didn't ask what had happened. All they knew was that she had left in dignity, and that she looked as though she was sleeping peacefully, and would do so for ever.

When they were downstairs discussing funeral arrangements, Mama spotted the squashed coffee pot and a coffee cup on the table. There was still a small amount of coffee in the cup. She picked up the coffee pot, the one Nainai had brought with her from France all those years ago, and shook it gently. Nainai must have made a pot of coffee before she went.

That day, they kept Nainai at home.

That night, they kept vigil over Nainai.

During the vigil, it was almost as though they had stopped feeling sad, and in the warm glow of candlelight,

Nainai looked so beautiful. Then they sang for Nainai, one song after another, French songs and Chinese songs. Ah Mei sang the odd little rhymes that her grandmother had taught her.

While she was singing, Ah Mei noticed Nainai's hand was clenched. As she gently prised it open, she could see words in her mind: *I want to go home!*

Ah Mei stopped mid-song.

The hearse arrived at ten o'clock the next morning.

Dabo held Nainai in his arms, and was about to carry her through the door, when another gang burst in. It was the same gang that had snatched the dragonfly eyes and beaten up Yeye.

How the gang had got together again was anyone's guess. But they never expected that Nainai might have passed on, and they were clearly disappointed.

The leader asked Dabo, "What's your relationship to her?"

Dabo smiled. "I am her son, her eldest child."

"But you don't look anything like her," said the gang leader.

"I am her son, her true flesh and blood," answered Dabo. "And she is my mother, the best mother in the world." Dabo looked at Erbo and Dagu and, in a loud voice, said, "Come on, let's go. Let's see Mama off!" Then he looked at Ah Mei and her parents. "Come on, let's go. Let's see Nainai off!"

The gang jumped aside, then left. They had obviously lost interest.

Ah Mei was holding the little leather suitcase. The night

before, she had transferred everything from the canvas case into this little leather suitcase. She wanted to give it back to Nainai. The adults didn't try to stop her: they could imagine Nainai on her long journey, carrying this suitcase.

A wide stretcher was taken out of the hearse. Nainai was placed carefully on top of it. As Dabo and Erbo were carrying the stretcher back to the hearse, Ah Mei suddenly turned around and ran back inside. She returned with a big red oil-paper umbrella in one hand, and a little red oil-paper umbrella in the other.

She placed them both by Nainai's side.

When Dagu, Mama and the aunties saw this, they began to cry.

The family walked with heavy footsteps. It was a dazzlingly sunny day, but in Ah Mei's mind it was raining. She and Nainai were holding their red oil-paper umbrellas, one big, one small, and as the rain became heavier, they started to run, giggling in the rain.

Historical Note

Dragonfly Eyes is a fictional story, set in France and China from the 1920s to the late 1960s. It follows the family life of Du Meixi, a Chinese man from Shanghai, and Océane, a Frenchwoman from Marseilles, their four children and ten grandchildren, against the background of war and political upheaval, particularly in China. The historical events are mentioned only lightly, but their impact on this international family is devastating.

After several idyllic years in France, the family relocate to Shanghai to help with the Du family silk business. When they first arrive, Shanghai is a thriving international city. But war in the 1930s and 1940s – first with Japan, then civil war – takes its toll on China, Shanghai and, therefore, the Du family. War ends in 1949, when the communists establish the People's Republic of China and start to rebuild the country: the New China. When political movements become especially heated during the 1960s – the Cultural Revolution – suspicion rises against the family, particularly against Océane, who, in many people's eyes, will always be a "foreigner".